bittersweet

ALSO BY ALICE MEDRICH

Cocolat: Extraordinary Chocolate Desserts

Chocolate and the Art of Low-Fat Desserts

Alice Medrich's Cookies and Brownies

A Year in Chocolate: Four Seasons of Unforgettable Desserts

ALICE MEDRICH

bittersweet

RECIPES AND TALES FROM A LIFE IN CHOCOLATE

Photographs by Deborah Jones

ARTISAN

NEW YORK

Published by Artisan
A Division of Workman Publishing, Inc.
708 Broadway
New York, New York 10003-9555
www.artisanbooks.com

Library of Congress Cataloging-in-Publication Data
Medrich, Alice
  Bittersweet : recipes and tales from a life in
  chocolate / by Alice Medrich
        p. cm.
  Includes bibliographical references and index.
  ISBN 1-57965-160-7
     1. Cookery (Chocolate) I. Title
TX767.C5M4297 2003
641.6'374—dc21   2003052303

Printed in Singapore
10   9   8   7   6   5   4   3   2   1

Book design by Vivian Ghazarian

This book was set in Helvetica Neue, Perpetua,
Saddlebag, and Trade Gothic

to Lucy

CONTENTS

I grew up on Hershey bars and M&Ms in a world of food vastly different from today's. The chocolate that we eat and cook with now is better and more varied than it was thirty, twenty, even ten years ago. It is also different in composition. It begs for the creation of new recipes and a fresh take on old ones.

WHEN CHEESE WAS ORANGE

The years have changed our palates too. We are hungry for more and bigger flavors in all that we eat, including chocolate desserts. Cooks need new approaches and a new understanding of chocolate. I have worked with this celestial ingredient all my adult life, participated in its renaissance, and cultivated its transformation from common candy to divine dessert. What happens next with chocolate is connected to what came before, and yet perhaps it is even more exciting. This book is my look at the past and a look to the future.

When I shop in the farmers' market, or when I eat in a restaurant, or buy sushi or a great bottle of wine or freshly roasted coffee beans or exquisite cheeses from anywhere in the world in my supermarket, I have to remind myself of a time when prepared foods from every cuisine, exotic ingredients, and spectacular chocolates were not abundant and easily available. But when I sold my first chocolate truffles in the early 1970s, take-out food was pizza or Americanized Chinese food or, in some cities, Jewish or Italian food from a delicatessen. Coffee had the strength of dishwater and cheese was always orange. We were not yet a nation addicted to fast food, but neither were we passionate about organic produce, the authentic tastes of foods from every corner of the globe, or handmade "artisan" foods. We loved chocolate, but our taste for it was childlike. Chocolate was fudge or a candy bar, plain, nutty or nougatty, or an assortment of boxed chocolates from Whitman's or See's. More than 70 percent of the chocolate purchased by Americans was milk chocolate. Home bakers melted gritty squares of one of two brands of bitter "baking chocolate" or spooned out cocoa to make cakes, brownies, and fudge.

A chocolate cake was a tall fluffy affair made with shortening rather than butter and slathered with swirls of sugary fudge frosting. The prettiest desserts were usually disappointing. (How many frilly cakes or fussy fondant-cloaked petits fours could a hopeful little girl taste before learning that they always looked better than they tasted?) When I opened my first shop, American desserts were still more sweet than flavorful and more decorative than delicious. Even the darkest chocolate contained less chocolate liquor (cocoa beans) and more sugar than it does today. Ganache was more of a foreign language, bittersweet rarely spoken. But in fewer than twenty-five years, everything changed.

Julia Child, and then a legion of baby boomers like me, brought home to America new tastes in food and new ideas about eating from life and travel in Europe or war in Asia. Wearing T-shirts and aprons rather than toques and starched jackets, would-have-been architects and teachers became butchers and bakers. We changed the way Americans ate and cooked. Some did it with small restaurants, wineries, cooking schools, and cookbooks; I opened my chocolate dessert shop. For me it had all begun in 1973, in Paris, with a single bite of a homemade chocolate truffle.

MME. LESTELLE'S FATEFUL TRUFFLE

The truffle was an unexpected jolt of pure bittersweet pleasure that left me momentarily speechless. I knew that I had tasted chocolate for the very first time. The truffle was intense, complex and earthy, dense and smooth. It was not candy, but a very tiny divine dessert. It was all about chocolate flavor rather than sweetness. Seriously sensual, it was a bittersweet poem. And it was fresh, as a true chocolate truffle must be, homemade by my elderly landlady on the rue Copernic, during a postgraduate year in Paris. Mme. Lestelle's truffle was the beginning of a year of tastes, little explosions that redefined my understanding of even the simplest foods. I tasted fragrant peaches and strawberries ripe beyond any previous experience of ripeness, chicken with so much flavor and a texture that, in retrospect, I compare with the first taste of pasta cooked "al dente" after a lifetime of mushy noodles. Cheeses (none of them orange) beguiled me. And wine. That truffle was only the beginning.

Back in Berkeley I seduced my friends with Madame's truffles. Hardly allowing graduate school studies to get in the way, and with a business card proclaiming "Alice's Chocolates (truffles, cakes, pâtisserie diverse)," I made French cakes and truffles at home and sold them at the Pig by the Tail Charcuterie, across the street from a new little restaurant called Chez Panisse. By 1976, my miniature chocolaterie had overflowed my home kitchen and, instead of starting my master's thesis in marketing, I opened a small chocolate dessert shop I called Cocolat. (I never did write the thesis; I lived it instead.)

The simplest French chocolate tortes and truffles were a revelation to my customers, as they had been to me. Dramatically bittersweet and far richer than anything Americans were accustomed to, Cocolat desserts transformed local standards. That influence rippled beyond the rarefied air of Berkeley and became part of the larger culinary revolution. Mme. Lestelle's bite-sized cocoa-dusted truffles created a local sensation, but my almost inadvertent invention of extravagantly large chocolate-dipped ganache truffles (see page 151) caused an explosion. When Zabar's in New York called to place an order, I first said, "No, truffles are too fragile and perishable to ship." But who could say no to Zabar's? Ultimately, I solved the shipping problem and Zabar's bought truffles. Then Gael Greene discovered them and wrote about them in *New York* magazine.

Cocolat increasingly became a destination for savvy chocolate lovers from all over the country. Europeans living in Berkeley shared the "secret" of Cocolat with visiting friends and relatives. One small shop eventually became seven, and then ten. *Gourmet* said, "Cocolat is to chocolate what Tiffany's is to diamonds." Meanwhile, "gourmet" food was becoming big business. Executives from food corporations came to see and taste what was going on at Cocolat. They came to sample desserts that tasted more of chocolate than sugar, and cakes made with butter and topped with fresh whipped cream or bittersweet ganache rather than powdered sugar frosting or sugary fudge. They came to see elegantly designed desserts, from tailored and simple to spectacular, without the old-fashioned bakery frills and fuss. And they came to try freshly made chocolate truffles, which didn't taste like ordinary candy. Cocolat-style desserts found their way onto menus across the country and into the pages of food magazines. Big chocolate truffles began to show up everywhere too, often to my chagrin, since they tasted nothing like a true truffle should. I didn't know whether to be proud or appalled when my dad reported seeing so-called chocolate truffles in a gas station mini mart.

CHOCOLATE FOR ADULTS

Mini marts not withstanding, the idea and the image of chocolate shifted from sweet candy to suave dessert. I don't remember hearing the phrase "chocolate for adults" before I used it to explain the desserts and truffles at Cocolat. In less than two decades, chocolate had become a serious adult luxury item, spoken of in the same way as Champagne and caviar. Chocolate truffles, flourless chocolate cakes, and chocolate mousse became household words and items, found everywhere from food magazines and cookbooks to television to restaurants. And, as a result, Americans were buying and using chocolate differently. Recipes called for good bittersweet or semisweet chocolate (and plenty of it) rather than the unsweetened "baking chocolate" typical of traditional American recipes.

Now that chocolate was a starring ingredient in desserts rather than just a flavoring, the quality and flavor and texture of the chocolate made more of a difference. Where there had been chocolate for baking (unsweetened and generic) and chocolate for eating (sweetened, smooth, and delicious), now your favorite bittersweet or semisweet chocolate bar was the perfect ingredient for making chocolate mousse or a chocolate torte or chocolate truffles. One manufacturer redesigned the labels of all its chocolate bars, making them more elegant, and added the phrase "for baking and eating" to its classic semisweet bar. A short time later, the same company introduced bars of bittersweet chocolate, "for baking and eating," previously sold only to professionals. Home cooks could find Belgian, French, and Swiss chocolates in specialty stores. Was it a coincidence that the cocoa bean content of American dark chocolates increased slightly and chocolate got smoother too? Americans were buying more dark chocolate than ever before, for eating and for baking.

Although recent surveys by the National Confectioners Association and the Chocolate Manufacturers Association indicate that 66 percent of Americans still prefer milk chocolate to dark, chocolate preferences are age-related. Of Americans aged forty-five to fifty, 73 percent now prefer dark chocolate, compared with 11 percent of eighteen- to twenty-four-year-olds. The momentum of the dark chocolate trend is probably best reflected in the fact that mainstream candy manufacturers are offering more dark chocolate versions of their most popular milk chocolate candy (such as Hershey's Kisses, KitKat bars, and Milky Ways).

By the late eighties, there were many more recipes in books and magazines that called for bittersweet or semisweet chocolate, and I was seeing more semisweet baking chocolate in the grocery store, next to the squares of unsweetened baking chocolate. This was dramatic evidence that even mainstream American baking habits had changed. However, unlike European chocolate for cooking, our American bittersweet and semisweet "baking chocolates" were grainy and the flavor too harsh for the chocolate to be eaten plain. The manufacturers got the message only half right: They understood that new-style recipes called for semisweet chocolate, but they clung to the notion that cooking chocolate and eating chocolate were two different things. I thought they missed the real trend: better quality and more variety.

THE NEW CHOCOLATES

Now, only a little over a decade later, there are many more chocolates to choose from and the quality has never been better. Home cooks can buy all kinds of imported and domestic chocolates, in specialty stores and by mail and even in supermarkets, that were once accessible only to pastry chefs and candy makers. In my town, where food things happen early (if not first), premium American, Swiss, French, German, and Dutch bittersweet, semisweet, white, and milk chocolates for eating and dessert making are stacked right beside those tedious baking squares in the supermarket. There are better-quality unsweetened baking chocolates and even tins of roasted cocoa beans. And no single chocolate tastes like any other. Any dessert maker today who uses only baking squares is missing a great culinary adventure: Ordinary chocolate makes good-enough desserts, but great chocolate makes fabulous desserts.

The very definition of chocolate is changing again. Like wine makers blending grapes, chocolate makers differentiate their products according to the way they choose and blend cocoa beans of different varieties and from different sources (some are even making chocolates exclusively with beans from a single source). There is no one best chocolate, just as there is no one best wine. One man's divinely smooth chocolate with nutty flavors may be too tame for the person who wants chocolate with lots of fruity acidity.

In addition to better quality and greater variety, the composition of chocolate has changed. The newest and most exciting examples are bittersweet and semisweet chocolates made with more cocoa beans and less sugar than before. These chocolates have a percentage listed on the label to indicate chocolate liquor or cocoa bean content. The higher the percentage, the stronger and more intense the flavor. For example, bittersweet chocolate marked "70%" contains almost half again as much ground cocoa beans and more than a third less sugar than the traditional style of bittersweet chocolate. Old-style bittersweet chocolate tastes mild and sweet compared to a bar of bittersweet 70 percent. But Americans are catching on fast to the pleasures of European-style flavors and stronger dark chocolates, and American manufacturers have begun to make their own new chocolates, blending cocoa beans differently and using a higher percentage of them as well.

Cooking with the new chocolates is the obvious next step, and one of the primary reasons for this book. These stronger chocolates provide more variety and excitement in desserts, but they do not always substitute perfectly in recipes that were created for the older, sweeter standard bittersweet and semisweet chocolates. To make our favorite recipes with the new chocolates, we need to crack the code for substituting one type of chocolate for another. But there is more to it than that. If our palates hadn't changed, we wouldn't be enjoying stronger and more interesting chocolates in the first place. We need a new approach to chocolate desserts—a new kind of recipe.

Desserts that seemed daringly bittersweet a decade ago, including my own, now often seem too rich and sweet. They don't do justice to the more interesting and better chocolates. Even in my favorite local restaurant, world renowned for exquisitely simple dishes that celebrate the perfection of each ingredient, the signature chocolate dessert is so rich in egg yolks and cream it lacks the stunning clarity of flavor characteristic of every other dish on the menu. To taste more chocolate, we don't need to increase the chocolate in recipes—we did that years ago. We do need to adjust the proportions of fat, dairy products, and sugar, not for reasons of healthy eating or dieting but for pleasure and flavor. Indeed, lessons I learned from creating low-fat recipes turned out to be true for all recipes: Less fat and less sugar actually bring flavors into sharper focus and allow nuances to be tasted. Cream can soften flavors too much, and egg yolks, usually so wonderful with dark chocolate, can be overdone as well. I found myself applying these lessons in all of my cooking. By the time I worked on the revision of *Joy of Cooking* a few years later, I was using the knowledge instinctively to sharpen flavors in recipes that tasted too tame for the twenty-first-century palate.

BAKING WITH THE NEW CHOCOLATES

I could not have been prepared better for working with the new more distinctive and complex chocolates. First as a casual consultant, later as a friend and board member, I watched the birth of the new American chocolate company Scharffen Berger Chocolate Maker. For me, what began as experimentation with a particularly interesting new chocolate led me to greater curiosity about all of the newer-style chocolates, including those from El Rey and Valrhona, among others. But I became increasingly frustrated at not being able to taste the specific characteristics, much less the nuances, of these chocolates in desserts. Even when restaurant chefs were asked to make special desserts to promote any of these chocolates, the desserts often didn't do justice to their specific flavors. As often as not, the desserts simply tasted like rich sweet chocolate desserts.

I wanted recipes that let the flavors in these new chocolates speak. When I began to play with recipes, I realized that I already knew how to make the chocolate flavors pop forward: strategic reductions in sugar, butter, and cream, simplifying recipes, and using fewer ingredients. I started applying this in cooking classes and in published recipes. After one of my "minimalist" recipes appeared in *Food & Wine,* I bumped into a well-known local chef in the produce market. He greeted me with, "Do you really make chocolate mousse with water instead of cream?" Yes, I do. I urged him to try it if he wanted to taste more chocolate flavor.

I was also beginning to choose different chocolates to partner different ingredients, for different recipes, for different occasions, or even just for fun—as a hostess chooses different wines to go with different food or company. This required that I taste chocolate with more attention, as though I had never tasted it before. It also required information that I could not find in books or from classes. It was not enough to understand how the chocolates differed, I had to understand how they behaved in all kinds of recipes. Why was it, for example, that I could substitute a bittersweet 70 percent chocolate in my favorite chocolate torte recipe and produce something delicious, with minimal tweaking, while the same substitution wrecked my best ganache? I wanted to work with all kinds of chocolates in all kinds of desserts and to help others do it as well. I approached the project in my usual trial-and-error mode, in the process learning how different types of recipes responded to varying the amounts of cocoa, sugar, and fat in different chocolates. Then I used what I knew about the composition of the chocolates to devise rough formulas that I could apply strictly or loosely, depending on the recipe, to substitute various high-percentage chocolates in my favorite recipes. Now I was playing with the chocolate in recipes like a musician playing variations; I was learning nuances of taste and texture that I had missed before. I was tasting chocolate for the first time—again.

BITTERSWEET

Thirty years after I tasted my first chocolate truffle, I have entered the next *Bittersweet* chapter. I find myself more interested than ever in flavor and simplicity, and my focus has shifted over the years, away from complex creations that are easy for pastry chefs to accomplish in professional kitchens but too time-consuming for busy home cooks. Instead, this book is about understanding the chocolate and rethinking recipes. It is filled primarly with simple recipes, sweet and savory, and new information for curious cooks who love chocolate and want to taste and use the newest varieties. Here I share the tools I created for myself, to allow other enthusiasts a chance to speak the language of chocolate more fluently: to experiment and convert recipes with ease and understanding. Readers will find a primer on working with chocolate, on making chocolate truffles, and on substituting one kind of chocolate for another. I've also included new or revised low-fat recipes, as well as savory dishes and recipes that include roasted cocoa beans, or cocoa nibs, the newest chocolate ingredient available to home cooks.

Along the way, I've shared memories and experiences, small tastes of my life with chocolate. Although my stories go back in time, the recipes themselves, even those for making childhood favorites, are infused with current knowledge and reflect a very contemporary taste for chocolate. I wish you all of the pleasures of chocolate, and I invite you to taste chocolate again, for the very first time. *Bon appétit.*

—ALICE MEDRICH, *Berkeley, California*

Remembering

*Change is the key to making the desserts
of memory—brownies, cookies, and ice creams
—taste as good as we remember them.*

PRECEDING PAGE: Classic Ganache Truffles (PAGE 146). **OPPOSITE:** Grappa, Currant, and Pine Nut Torte (PAGE 118). **ABOVE:** Cream Scone with Chocolate Chunks (PAGES 288).

Rich Hot Chocolate (PAGE 204). **OPPOSITE, CLOCKWISE FROM TOP:** Nibby Nut and Raisin Cookies (PAGE 312); Nibby Pecan Cookies (PAGE 307); Currant and Nib Rugelach (PAGE 314); Bittersweet Decadence Cookie (PAGE 286); Real Chocolate Wafers (PAGE 284); Nibby Hazelnut Cookies (PAGE 307).

OPPOSITE, LEFT TO RIGHT: Black-Bottom Pecan Praline Bars (PAGE 98); Lacy Coconut-Topped Brownies (PAGE 99); Macadamia Shortbread Brownies (PAGE 97). **ABOVE, CLOCKWISE FROM LEFT:** Cocoa Nib Ice Cream (PAGE 81); Milk Chocolate Lover's Cinnamon Ice Cream (PAGE 82) with crushed walnut praline (PAGE 245); Bittersweet Chocolate Ice Cream (PAGE 77).

Bittersweet Decadence Cookie (PAGE 286). **OPPOSITE:** Rich Hot Chocolate (PAGE 204) and Almond Sticks with Cocoa Nibs (PAGE 311). **FOLLOWING PAGE:** Making Chocolate Pecan Pie (PAGE 276).

Before You Start

WORKING WITH CHOCOLATE, DESSERT MAKING, AND BAKING are each different from cooking. Small, simple, but often nonintuitive details can significantly alter results. Unlike the cook, the baker can rarely taste and adjust or repair as he or she mixes a batter or creates a dessert. Knowing which details are important sets you free to be as creative and playful as you like, without any sad surprises.

Details That Make a Difference

MISE EN PLACE

Mise en place is a French phrase that means "put in place," or "set up." Professional chefs could not survive in a busy kitchen without relying on this practice. When you see TV chefs with all their ingredients measured in little dishes before any cooking begins, you are seeing mise en place!

The ritual of setting out and measuring ingredients focuses you. It clears your mind and promotes attention and connection to the task at hand. It allows you to determine before you start a recipe that you have all of the ingredients and equipment you need. You are less likely to measure incorrectly or forget to include an ingredient in a batter, regardless of any distractions.

Many desserts and chocolate confections turn out best when the recipe steps are performed without interruption. Mise en place ensures that once you begin a recipe, you will not have to run to the store, search the sandbox for your sifter, or rummage in the pantry for a particular pan while your melted chocolate hardens or your batter deflates. Mise en place makes both baking and dessert making more pleasurable and more successful.

MEASURING

Some inaccurate measurements will not always spoil a dessert. You can use a liberal hand with certain ingredients such as raisins, nuts, chocolate chips, coconut, or even vanilla, and you can normally substitute dried fruits and nuts in equal measure one for another.

But, for tender cakes with a perfect crumb, you must measure the baking soda, baking powder, salt, and, most of all, the cocoa powder and flour *carefully*. Even, or especially, in the simplest recipes, baking is not as forgiving as cooking. If cakes are tough, dry, doughy, or leaden, chances are your flour measurement is at fault.

A cup of all-purpose flour can weigh anywhere from 4 to 6 ounces, depending on whether or not it is sifted before measuring or packed firmly or less so into the cup. That 2-ounce (50 percent!) discrepancy can make the difference between a moist, light poem-of-a-cake and a highly effective doorstop.

How to Measure Flour

When a recipe says "1 cup all-purpose flour," this means 1 cup of all-purpose flour measured, without first sifting, as follows: If it is compacted, the flour should be stirred briefly in the sack or canister with a spoon. Spoon the flour lightly into a 1-cup dry measure until it is heaped above the rim. *Do not* shake or tap the cup to settle the flour! Sweep a straight-edged knife or spatula across the rim of the cup to level the flour. A cup of unsifted all-purpose flour measured this way weighs almost 5 ounces; a cup of unsifted cake flour weighs 4 ounces.

If a recipe calls for "1 cup sifted flour," the flour should be sifted before measuring: Set the measuring cup on a sheet of wax paper. Use a fine-mesh strainer (my preference) or a sifter to sift the flour over the cup until it is heaped above the rim. *Do not* shake or tap the cup to settle the flour! Sweep a straight-edged knife or spatula across the rim of the cup to level the flour. A cup of sifted all-purpose flour measured this way weighs 4 ounces; a cup of sifted cake flour weighs $3^{1}/_{2}$ ounces.

NOTE: Ignore the "presifted" label on flour sacks. Presifting eliminates any foreign matter, but the flour gets compacted again en route to your grocer's shelf.

How to Measure Cocoa Powder

Normally my recipes call for unsifted cocoa. If your cocoa is very lumpy and compacted, press out most of the lumps with the back of a spoon, then stir it a little to loosen it before measuring it like unsifted flour (see above).

If sifted cocoa is called for, use a medium-fine strainer to sift and measure it as for sifted flour (see page 26).

Dry and Liquid Measures

Dry measures are measuring cups designed to measure dry ingredients. When using dry measures, you use a 1-cup measure to measure 1 cup, a $^1\!/_2$-cup measure to measure $^1\!/_2$ cup, and so forth. Unless the recipe calls for a "packed" or "lightly packed" cup, heap dry ingredients above the rim, as described for flour, without packing them down; *do not* tap or shake the cup to settle the ingredient. Sweep a straight-edged knife or spatula across the rim of the cup to level it.

Liquid measures are clear glass or plastic containers designed to measure liquids; they have pouring spouts and lines up the sides to indicate measurements. Set the measure on the counter before pouring in the liquid—you can't hold it completely level in the air. Lower your face so you can read the measurement at eye level as you pour in the liquid.

MIXING

For best results, use the specific type of mixing utensil suggested in each recipe. Mixing with a rubber spatula does not produce the same batter texture as mixing with a wire whisk. Folding, stirring, beating, and whisking all produce different results. When a recipe calls for mixing (or folding or stirring, etc.) "just until the ingredient is incorporated," this means that extra mixing may deflate the batter, result in a tough cake, or cause other problems.

Add and mix ingredients in the order called for. The order in which key ingredients are mixed can be critical. If a recipe calls for stirring A into B, it is safest to assume, especially when working with chocolatey batters, that stirring B into A will not produce the same result.

In order to blend flour and other dry ingredients into batters without excessive mixing, many recipes call for whisking the flour and the other dry ingredients (such as leavening, spices, and salt) together first. For very delicate cakes such as sponge or génoise, the dry ingredients are sifted two or three times as well. Whisking and/or sifting fluffs and aerates the dry ingredients so they blend easily and thoroughly into the batter or dough with very minimal mixing.

To prevent overmixing, recipes may call for turning the mixer off before adding the dry ingredients to a dough or batter. Then the mixer is turned back on to a low speed to prevent the ingredients from flying out.

Tough or Tender?

Tenderness in cakes, cookies, and pastry is often a matter of proper measuring, mixing, and timing. Toughness can result from measuring flour inaccurately, using too much flour or the wrong flour (bread flour or whole-grain flour rather than all-purpose or cake flour), or too much mixing after the flour has been moistened in the batter. Baking for too long or at a temperature that is too high or too low can also cause tough cakes, cookies, and pastry.

Hot and Cold

The texture of cakes and other desserts can be critically affected by the temperature of the individual ingredients called for in the recipe. Mixing cool or cold ingredients into tepid chocolate can cause a batter to harden precipitously. When a recipe calls for butter, milk, eggs, or any usually refrigerated ingredient to be at room temperature, that means at about 65° to 70°F. The ingredient should still be cool, not warm. Remove such items from the fridge early, or bring them to room temperature more quickly as follows:

- Put eggs (still in the shell) in a bowl of warm water or crack them into a stainless steel bowl (which conducts heat better than glass) set in a larger bowl of warm water and whisk gently until blended, then let stand until no longer cold.

- Microwave milk or another liquid in a glass measure on Low (30%) power or Defrost for just a few seconds, or set the measure in a bowl of hot water, just until no longer cold.

- Cut butter into chunks and microwave on Low (30%) power or Defrost, a few seconds at a time, until pliable but *not* melted.

BAKING

Always preheat the oven for 15 to 20 minutes so that it reaches the correct temperature before you bake. Remember that heat rises, so baking something in the top of the oven will produce a different result from baking it in the bottom. Follow the recipe instructions for rack placement in each recipe. I usually position a rack in the lower third of the oven so that a cake placed on the rack is just below the center of the oven. When baking a thin sheet cake or a single sheet of cookies, I position the oven rack in the center.

Unless the instructions are otherwise, baked items should be cooled on a rack. They should always be cooled completely before covering or wrapping. Wrapping baked goods before they are completely cool produces a damp, soggy texture and encourages the growth of mold and bacteria.

Equipment

Bowls

I use stainless steel and glass mixing bowls for different purposes. Stainless is best for melting chocolate in a water bath, for example; glass for melting it in the microwave. Bowls that are nearly as deep as they are wide keep dry ingredients from flying out and are best for beating egg whites. One- and two-quart glass measures with handles also make wonderful mixing bowls and are perfect for melting or tempering chocolate in the microwave.

Cake Decorating Turntable

A heavy well-balanced lazy Susan or decorating turntable is the best tool for frosting and decorating cakes, but a lightweight plastic one will do in a pinch. Ateco turntables are available at restaurant supply and kitchenware stores or by mail (see Sources, page 366) and they last a lifetime (so far). A 12-inch metal banding wheel from a ceramics supply shop is just as good, at about half the cost.

Cake Pans

Experienced bakers normally avoid stainless steel pans because stainless steel does not conduct heat evenly. However, there are some new heavy-gauge stainless pans with aluminum cores to ensure even heating; they are beautiful but quite expensive. For layer cakes and sponge cakes, I avoid glass pans and pans with dark finishes, even if they are nonstick. These tend to overbake the edges and bottoms of light and tender cakes, sometimes even before the inside is done. Richer or heavier pound cakes and loaf cakes are different—the deep golden brown crust produced by heavy (often decorative) dark tube and loaf pans is both delicious and beautiful to see. Always read the information that comes with these pans; you may be advised to lower the baking temperature by 25 degrees, which is also good advice if you must bake in a glass pan.

I use 8- and 9-inch round and square pans and 9-by-13-inch rectangular pans, all 2 inches deep. For springforms, I use pans with true 8- and 9-inch diameters (rather than European pans with metric sizes) and a depth of a full 3 inches. Even better than traditional springform pans are Magic Line "cheesecake pans" with removable push-up bottoms, in depths of 2 and 3 inches.

Baking Sheets and Jelly-Roll Pans

Medium- to heavy-weight aluminum baking sheets and jelly-roll pans will not warp or bend and they cook evenly, without hot spots. I avoid dark or nonstick surfaces, which toughen and overbake tender cakes and cookies; nor do I like cushioned pans, because they yield uninterestingly uniform cookie textures. Professional aluminum "half sheet pans," which measure 12 by 17 by 1 inch, fit most home ovens and perform much better than lighter-weight 11-by-17-inch home-kitchen jelly-roll pans. You can buy them at specialty cookware stores, restaurant supply stores, and warehouse grocery discount stores.

Cooling Racks

Racks for cooling cakes and cookies speed up the cooling process and keep baked goods from getting soggy. To save counter space, I have a multitiered rack that holds either four half-sheet pans or four cooling racks. The rack folds away when not needed.

Silica Gel

Silica gel is an inert, nontoxic, granular form of silica, and the highest-capacity absorbent available. Packets of silica are packed in pill bottles and with leather goods, electronics, and myriad other products. Similarly, silica gel can be used to keep cookies crisp in an airtight container and to prevent decorative caramel pieces, carmelized nuts, or praline from becoming sticky from the moisture in the air. Store silica gel in an airtight container. Once saturated with moisture, it can be reactivated (again and again) by baking it in a 250°F oven for $1\frac{1}{2}$ hours. Order silica gel from special cake decorators suppliers, such as Beryl's (see Sources, page 366).

Food Processor

The processor is invaluable for pulverizing nuts or chocolate, transforming ordinary granulated sugar into extra-fine sugar for meringue making, making fruit purees, and mixing some tart and cookie doughs. I keep a mini processor on hand too, for small quantities.

Measuring Cups

For measuring liquids, I have 1-cup, 2-cup, 4-cup, and 8-cup measures. The two larger sizes double as mixing bowls. For measuring flour and dry ingredients, I keep at least one set of metal or sturdy plastic measuring cups including $\frac{1}{8}$-, $\frac{1}{4}$-, $\frac{1}{3}$-, $\frac{1}{2}$-, and 1-cup measures.

Microwave Oven

I find the microwave to be an essential tool for a variety of tasks from melting chocolate to reheating anything to bringing refrigerated ingredients like eggs, butter, or milk to room temperature.

Mixers

I use a KitchenAid 5-quart mixer for larger jobs and a hand-held mixer for smaller ones. I keep extra sets of beaters for both mixers so that I do not have to wash them between beating a batter and egg whites, etc.

Parchment Paper and Wax Paper

Baker's parchment paper is much cleaner and more reliable than grease on the bottom of cake pans, and it can be used to line cookie sheets as well. Everything from meringues to macaroons releases easily from parchment paper. I still keep wax paper (cheaper than parchment!) in my kitchen for all kinds of miscellaneous tasks that do not require the special characteristics and expense of parchment: e.g., a landing place for sifted flour, and so forth.

Pastry Bags and Tips

Pastry bags made of nylon or polypropylene are better than cloth or canvas bags because they wash easily and do not become stiff and cracked or sour smelling. Whipped cream does not weep through these bags either. Disposable plastic pastry bags eliminate the need to wash altogether. A large 16- to 18-inch bag is handy for piping a batch of meringue. A 10- to 12-inch bag is good for smaller quantities. Since pastry bags should not be filled much more than half-full, a bag that is a little too big is better than one that is too small.

PASTRY TIPS Ateco is the universal brand. A useful assortment of tips might include plain round tips varying in diameter from ⅜ to ¾ inch as well as several star tips.

Pastry Brushes

Natural boar's-bristle brushes are the best. Keep separate brushes for pastry and savory dishes, unless you want your desserts to taste of garlic or barbecue sauce.

Rolling Pin

Choose a pin that is comfortable for you: with or without handles, heavy or lightweight. I find that a straight rather than a tapered pin works best for beginners. Absent a rolling pin, you can improvise with a length of thick dowel or pipe, or a tall bottle.

Scale

Many fine chocolates do not come in premeasured squares, so a scale is really a must. Once you get used to using one, you will wish that all recipes were written by weight instead of cup measures. I like a scale that enables me to put any bowl or pot on it, reset to zero, and weigh the ingredients—without dirtying an extra container. Cookware stores sell a variety of scales, or you can even use a digital postal scale, as I do.

Scissors

Keep a good pair in the kitchen for cutting parchment paper, etc.

Serrated Bread Knife

A knife with a 12-inch blade is ideal for cutting a sponge cake or génoise into horizontal layers, but a shorter blade will also do.

Skewers and Toothpicks

For testing cakes, wooden (barbecue) skewers are cleaner than broom straws and longer than toothpicks. Moist batter and crumbs stick to a wooden skewer or toothpick much better than to a metal cake tester, so that you can see exactly how gooey or dry your cake is within.

Spatulas

RUBBER AND HEATPROOF SILICONE SPATULAS Three sizes will meet every contingency: Use the largest for folding meringue into delicate batters and scraping large bowls. A mini spatula teases tiny quantities from small containers. Medium handles everything in between. Rubber spatulas melt and discolor if used over heat. The new silicone spatulas, on the other hand, are miraculous for cooking everything from custards to caramel; they have replaced wooden spoons in my kitchen.

METAL SPATULAS For frosting cakes, I like a stainless steel spatula with a straight 8-inch-long blade that is rounded at the end. For spreading cake batter in a sheet pan, I like an offset spatula (the blade has a bend in it right after the handle) with a blade at least 8 inches long.

Strainers

I hate cleaning and storing sifters. A large fine-mesh strainer does the job for flour and other dry ingredients. It requires only one hand, and it shakes out and cleans easily. Fine-mesh strainers are also best for dusting desserts with powdered sugar or cocoa. I keep on hand a couple of good fine-mesh stainless steel strainers, as well as several inexpensive strainers with plastic rims in a variety of sizes.

Tart and Tartlet Pans

I use a 9$\frac{1}{2}$-inch tart pan with a removable bottom, fluted edges, and a shiny reflective surface rather than one made of darkened steel.

I keep several sizes of shiny, not dark, tartlet pans. Those that measure 3$\frac{1}{2}$ to 4 inches across the top are most useful for making single servings. (It takes 1 ounce of tart dough to line the former and about 1$\frac{1}{2}$ ounces or a little less to line the latter.)

Thermometers

INSTANT-READ THERMOMETER Inexpensive instant-read thermometers are available in cookware and hardware stores. These thermometers, which have a range of 0° to 220°F, are perfect for cooking custards, working with chocolate, or checking when eggs, butter, and milk, etc., for baking are at room temperature (70°F). But digital thermometers are more convenient and fun. I like the combination timer/ thermometer made by Polder with a range of 32° to 392°F (0° to 200°C). It has a probe attached to a wire that can be inserted into a pot of candy on top of the stove or a roast or loaf of bread in the oven. The temperature registers on an easy-to-read digital display that sits on the counter, and it can be set to beep when the desired temperature is reached. This is the best thermometer for recipes that require heating and stirring eggs to a particular temperature: Just hold the probe in the bowl with one hand and stir with the other until the beeper goes off.

OVEN THERMOMETER Even the best recipes suffer if baked at the wrong temperatures. Use a thermometer to check your oven every now and again to see that it remains accurate. If necessary, either have it calibrated or compensate for any discrepancy yourself until you can get someone to adjust it.

Timer

Whether it's the tick-tick, ding-ding type or a digital buzzer, a timer is an essential kitchen tool.

Wire Whisks

A whisk is an essential hand tool, and not just for beating. Whisks are better than kitchen forks for mixing dry ingredients together thoroughly or fluffing up flour before it is added to a batter.

Zester (Microplane)

Hate zesting, removing the thin colored top layer of citrus peel? A Microplane zester is modeled on a fine woodworker's rasp. Rather than "scrubbing" the fruit, and your knuckles, back and forth against a grater, simply draw the zester lightly across the fruit, in one direction, like a violin bow across strings. The Microplane lifts off the thinnest shreds of zest—effortlessly and without any bitter white pith or scraped knuckles. Rather than dreading the task, you will look forward to any recipe that calls for zest.

Ingredients

Baking Powder and Baking Soda

Cakes may be leavened with baking powder or baking soda, or both. Baking powder has an expiration date because it loses its oomph if not fresh and stored in a tightly sealed container. You can check to see if baking powder still has its power by adding a teaspoon or so to about a quarter cup of hot water—if it bubbles vigorously, it's still good. If in doubt, splurge on a new tin.

Butter

I use butter for baking because it tastes better than shortening or margarine. I always use unsalted butter; salted butter contains $\frac{1}{4}$ teaspoon of salt per stick, and it will make many butter-rich chocolate desserts taste much too salty. If using salted butter in a recipe where butter is not a major ingredient, subtract $\frac{1}{4}$ teaspoon of salt for each stick of butter used.

If you are baking for the Jewish holidays and strictly observing dietary laws, for nondairy meals, substitute unsalted pareve margarine for butter. If you must for whatever reason use margarine or shortening instead of butter, avoid tub margarine, butter substitutes, and spreads, which may contain a very high percentage of water. These ingredients are not made for baking and results will be unpredictable. Do not expect predictable results from substituting vegetable oils for solid fats either.

SPECIALTY BUTTERS Some of the finest French and other butters available in gourmet shops and upscale markets have less water in them than brands that we are accustomed to. If you substitute these delicious butters in baking, please take into account that ordinary butter contains 15 to 20 percent water, while brands such as Plugrá contain 5 percent (or less). When substituting these "drier" butters, I usually decrease the amount of butter in the recipe by 10 to 15 percent.

Chestnuts

If you don't want to roast or steam your own, the best cooked whole chestnuts come in vacuum packages in better supermarkets and gourmet stores. Those in jars are not quite as good, but they are still acceptable. Do not confuse them with sweetened chestnuts or chestnuts packed in syrup. You can also use Faugier chestnut puree (ingredients are listed as: chestnut puree, water, corn syrup), which is essentially unsweetened except for the tiny amount of corn syrup. Do not confuse the latter for sweetened chestnut puree, also called chestnut spread, that comes in cans or jars.

Chocolate

See pages 43–64.

Cocoa

See pages 48–51.

Coconut

Sweetened shredded coconut is available in the baking aisle of the supermarket. Unsweetened dried shredded coconut is more often found in specialty or gourmet markets, or in natural or health food stores.

Coffee and Espresso

If a recipe calls for freshly ground coffee beans, use freshly roasted beans from a gourmet coffee purveyor, and grind or crush them yourself if possible. Bypass that vacuum-packed can of ground coffee from the supermarket.

For recipes that call for instant espresso powder, I use Medaglia d'Oro. To substitute regular instant coffee powder or freeze-dried instant for expresso powder, use 25 to 30 percent more than the recipe calls for.

Cream

The freshest, cleanest-tasting cream is simply pasteurized, rather than "ultrapasteurized" or "sterilized," and it contains no added ingredients. Some ultrapasteurized and sterilized creams, which have been processed for longer shelf life, no longer taste as cooked or as much like canned milk as they used to, so I am less adamantly against them than I was. But I still buy regular pasteurized whenever possible, and I prefer cream without the stabilizer carrageenan, although it does make smoother whipped cream.

Eggs

Use Grade AA large eggs for the recipes in this book. Buy eggs from a source that keeps them refrigerated, and do likewise at your house. When recipes call for eggs at room temperature, remove them from the refrigerator an hour or so ahead, or warm them quickly in a bowl of warm water.

Extracts

Always use pure extracts. Artificial flavorings are not worthy of the time and other good ingredients that you put into your favorite recipes.

Dried Fruits

These should be moist, plump, and flavorful. Whole pieces are always better, fresher, and moister than prechopped or extruded pellets. If they are sticky, chop or cut them with an oiled knife or scissors.

Flour

The recipes in this collection were tested and developed with either bleached all-purpose flour or cake flour. The type of flour and method of measurement can make a critical difference in the outcome of cakes and desserts.

Liqueurs and Spirits

When recipes call for spirits, such as brandy or rum, it is not necessary to use the finest and most expensive, but choose a brand that you can sip without grimacing, or omit the liquor altogether. If you omit the liquor used as a flavoring, there is no need to substitute another liquid in its place in most recipes. However, omitting the liquor used to flavor truffle centers will make the ganache centers firmer; this can be corrected, if desired, by adding a little extra cream or by using a little less chocolate. I do not use liquor flavorings or extracts, as they taste artificial.

EAU-DE-VIE DE FRAMBOISE Not to be confused with sweet pink raspberry or black raspberry liqueurs such as Chambord, eau-de-vie de framboise is a clear high-proof distilled fruit brandy made exactly the way kirsch is made, but with raspberries instead of cherries. St. George Spirits is my favorite brand.

Nuts

For freshness and flavor, buy nuts raw, rather than toasted, and in bulk from stores that have lots of turnover, rather than packaged from the supermarket. Larger halves and pieces stay fresher longer; it's better to chop them yourself. Nuts keep well in the freezer, packaged airtight.

Fresh nuts are delicious raw, but toasting brings out such rich flavor that almonds and hazelnuts are virtually transformed. Toasted nuts are also extra crunchy.

To toast nuts, spread them in a single layer on an ungreased baking sheet. Bake in a preheated oven (350°F for almonds and hazelnuts; 325°F for pecans and walnuts) for 10 to 20 minutes, depending on the type of nut and whether they are whole, sliced, or slivered. Check the color and flavor of the nuts frequently, and stir to redistribute them on the pan. Almonds and hazelnuts are done when they are golden brown when you bite or cut them in half; pecans and walnuts when fragrant and lightly colored.

To rub the bitter skins from toasted hazelnuts, cool them and then rub the nuts together until most of the skins flake off. When chopped toasted nuts are called for, toast them whole or in large pieces and chop them after they cool.

To pulverize or grind nuts in a food processor without making paste or nut butter, start with a perfectly dry processor bowl and blade, and have the nuts at room temperature. Frozen or cold nuts will release moisture that will turn the nuts to paste, as will nuts still hot from the oven. Use short pulses, stopping from time to time to scrape the corners of the processor bowl with a skewer or chopstick. If you observe these rules, there is no particular need to add some of the flour or sugar from the recipe to the nuts to keep them dry, although you may do so as an extra precaution.

Spices

For the best and brightest flavors, use spices that still smell potent in the bottle. For the recipes in this book, I prefer true Ceylon cinnamon (called *canela* in Mexico), which has a more complex, almost citrusy, flavor than the more familiar hot, spicy cassia cinnamon that Americans know best. When you buy cinnamon sticks, you can recognize the variety by color and texture: Cassia sticks are reddish brown and as hard as wood; they are often used as stirring sticks for holiday drinks. Ceylon or *canela* cinnamon sticks are buff-colored rolls of papery bark that are easy to crumble and can be chopped with a heavy knife. Look for Ceylon cinnamon or *canela* in specialty food stores or Latin markets, or order it by mail from Penzeys Spices (see Sources, page 366).

Sugar

I use cane sugar rather than beet sugar for baking and dessert making. Chemically the two substances are exactly the same, yet too many bakers and pastry chefs that I know have reported differences and disappointments with beet sugar. All of the recipes in this book were tested with C&H pure cane sugar (granulated, golden brown, or dark brown) purchased in the supermarket. After having several cakes fall, I now avoid sugar with added fructose. (Granulated sugar is, by definition, a combination of sucrose and fructose, but when fructose is on the ingredients list, it means that extra fructose has been added.)

Sugars seem to vary in coarseness in different parts of the country. Coarse sugar makes cookies less tender and may cause butter cakes to collapse as well. If your sugar is as coarse as regular table salt and/or your cookies are tough or your butter cakes sometimes sink, switch to "bar sugar," fine granulated sugar, or even superfine sugar—or simply process your regular granulated sugar briefly in the food processor before using it. (Or use C&H bakers' sugar.)

Light (golden) brown and dark brown sugars impart wonderful caramel or butterscotch flavor to desserts. I usually specify my preference for light or dark brown sugar, but you can use them interchangeably. Brown sugar should be lump-free before it is added to a batter or dough, as it is unlikely to smooth after it is added. Soft lumps can be squeezed with your fingers or mashed with a fork. If the sugar is quite hard or has hard lumps, save it for your oatmeal. If you soften the sugar by warming it, the warm sugar may cause a batter to separate or curdle: Make applesauce instead. Brown sugar is measured by packing it fairly firmly into the measuring cup.

Vanilla

EXTRACT I use only pure vanilla extract. There are no rules, really, but when I want classic vanilla flavor or a subtle backdrop in chocolate desserts, I choose Bourbon vanilla from Madagascar or Mexican vanilla. When I want a more floral or exotic flavor, I use Tahitian.

POWDER Vanilla powder is a good way to get vanilla flavor without adding any liquid to the recipe. I found it helpful in flavoring a low-fat cheesecake batter without adding unwanted extra moisture. But the seeds from a real vanilla pod or the ground-up pod itself is even purer and more exciting.

BEANS These are slightly more time-consuming to use, but luxurious. Split the bean lengthwise and scrape the seeds into a batter, dough, or custard. In the latter case, be sure to steep the whole pod in the liquid as well, then retrieve and discard it later. I also use ground-up whole vanilla beans in cookie dough, cheesecake batter, and ice creams. If you can't find jars of ground vanilla beans (not to be confused with vanilla powder), you can chop a whole bean and grind it as fine as possible in a coffee or spice grinder.

A Chocolate Primer

HOW CHOCOLATE IS MADE

The world's supply of chocolate is produced from cacao cultivated in a narrow band that encircles the globe, twenty degrees north and south of the equator and in Hawaii. Cocoa beans, the seeds of the cacao tree, are the source of all forms of cocoa and chocolate. The rich, heady, sensual chocolate that we know and love is the result of a complicated processing of these beans, not unlike the miracle of art and science that transforms grapes into wine.

Cacao trees grow only to about twenty feet high. White blossoms, followed by colorful fruit, form directly on the spindly trunks and lower branches, giving cacao groves the exotic appearance of a movie set for a tropical fantasy. The fruit, elongated heavy grooved pods from eight to twelve inches long, may be deep ocher, red, green, or taupe, depending on ripeness and variety.

After harvesting, the pods are split open with a machete to reveal a cluster of twenty-four to forty seeds embedded in a viscous white pulp. At this point, the pulp has a fresh, cool, mildly sweet fruity flavor, somewhat reminiscent of a fresh litchi nut, while the seeds themselves have very little flavor. The seeds and pulp are scooped out, transferred to boxes, and covered with mats or palm or banana leaves (or sheets of plastic) to ferment. This takes about four days, during which time workers frequently turn the heaps with shovels to promote even fermentation. As the pulp ferments, it is converted to alcohol, then acetic acid (vinegar), which in turn transforms the meat of the cocoa beans and creates flavor precursors that later, with care and skilled manufacturing techniques, become the incomparable rich complex flavors of the chocolate.

The fermented pulp ultimately drains away, leaving behind the moist fermented beans. The beans are spread out to dry for several more days (ideally in the sun) before they are bagged and shipped to chocolate factories. Proper fermentation and drying are critical to the quality and flavor of the chocolate that will ultimately be produced from the beans. If you have ever tasted chocolate that tastes smoky, for example, it may mean the beans were dried over a fire rather than in the sun. Harsh-flavored chocolate may be a result of inadequate fermentation, while a moldy flavor signals moldy beans from insufficient drying or badly managed fermentation.

Although properly fermented and dried beans, still considered raw, now contain the essential elements for chocolate flavor and quality, at this stage they barely taste of chocolate. The chocolate flavor and quality potential is realized—or not— at the chocolate factory. Here, in separate batches, beans from different parts of the world, with different flavor profiles, are inspected for quality, cleaned, roasted, and then winnowed to remove their thin shells, or hulls. The roasted beans shatter into fragments in the process of winnowing. They are called nibs. Although some boutique manufacturers make single-source chocolates, it is more usually the case that nibs from different origins are fragments blended to create the desired chocolate flavor. Once blended, the nibs are finely ground to a thick paste called chocolate liquor. Chocolate liquor hardened into bars or squares is the unsweetened baking chocolate we buy in supermarkets. It is also the defining ingredient in all other forms of chocolate.

Chocolate liquor has two significant components: fat, called cocoa butter, and nonfat dry cocoa solids. Cocoa butter is a unique fat that is responsible for both the challenges of working with chocolate and the luxurious sensation of eating it. It is the complex crystal structure of cocoa butter that requires that we temper chocolate in order to harden it properly. Even when solid, cocoa butter melts close to our body temperature, which gives chocolate its most sensual characteristic—it literally melts in our mouths. But, for all of that, cocoa butter is nearly tasteless. Most of the chocolate flavor is in the other component of chocolate liquor, the nonfat dry solids—which you could think of as fat-free cocoa powder.

Chocolate liquor is the necessary ingredient of any kind of chocolate, but extra cocoa butter is usually added to enhance flavor, fluidity, and smoothness when making sweetened chocolate. Where does the extra cocoa butter come from? Cocoa butter is obtained in the process of manufacturing cocoa, when most of the fat is extracted from the chocolate liquor with a hydraulic press. Then the remaining partially defatted liquor is pulverized into cocoa powder. (Some special-purpose chocolates used by pastry chefs may have extra cocoa powder added instead of extra cocoa butter.)

Cocoa butter, so necessary in manufacturing chocolate, is also an important ingredient in the cosmetics industry. What a chocolate lover may regard as the process of manufacturing cocoa is more accurately a process for extracting cocoa butter, the more valuable commodity. In the larger economic picture, cocoa powder is a by-product of cocoa butter extraction!

Sugar, vanilla, or vanillin and a little lecithin are also added to the chocolate liquor to make sweetened chocolates, including bittersweet and semisweet. Dried or condensed milk or cream is added to make milk chocolate. The best white chocolate is made similarly to milk chocolate, but starts with cocoa butter only instead of chocolate liquor. (Because it doesn't contain chocolate liquor, white chocolate is not technically considered chocolate.)

Fine chocolate destined for eating and candy making, and baking too, is then conched: The chocolate liquor, sugar, and other ingredients are mixed and scraped against a slightly rough surface. The friction of the conch heats the chocolate and drives off unwanted volatile flavors and aromas, further improving the taste of the chocolate. Fine chocolate may be conched for twenty-four to forty-eight hours or more—each manufacturer makes a judgment call here. Long conching is a necessary, though costly, step in the manufacture of the finest chocolates, and to a point it improves both flavor and texture. Past that point, though, conching can eliminate desirable flavors and make the chocolate so smooth that it feels slimy on the palate. After conching, the chocolate is tempered, molded, cooled, and packaged.

Blended Versus Single-Origin and Varietal Chocolates

Chocolate manufacturers normally blend cocoa beans from more than one source. Like wine grapes and coffee beans, cocoa beans from different parts of the world, or even from different plantations in the same region, have different tastes. Blending allows the chocolate maker to create a signature flavor that becomes associated with and defines that brand.

Chocolate that is not made from a blend of beans is referred to as varietal or single-origin chocolate. The terms tend to be used interchangeably, although, strictly speaking, a varietal chocolate would be made from only one of the three (some say four) cacao species, while single-origin chocolate would imply chocolate made with cocoa beans, regardless of species, from a single region, area, or farm. *Varietal* is a questionable term, however, since cacao species are no longer pure or completely distinct from one another; still, cacao from a single region may be the closest thing to a single species that exists today. In any case, the terms are now used to refer to chocolate made with cocoa beans from a single place.

The traditional view is that a chocolate made from varietal or single-origin cocoa beans is unbalanced or incomplete and that blending is the real art of chocolate making. The argument is supported by a very practical reality. Cacao is a Third World crop subject to weather, soil conditions, farming practices, economics, and local politics; it varies in quality and abundance from season to season. Chocolate makers who blend beans from different sources can adjust their blends and manufacturing process to compensate for the variations in the beans. If beans from one source are more acidic or fruity than usual, a lesser proportion may be used in the blend. If other beans are scarce or the quality is poor, they might be replaced by beans with similar characteristics from another source. The blend is ever-changing as the chocolate maker tries to balances acidity, high and low flavor notes, fruit, spiciness, and the like to produce a relatively consistent, pleasing flavor. On the economic side, blending is also a hedge against price fluctuations.

But there are now fascinating single-source bittersweet and semisweet chocolates made with cacao from a single region, or even one farm. Varietal wines and single-origin, even single-estate, coffees and teas are well known to us, but the idea is newer with chocolate. It reflects an increasingly sophisticated taste and curiosity, an appreciation for chocolate flavors that are not just sweet. It also suggests a growing awareness of what is called *terroir*—the unique contribution of locale, of soil and climate—to the flavor, aroma, and texture of food. Single-origin chocolates allow us to taste chocolate flavors that do not otherwise stand alone. Imagine if you were passionate about the symphony and you heard, for the very first time, the solo voice of a cello. Or, if the only wines you had ever tasted were blended from different grapes, how could you resist the chance to taste a chardonnay or Zinfandel for the first time? Single-origin chocolates educate the palate and mind; they broaden our understanding of what chocolate tastes like, making it abundantly clear that there is no single definition of chocolate flavor. (See Sources, page 366, for mail-order information.)

As compelling as the idea of single-origin chocolate is, there can be problems with consistent quality from batch to batch. I have tasted divine single-source chocolates, only to be disappointed when I taste the same maker's chocolate again weeks or months later.

Even if they never become thoroughly mainstream, single-source or varietal chocolates could ultimately improve the quality of cacao, and thus all chocolate, worldwide. Manufacturers dependent on specific cacao sources pay more to ensure quality and availability. If cacao becomes more profitable, farmers plant more of it, cultivate it more carefully, and give more attention to the critical fermentation and drying processes. A more profitable crop should also result in better conditions and pay for cacao workers, so everyone benefits. In the meantime, we may have to let go of the belief that consistency is the paramount value in chocolate and embrace the notion that, like wine, a good varietal chocolate has certain characteristic flavors but cannot taste exactly the same from batch to batch.

TYPES OF CHOCOLATE

These are the various types of chocolate I call for in the recipes in this book.

COCOA NIBS Nibs, the newest chocolate ingredient available to cooks, are roasted, hulled, and broken cocoa beans, the very essence of chocolate. They are crunchy and relatively bitter, and have within them deep primal chocolate flavors ranging from toasted nuts to wine to berries, tropical fruit, or citrus, to grass or spice.

They encompass every possible nuance of flavor found in chocolate, as well as some flavors normally eliminated in the chocolate-making process. Crushed, ground, chopped, left in their natural form, or infused, nibs add something special to any number of sweet as well as savory recipes.

UNSWEETENED CHOCOLATE, AKA CHOCOLATE LIQUOR *Chocolate liquor* is the professional term for unsweetened chocolate. It is nothing more than ground cocoa nibs— pure roasted and hulled cocoa beans to which a little vanilla is sometimes added. Because they are like nuts in structure and in fat content, cocoa nibs become an oily semiliquid paste with the friction and pressure of the grinding process, just as peanuts become peanut butter. Unlike peanut butter, chocolate liquor hardens when tempered and cooled. Home cooks buy it in familiar baking squares or bars labeled unsweetened baking chocolate. Meanwhile, chocolate liquor is the essential ingredient in any type of chocolate, from the most intense bar of bittersweet to the sweetest milk chocolate. Only white chocolate, which is not really chocolate at all, does not contain chocolate liquor. (As mentioned earlier, chocolate liquor is comprised of two important components: cocoa butter, which is the fat, and nonfat dry cocoa solids, which can be thought of as completely fat-free cocoa powder.)

COCOA POWDER The cocoa powder that we use to make hot cocoa or desserts is made by removing 75 to 85 percent of the cocoa butter from chocolate liquor (see page 44) and then pulverizing the partially defatted mass that remains. With all of the flavor and none of the fat, cocoa is essentially a concentrated form of cocoa bean. And, because cocoa beans are naturally tart and acidic (characteristics that provide fruitiness and complexity in chocolate), those qualities are exaggerated in cocoa powder. The tendency for cocoa to be harsh is exacerbated by the fact that the best cocoa beans are normally reserved for producing chocolate. With rare exception, cocoa is made from beans of lesser quality.

There are two types of cocoa: natural (or nonalkalized) and Dutch-process (or alkalized). Natural cocoa powder is described above. It is bitter and strong. The best-quality natural cocoa is complex and fruity and wonderfully flavorful. Natural cocoa, with its harshness tamed by sugar in the recipes, delivers a strong hit of flavor in American favorites such as brownies and fudge. It also makes flavorful cakes and cookies with a tender crumb, excellent beverages, and remarkable chocolate desserts with less than the usual amount of fat.

Dutch-processing was developed in an attempt to improve natural cocoa powder. We can't know what cocoa beans were like in 1828, when Conrad Van Houten figured out how to squeeze the fat from them to make cocoa powder in the first place, but we can bet that the results were pretty harsh. He went on to invent the process, still used today, for treating cocoa with chemical alkalis to make it less harsh and acidic. (It was once also believed to render the cocoa more soluble in liquids, but this has turned out not to be true.)

Dutch-processing, or Dutching, gives cocoa an appetizing rich, dark reddish brown color that we intuitively (if erroneously) associate with deep flavor. In reducing acidity, Dutching strips some of the natural fruit flavors, high notes, and complexity from cocoa. The process also adds a different flavor to the cocoa, whether it is the flavor of the chemical itself or something produced in the marriage of the chocolate with the chemical. Regardless, this flavor, mingled and perhaps confused with chocolate flavor, has developed a following of its own. Extreme Dutching gives cocoa a charcoal black color and distinctive, although not particularly chocolatey, flavor. This "black" cocoa is responsible for the color and flavor of a popular sandwich cookie, which happens to be the highest-grossing cookie sold in supermarkets!

Fans of Dutch-process cocoa extol its rich color, toasted, nutty flavor, and coffee notes. Detractors find the taste dull, dusty, chemical, uniform, and lacking in fruit. I hope the current trend toward more rather than less Dutching (to produce darker and darker cocoa) will be a passing fad. When I use a Dutch-process cocoa, I prefer one that is moderately rather than highly alkalized. I like Valrhona, Pernigotti, Droste, and Guittard Jersey.

Dutch-process cocoa has enjoyed a surge in popularity in the last generation or so, possibly because European chefs use it or because of its color or because there have been so few high-quality natural cocoas. Usually, however, when a recipe specifies Dutch-process cocoa, it represents the preference of the chef or author, or a trend, rather than a requirement for success with the recipe. Some chefs, myself included, use both natural and Dutch-process cocoa.

You can go wrong by switching cocoas in a recipe that includes baking powder or baking soda because these leavenings react with the acidity of the cocoa. But in recipes without leavenings, natural and Dutch-process cocoas can be substituted for one another, and I absolutely encourage you to experiment and to choose cocoa for its flavor rather than its color.

If you roll truffles in cocoa, Dutch-process may look darker and more luscious than most natural cocoas, but I suggest that you close your eyes and put a little cocoa on your tongue before choosing. I used to roll my truffles in Dutch-process cocoa, but tasting converted me to Scharffen Berger Natural Cocoa Powder. Tasting is so important. If you can't tolerate cocoa on your tongue, make a cup of very lightly sweetened hot cocoa or a batch of brownies with several brands and styles to find your favorite. The recipes in this book tell you when you must use a particular cocoa, when you can choose, and what my preferences are.

Most cocoas, both natural and Dutch-process, vary in fat content from 10 to 24 percent. In general, supermarket natural cocoas contain only 10 to 12 percent cocoa butter, which almost automatically puts them at a quality disadvantage when compared to Dutch-process cocoa. Except for Hershey's European Style, which has somewhat less, Dutch-process cocoas tend to contain 20 to 24 percent cocoa butter. Premium natural cocoas with 20 to 24 percent cocoa butter are available from specialty retailers and by mail-order and they are definitely worth trying (see Sources, page 366). There are also nonfat and low-fat cocoas with less cocoa butter, but in general, the best-quality cocoas are those with the highest fat, and they should be used for their superior flavor even in low-fat recipes.

Dutch-process cocoas may or may not be labeled "Dutch-process," but the ingredient statement should say "cocoa processed with alkali." Natural cocoa is rarely labeled with the word *natural* on the package; the ingredient statement will simply say "cocoa" or "unsweetened cocoa powder." Absent the words *alkalized* or *Dutch-process* on a label, you should be able to assume that the cocoa is natural. However,

I have seen packages that are not correctly labeled. The highly regarded Maison du Chocolat cocoa, which is Dutch-process, carries no indication of it on the label. Similarly, although the industrial bulk package of Valrhona cocoa indicates that it is Dutch-process, the retail package does not.

Ghirardelli, Hershey's (regular, not European Style), and Nestlé are all natural cocoas readily available at supermarkets. Most supermarkets also carry Droste, the best of the widely available Dutch-process cocoas. For better-quality cocoas such as the superb Scharffen Berger (natural), Merckens (natural or Dutch-process), Valrhona (Dutch-process), Pernigotti (Dutch-process), Bensdorp (Dutch-process), Guittard (natural) or Guittard Jersey (Dutch-process), you have to go to specialty stores or order by mail (see Sources, page 366).

BITTERSWEET AND SEMISWEET CHOCOLATES These are the most dynamic and exciting chocolates to eat and bake with, and an important reason for this book. Although the official definition of bittersweet and semisweet chocolates has not changed in recent years, the chocolates in this category are now more varied than ever before. Technically, today's bittersweet and semisweet chocolates may contain anywhere from 35 percent to well over 70 percent chocolate liquor. Chocolates with a higher percentage of chocolate liquor are a gift to lovers of bittersweet and a testimony to changing tastes, but they are a challenge for home bakers or confectioners: It is no longer safe to consider all bittersweet and semisweet chocolates interchangeable in recipes.

The chocolate industry makes no distinction between bittersweet and semisweet chocolate. By federal regulation, both must simply contain a minimum of 35 percent chocolate liquor. In reality, and for some time now, American and some foreign manufacturers have observed an unofficial minimum of about 50 percent chocolate liquor. Until recently, most bittersweet and semisweet chocolates, including premium American brands and some European ones, contained an average of 55 percent (with a low of 50 and high of about 58 percent) chocolate liquor. These are the mainstream bittersweet and semisweet chocolates that have been most readily available on grocers' shelves and most widely used by home cooks. Sugar makes up the remainder (i.e., nearly half) of these bars, except in brands that contain small quantities of milk solids (up to 12 percent is allowed). With roughly the same ratio of ingredients, traditionally a standard bittersweet chocolate may be no less sweet than a standard semisweet, and any of these chocolates could be used interchangeably in recipes.

But now, the increasing number of imported and boutique chocolates containing at least a little and often a lot more chocolate liquor has effectively, if not officially, redefined bittersweet and semisweet chocolate. *High-percentage chocolates* is not yet an official category, but the term is a handy way to describe bittersweet and semisweet chocolates with more than the standard percentages of chocolate liquor, less sugar, and no milk solids. The percentage tells how much of the bar, by weight, is chocolate liquor; the remainder of the bar is sugar. Although most of these chocolates are imported, American manufacturers have begun to make them too.

Chocolate that contains 70 percent (or more) chocolate liquor behaves differently in recipes from chocolate containing only 55 percent liquor. Bakers and dessert makers accustomed to standard chocolates need to make adjustments to recipes when using chocolate with more than 62 percent chocolate liquor. Higher-percentage chocolates make cake or torte batters a little thicker and cakes made with them may be done a little sooner or seem drier than before; ganaches may curdle or separate. A major goal of this book is to explain how chocolates with different percentages of chocolate liquor affect recipes—and to encourage their use. The Chocolate Notes that accompany each recipe explain how you can use high-percentage chocolates successfully. For a more comprehensive understanding, see A Dessert Maker's Guide to High-Percentage Chocolates (page 344) in the Appendix.

How do you know the percentage of chocolate liquor in a particular bar of chocolate? Imported chocolate bars often have the percentage of chocolate liquor (also referred to as cacao, cocoa masse, cocoa mass, cocoa, cocoa solids, dry cocoa solids, or simply cocoa beans) displayed prominently on the label (see Composition of Unsweetened, Bittersweet, and Semisweet Chocolate Bars, page 346). A few of the newest American chocolates are labeled. And chocolates labeled "extra bittersweet" usually contain a higher percentage of chocolate liquor. But the majority of American chocolates are the standard chocolates described on page 51, usually containing between 50 and 58 percent chocolate liquor. If you are curious about a particular chocolate, see the list on page 58 for chocolates in the standard percentage range.

Is a high percentage of chocolate liquor an indication of quality? That is a common belief in Europe, and it *should* be true. Chocolates with more chocolate liquor and less sugar cost more to make because cocoa beans are more expensive than sugar. Also, there is less sugar to hide harsh or unpleasant flavors, so the quality of the cocoa beans should be that much better.

SWEET CHOCOLATE AND SWEET DARK CHOCOLATE I do not use these types of chocolate in recipes.

MILK CHOCOLATE Made of sugar, milk solids (at least 12 percent), chocolate liquor (at least 10 percent), added cocoa butter, and butterfat, milk chocolate is softer and milder than dark chocolate and has a pronounced flavor of milk or cream, often with caramel undertones. Most milk chocolate is eaten plain or in candies rather than used for baking, but it can be used in frostings and fillings or mousses. It is worth choosing a brand that you enjoy eating. I like the milk chocolates made by Callebaut and El Rey, the former for its rich balance of caramelized creamy chocolate flavor and the latter for its complexity and earthiness. Other quality imported milk chocolates are Valrhona and Lindt. Guittard and Ghirardelli are good American-made milk chocolates.

WHITE CHOCOLATE/WHITE CONFECTIONERY COATING According to the FDA, chocolate must contain chocolate liquor, which is made up of cocoa fat (called cocoa butter) and nonfat dry cocoa solids (the main component of cocoa powder). Even when it is made with cocoa butter, so-called white chocolate does not contain nonfat dry cocoa solids. Without both, it is not considered to contain chocolate liquor and cannot be called chocolate; it is officially known as "white confectionery coating." However, all white confectionery coatings are not created equal. While the better ones are made with cocoa butter, others are made with vegetable fats such as partially hydrogenated palm kernel, palm, soy, and/or cottonseed oil instead. The differences are palpable.

White chocolate made with cocoa butter is a creamy off-white to buttery yellow or ivory, never stark white. Because cocoa butter melts at body temperature and carries nuances of chocolate flavor, it adds the melt-in-the-mouth texture, the chocolatey aroma, and the quick release of flavor characteristic of fine chocolate. The ingredients of such white chocolates (sugar, cocoa butter, milk or cream, and vanilla) and the manufacturing process are the same as those for milk chocolate, but without the dry cocoa solids. Confectionery coatings made from other fats do not compare; they are almost stark white and taste only like ultrasweet candy.

Since the term *white chocolate* persists, regardless of the FDA, I wish it could be officially reserved for white confectionery coatings made with cocoa butter. To make sure you are buying white chocolate with cocoa butter, read the label. Cocoa butter should be the only fat other than butter or milk fat listed. Callebaut, El Rey, and Lindt are the brands of white chocolate that I like best.

Like milk chocolate, white chocolate is best in candies, fillings, frostings, mousses, and other uncooked desserts. Any recipe in this book that calls for white chocolate means chocolate that has cocoa butter as its only vegetable fat.

CHOCOLATE CHIPS, MORSELS, AND CHUNKS Chocolate chips, morsels, and chunks are formulated to look, taste, and perform best in cookies or cakes, where it is desirable that they remain intact. They are made with less cocoa butter than the best bar chocolate, so when they get hot, they hold their shape rather than melting into puddles to burn on a hot cookie sheet. Chocolate chips et al are also much sweeter and coarser than most bar chocolates. They only seem smooth and not-too-sweet in contrast to the coarser texture and sweeter taste of the cookie or cake they are imbedded in.

I do not recommend substituting chocolate chips/morsels/chunks for bar chocolate in any recipe that calls for the chocolate to be melted and blended with other ingredients. The very characteristics that make them successful for their intended purpose work against them here. When melted, they are thick and viscous and hard to handle, and they deliver too much sweetness and too little chocolate flavor.

On the other hand, although there is a risk of scorching, I do sometimes use chopped bar chocolate rather than chocolate chips when I want less sweetness and a more sophisticated chocolate flavor. A number of other pastry chefs and bakers do the same, and, in response, some chocolate manufacturers have begun making "gourmet" chips or chunks that are smoother, less sweet, and richer in cocoa butter.

PASTILLES, BUTTONS, PISTOLES, CALLETS, AND RIBBONS You may see these in specialty shops or mail-order catalogs (see Sources, page 366). Not to be confused with chocolate chips, these small drops, morsels, wafers, ribbons, or bits of chocolate (white, milk, semisweet, or bittersweet) were designed to be melted. Originally created for chefs and commercial bakers and chocolatiers, they eliminate the step of chopping chocolate before melting it. They are wonderfully convenient, but they vary in type and quality from excellent to ordinary, depending on the manufacturer.

PREMELTED CHOCOLATE IN PREMEASURED POUCHES Don't even think about it!

UNDERSTANDING BITTERSWEET AND SEMISWEET CHOCOLATE LABELS

Bittersweet and semisweet chocolate labels can be confusing. First, there is no official distinction between bittersweet and semisweet chocolate (see Bittersweet and Semisweet Chocolates, page 51). Second, manufacturers use several different terms for cocoa bean content. As you read further, remember that roasted cocoa beans are roughly half fat (cocoa butter) and half nonfat dry cocoa solids (which you can imagine as fat-free cocoa powder), and that extra amounts of either component may be added to chocolate separately.

Chocolate liquor is the usual American term for cocoa bean content, but other terms include *cocoa mass* (or *masse*), *cacao* or *cacao beans, cocoa beans, cocoa, cocoa solids,* and *dry cocoa solids.* Technically, these terms do not all have exactly the same meaning in all contexts, but when they appear with a percentage on a label, they mean just one thing: roasted cocoa beans, including any extra cocoa butter or nonfat dry cocoa solids added.

Meanwhile, *cocoa, cocoa solids,* and *dry cocoa solids* all have other meanings in other contexts. While *cocoa* sometimes (and customarily in England) means chocolate liquor or the commodity cocoa beans, it otherwise refers to the powdered product we use to make beverages or sprinkle on truffles, made from chocolate liquor after most of the fat is removed. This is like using the word *milk* at times to mean "milk" and at other times to mean "cream." Similarly, *cocoa solids* and *dry cocoa solids* are sometimes used to mean chocolate liquor, but other times they mean only the fat-free component of chocolate liquor—more accurately called nonfat dry cocoa solids.

Ingredient statements are another matter. Total cocoa bean content may be reflected in a single term such as *chocolate liquor* (or *unsweetened chocolate, cocoa liquor,* or any of the other terms mentioned above), including any added cocoa butter or nonfat dry cocoa solids, or added cocoa butter and nonfat dry solids may also be listed separately. Whether or not these are listed separately in the ingredient list, they are always considered part of the percentage when a percent appears on the front label.

STORING CHOCOLATE AND COCOA

Bittersweet, semisweet, and unsweetened chocolate will stay good for at least a year if wrapped airtight and kept cool, away from moisture and odors (*never store packages of chocolate in the cupboard with spices or other aromatic foods*). I try not to let chocolate sit that long.

Milk chocolate and white chocolate get stale and develop off flavors much more quickly. Buy only what you will use within about two months, or divide a larger quantity into portions and freeze the extra, wrapped airtight in foil and/or plastic and then enclosed in an airtight freezer bag. To avoid condensation on the chocolate, thaw it completely before removing it from the freezer bag and unwrapping.

Store cocoa in an airtight container in a cupboard away from herbs and spices or other aromatic substances. The full dimension of cocoa flavors fades over time, so it is best to use it within a few months, or a year at most.

CHOOSING CHOCOLATE (OR COCOA)

Buy chocolate that you like and can afford, of course, but do branch out a little. I wrote this book to inspire more chocolate dessert lovers to stray from the more familiar baking chocolates on the supermarket shelves. Good or great chocolate makes better, more complex, and more interesting desserts. Today the distinction between chocolate for eating and chocolate for cooking has become completely blurred, and we have more choices than ever before. Plain bittersweet and semisweet chocolate bars—without nuts, raisins, bits of toffee, or other distracting embellishments—may or may not be labeled for baking or eating, but they are perfect for either. To decide what chocolate you want to eat or cook with, you owe it to yourself to taste a wide variety.

You can begin to learn your own style and preferences by trying the following highly regarded brands: Callebaut, El Rey, Guittard (especially the E. Guittard line), Michel Cluizel, Scharffen Berger, and Valrhona. Each manufacturer makes more than one chocolate, often using different bean blends or percentages of chocolate liquor; you may like one particular chocolate more than another, even in the same brand. Branch out and try other brands too.

Keep in mind that the simplest recipes—those with the fewest ingredients—are the best ones for showing off individual characteristics and nuances of an interesting chocolate. When budget is an issue, use a basic good-tasting chocolate in any recipe with loads of sugar, flour, and fat (cookies, cakes, sweet candies like fudge, and brownies), and save the finest and most complex chocolates for truffles, mousses, sauces, etc.

The Chocolate Notes (see About the Chocolate Notes, page 65) that follow the recipes will help you use a wide range of chocolate, from standard, easily available brands to artisanal chocolates that are intensely bittersweet.

WHAT ARE STANDARD BITTERSWEET OR SEMISWEET CHOCOLATES? It is not necessary to buy imported, high-percentage or difficult-to-find chocolate to use this book. Most of the recipes in this book call for "standard" bittersweet or semisweet chocolate commonly found in supermarkets—with separate instructions (in the Chocolate Notes) for substituting specialized chocolates if you so desire.

The standard chocolates I refer to include American-made bittersweet or semisweet chocolates without percentages marked on the front or back of the package, or any American or imported bittersweet or semisweet chocolate labeled with a percentage that does not exceed 60 percent. Standard chocolate does not mean inferior or ordinary chocolate. It means chocolate with a cocoa bean content between 50 and 60 percent. Here are some examples, both ordinary and sublime, in alphabetical order.

> Baker's Bittersweet or Semi-Sweet
> Callebaut Bloc bittersweet (55%, in the 17.5 ounce package)
> Côte d'Or
> Cuba Venchi Fondente (56%)
> E. Guittard
> El Rey Bucare Dark (58%)
> Ghiraradelli Bittersweet or Semi-Sweet
> Guittard French Vanilla
> Guittard Gourmet Bittersweet
> Hershey's Semi-sweet
> Hershey's Special Dark
> Lindt Excellence Swiss Bittersweet (not Excellence 70%)
> Lindt Surfin
> Nestlé Semi-Sweet
> Rapunzel Semisweet (55%)
> Valrhona Equatoriale Dark (58%)

Chocolate in the 60 to 62 percent range can sometimes be substituted for standard chocolates as well. Consult the Chocolate Notes after the recipes for specific advice.

When asking about or looking for chocolate in stores, be aware that the companies that make them—especially those made for professional use—usually make several chocolates with different percentages. Look at the percentage on the label (if it is listed) as well as the brand name. If you buy bulk or broken chocolate labeled only with a manufacturer's brand name, find out which specific chocolate it is and what the percentage is before you buy it.

QUALITIES TO LOOK FOR

APPEARANCE Properly processed and stored chocolate should be glossy with no surface blemishes. The interior, though less glossy, should be dark and evenly colored, without a stratified or cakey appearance.

Improper storage, including moisture, heat, or even temperature fluctuations, can cause "bloom"—a dull grayish or mottled appearance, with or without streaks or spots—on the surface of the chocolate. If the chocolate has been jostled or tumbled with other pieces of chocolate, it may become scuffed or scarred; this should not be confused with bloom. Neither bloom nor scuffing indicates spoilage. But the damage can diminish your aesthetic enjoyment of the chocolate, and severe bloom can change its texture, mouthfeel, and flavor. These flaws are inconsequential, however, if the chocolate is to be melted and made into a confection or dessert, or retempered.

The large thick bars of chocolate supplied to chocolatiers and pastry chefs—and often broken up and sold in random weights to home bakers—are sometimes less than perfectly tempered in the center, due to inadequate cooling during the manufacturing process. This is nothing to worry about, though, because the bar is destined to be remelted and transformed into a confection or dessert, or retempered for molding or dipping.

TEXTURE Good chocolate should break with a crisp "snap"; it should not crumble or break in layers, although this may occur if chocolate is improperly stored. Milk chocolate and white chocolate are a little softer than darker chocolate, but they too should break with a snap.

AROMA Different chocolates smell different from one another, but good chocolate should always have a pleasing natural "chocolatey" aroma, unmarred by the smell of paper or wrapping materials. And, obviously, there should be no rancid or other off or foreign smells.

MOUTHFEEL *Mouthfeel* is the "technical" term for what chocolate (or another food) feels like in your mouth. Cocoa butter has a melting temperature so close to our own body temperature that it increases the sensual appeal of this special food. Chocolate should melt readily as it is warmed by your tongue and palate. It should feel smooth and creamy as it melts, not slimy or greasy, grainy or powdery.

TASTE This, of course, is subjective. Chocolates are as varied as wines, coffees, or cheeses. No one can tell you what *you* like. What is divinely fruity and bittersweet to one may be too strong and sour for another. The more you taste and expose yourself to the varieties of chocolate, the more different chocolates you will enjoy. Your own taste criteria may even change over time.

MELTING CHOCOLATE

If you ask six pastry chefs or chocolatiers how to melt chocolate, you will get six different answers. Indeed, there are various ways to do the job, and we all have our preferences. The three main methods are the *double boiler,* the *water bath* (heatproof bowl in a pan of hot water), and the *microwave*. Each of these methods enables you to melt chocolate without scorching it, but none of the three can prevent you from burning it if you are not attentive!

There are only a couple of absolute rules—the rest is simply common sense and paying attention. It takes very little time and very little heat to melt chocolate. Unless you are otherwise instructed, all you are trying to do is *melt* the chocolate, until it is fluid and warm (not hot) to the touch. If you have to pull your finger away, even if the chocolate is not yet scorched, you've probably gone further than you should have. Melted chocolate at any temperature between about 100° and 120°F usually blends easily into batters, whereas melted chocolate that is too hot may disturb the emulsion in batters and ganaches, or melt or heat other ingredients unnecessarily. However, although 120°F is a "soft" ceiling often given to keep inexperienced cooks from abusing chocolate, exceeding 120°F does not have to be fatal. Contrary to what you may have read, melted bittersweet and semisweet chocolates can survive temperatures up to approximately 200°F (unless they contain milk solids). But there is rarely a reason to get anywhere close to that temperature. White and milk chocolates are entirely different animals.

They can and will burn at somewhere near 130°F; I try not to exceed 115°F. If you keep your attention on the melting chocolate, stay in touch with the temperature by dipping in a finger frequently, and remove the chocolate from the heat sooner rather than later, you will never burn chocolate, and the entire dance will soon become second nature.

A *double boiler* is the chocolate-melting method most commonly cited in recipes, but it is not necessary, and I prefer not to use one. As a teacher, I worry that students assume that melting in a double boiler is foolproof: It isn't. Remember that steam is even hotter than boiling water. Unless your double boiler is glass, the water is hidden from view, so you are less likely to notice whether it is boiling furiously (too hot), or only simmering gently (much better). So how can you be attentive? In addition, why limit yourself to the same size container whether you are melting two ounces of chocolate or twenty?

My melter of choice is a *water bath*. In my kitchen, it is a wide (at least 12-inch) skillet of not even simmering water, into which I can set a heatproof bowl (usually stainless steel) of any size I like. The wide skillet ensures that the rim of the bowl does not extend to the edge of the bath or beyond it, so it won't get too hot either for the chocolate or for you to hold when you are stirring. A wide skillet also keeps the water in view, so that I always know when it starts to simmer or boil. As long as I am attentive, the bath is very fast and easy to control.

If you feel you must create a makeshift double boiler by placing a bowl over a pot of water, be sure most of the bowl fits into the pot. A wide bowl over a narrow pot is a sure way to scorch the chocolate around the sides of the bowl, where it extends beyond the pot. And you are likely to burn your fingers on the rim as well. If and when I do use a double boiler, I flout the rule that says that the bottom of the top container must never touch the water: I make sure that the water not only touches the bottom but extends up the sides of the insert to wrap the lower half of the container in warmth! The ban on water touching the insert is a misplaced precaution that distracts from more important details, such as the temperature of the water and of the melting chocolate.

I also like to use a *microwave* for melting chocolate. It is clean and dry, so there is no risk of splashing or dripping water. It works perfectly as long as you zap in stages and, especially important, always stir in between whether the chocolate looks melted or not: Never try to melt all of the chocolate in one zap.

The following guide is based on my experience with an 800-watt GE Spacesaver II microwave. I melted the chocolate alone in a dry bowl, without any other ingredients. If your chocolate pieces are larger or smaller than mine, or if your microwave is more or less powerful, times will be different. Once there are only a few unmelted pieces left in the bowl, it is best to finish by stirring rather than microwaving the chocolate again.

Chop *semisweet*, *bittersweet*, or *unsweetened chocolate* into pieces no larger than almonds. Chop *milk chocolate* or *white chocolate* very fine or process it in a food processor to the size of coarse bread crumbs. In a microwave-safe glass container, heat chocolate on Medium (50%) power for the time indicated on the chart that follows, without interruption. These times are intended to melt the chocolate only partially. Stir well, even if it looks as if less than half of the chocolate is melted. Then, if necessary, add 5- to 10-second increments of additional heat for milk or white chocolate or 10- to 15-second increments for dark chocolate. Stir well after each zap. Stirring hastens melting and prevents you from overheating the chocolate.

STARTING TIMES (AFTER STIRRING WELL, ADD 5- TO 15-SECOND HEAT INTERVALS)

1 ounce	} 1½ minutes on Medium (50%) power
2 to 3 ounces	} 2½ minutes on Medium (50%) power
4 to 5 ounces	} 3 minutes on Medium (50%) power
6 to 8 ounces	} 3½ minutes on Medium (50%) power

CAUTION: Do not use these timings if you are melting chocolate with water, cream, or butter. Liquids and butter heat up fast and will melt the chocolate much more quickly.

Following are what I consider the three essential rules for successful chocolate melting, whichever method you use.

1. **AVOID MOISTURE**. Unless you are melting chocolate with adequate liquid or some other ingredient such as butter, make sure that the cutting board, knife, melting container, and stirring implements are perfectly dry. Just a little bit of moisture can seize the chocolate (see page 355). Don't cover the container of chocolate while it melts to protect it from steam—this may produce its own moisture in the form of condensation. If you are using a water bath, be careful to avoid inadvertently splashing or dripping water into the chocolate, but don't worry about the steam drifting up from the skillet. I have never seen rising steam change its mind and dive back down into a bowl of uncovered chocolate just for spite!

2. **CHOP THE CHOCOLATE**. Because it exposes a lot of surface area, chopping helps you control the melt and prevent burning. Smaller pieces melt faster, over lower heat, and they don't get too hot in the process, so long as you are watching and remove the chocolate as soon as or just before it is melted. How finely you chop depends on your patience and whether you want to spend more time at the front end with the knife, or more time later with the spatula stirring larger pieces over the heat. There are only two circumstances in which I take the time to chop chocolate really fine: I chop white chocolate and milk chocolate very fine because if these chocolates get too hot, they won't melt evenly but will instead thicken, turn gritty, and burn (see page 64). Fine pieces ensure a very quick, smooth melt with minimal heat. I also chop chocolate fine when a recipe calls for pouring a relatively small amount of hot cream (or other liquid) over the chocolate in order to melt it. In this case, it is simple common sense. If the chocolate is not chopped fine enough, it won't melt before the cream cools, and then you will have to spend time reheating it. In my recipes, I specify finely chopped chocolate only when it's necessary. Otherwise, medium or coarsely chopped chocolate works well. I use a chef's knife, serrated knife, or a pronged chocolate breaker. People who do not mind cleaning food processors can use one to chop chocolate, although the chocolate must first be coarsely chopped to prepare it for the processor. I don't use the processor unless I need a large quantity of very finely chopped chocolate; then it's great.

3. **STIR FREQUENTLY, PAY ATTENTION, ADJUST THE HEAT AS NECESSARY, AND PLEASE DIP YOUR FINGER**. Because I don't like double boilers, I always let the water touch the bottom

of the chocolate container, never worry about steam, and have little patience for chopping chocolate, you might conclude that I handle chocolate rather cavalierly. On the contrary. I am extremely attentive and quite finicky where it matters.

I stir melting chocolate frequently, whether I'm using a microwave or a water bath. Frequent stirring melts the chocolate faster and with less heat because it equalizes the temperature in the bowl and allows the warm fluid chocolate to help melt the remaining pieces.

I often turn the heat off under the bath well before the chocolate is melted and let the hot water finish the job. Even if I have turned the heat off, I try to remove the chocolate bowl from the bath early and stir to finish the melting. Once chocolate is melted, it's best to get it out of the bath because even with the burner turned off, the temperature of the chocolate will continue to rise if it sits in the hot water. If the chocolate cools off too much before you need it, just return it to the bath for a few seconds before using it. All of this becomes second nature once you realize that there is no precision involved and that dipping your finger frequently will tell you what you need to know.

An Extra Word About White Chocolate and Milk Chocolate

Milk chocolate is delicate, white chocolate even more so. These chocolates seem to need slower heating and more careful treatment, especially with small quantities. In my experience, they remain most fluid and easy to handle at temperatures below about 115°F. If I'm using only a small quantity, I chop the chocolate very fine, bring a water bath to a simmer, and turn it off. A full minute later, I set the bowl of chopped chocolate in it, and melt it with almost constant stirring. For larger quantities, a series of zaps in the microwave (on Low [30%] or Medium [50%] power) is easier. You can chop the chocolate less fine as long as you stir it frequently between zaps, even when it doesn't look at all melted. Signs of overheating or abuse are thickening and fine grit, although these may also be signs of old or poorly stored chocolate—but the negative result is the same.

About the Chocolate Notes

The Chocolate Notes that accompany almost every recipe in this book grew from the informal notes I began taking several years ago to reflect my experiences with the higher-percentage chocolates. Initially with dismay, then with growing interest, I began to realize that my tried-and-true recipes did not always turn out well when I made them with the wonderful new chocolates. Some cakes were dry, mousses gummy, ganaches curdled. I was using better chocolate but not always making better desserts.

To solve the problems that arose, I began making adjustments by trial and error, noting the results for each of the high-percentage chocolates I used. Later, when I finally thought to put what I knew about the composition of the chocolates into a kind of chart, the obvious fact that the percentage of sugar decreased inversely as the percentage of chocolate liquor increased became even more obvious. But then I realized that the increase in chocolate liquor meant that less extra cocoa butter was being added to the chocolate to adjust its flavor and fluidity—so the percentage of nonfat dry cocoa solids increased at a greater rate than that of cocoa butter. This fact is critical to understanding the behavior of high-percentage chocolates in recipes. In short, the effect of using a high-percentage bittersweet chocolate in a recipe rather than a standard bittersweet or semisweet one is not like simply adding more chocolate. It's like adding a little cocoa powder and subtracting sugar from the recipe at the same time. I ultimately created formulas to "translate" recipes that called for the old standard bittersweet or semisweet chocolate into successful recipes using the higher-percentage bittersweet chocolates. Each formula tells how much less chocolate to use, how much more sugar to add, and how to adjust the butter. The outcome will have about the same amount of nonfat dry cocoa solids, total sugar (sugar in the chocolate and granulated sugar combined), and total fat (butter in the recipe and cocoa butter combined) as the original recipe.

Not only does translating recipes like this generally work, to my greater delight, it does not necessarily produce results identical to the original recipe. Differences are due to the fact that granulated sugar and regular dairy butter affect the texture and melting characteristics of desserts differently than the finely milled sugar in the chocolate and the fat from the cocoa beans. The quartet of brownies on pages 93–94 is a fascinating example of four delicious recipes, each made with about the same amounts of nonfat dry cocoa solids, fat, and sugar, yet each with a different texture, crust, and appearance.

No matter how much I loved the brownies and what they taught me, there is much more to the story than balancing recipes mathematically. My main interest in using higher-percentage chocolates is to make more distinctive, less sweet, and more flavorful desserts. Formulas are only starting points, and the Chocolate Notes will take you far beyond them. I almost always round off the chocolate upward, never add the full sugar adjustment, and only sometimes adjust butter. But you will also see that the notes are not consistent from one recipe to another, because recipes are not equally sensitive to variations in chocolate. Also, some recipes require small changes in technique when using higher-percentage chocolates. Rather than simply doing the math, I have tested and tinkered to get the tastes and textures just the way I want them. Recipes that are more forgiving have fewer notes than recipes where matters of texture are especially delicate. I give the most explicit instructions where it makes the biggest difference. I did not intend to cover every single contingency, but rather, to set you on a well-lighted path with a good map. Common sense fills in the gaps. If I say that a recipe works well with any bittersweet or semisweet chocolate with up to and including 62 percent chocolate liquor, your results with 62 percent, of course, will be the least sweet. And if the notes call for 5 ounces of bittersweet 70 percent or 7 ounces of semisweet 62 percent, you will not go wrong by taking the middle ground, using 6 ounces of bittersweet 64 percent chocolate, even if I do not mention it in the notes.

The final key to the Chocolate Notes is this: I like the higher-percentage chocolates precisely for their intensity, so wherever possible, the adjustments for high-percentage chocolates yield increasingly bittersweet results as the percentage increases. This means that each recipe allows for a range of sweetness and intensity depending on the chocolate you choose. Arguably inconsistent, in reality, this scheme captures the richness of my testing and experimentation far better than applying a formula across the board (which I did only for the brownies and a few other recipes). To substitute a high-percentage chocolate for a sweeter standard chocolate without more bittersweet results, consult the formulas on pages 350–351 instead of the Chocolate Notes.

A NOTE ABOUT THE RECIPES WITH LESS FAT

Recipes with reduced fat are sprinkled throughout this book. They are easily spotted by the simple ❖ beside their titles. The recipes conform to the following self-imposed guidelines: Servings have less than 300 calories, less than 10 grams of fat, and usually less than 30 percent calories from fat. Because a limited amount of chocolate is used in these recipes, it is worth your while to choose chocolate with superb flavor. Please don't use low-fat or dietetic chocolate. All of the lower-fat recipes work well with standard bittersweet or semisweet chocolate or high-percentage chocolates up to and including those with 72 percent chocolate liquor. It is not necessary to modify recipes when using the latter; in fact, your results will be even better, although the percentage of calories from fat may slightly exceed 30 percent in some cases. For the story, a few tips, and the philosophy behind these recipes, see pages 191–193.

The Frog Hollow nectarines I recently brought home from the Monterey Market reminded me of peaches I had bought thirty years before in the Marché St. Didier, at the height of one Parisian summer. The fruits of memory were so perfectly ripe they teetered on the brink. They were so delicate, in my mind's eye, I see myself carrying them home on open palms, like a perfumed offering, although I know I couldn't really have done that and

CHOCOLATE AND THE NECTARINE

carried the rest of the shopping too. We ate those peaches for dessert, knowing they might not even last the night.

Thirty years later, I am in Berkeley sharing organic nectarines with my thirteen-year-old daughter, Lucy. We sit with the fruit and a paring knife and a plate. On the table there is no Flaky Nectarine Tart or Fresh Nectarine Ice Cream, nothing to suggest Mom is a pastry chef. Just the fruit and the knife. I tell her another slice of the Paris story and that leads to talking about perfect simple foods. Which, inevitably for me, leads to talking about chocolate. I suggest that putting exquisite chocolate with a perfect nectarine might ruin both.

The suggestion was hypothetical. Lucy knows that a perfect ripe nectarine wants no chocolate, needs no chocolate. But when I mentioned chocolate sauce (as another hypothetical example), she did look interested. I thought out loud that it might be possible. It would require the right chocolate, and the right sauce. I got up and mixed three tiny portions of sauce using the tart, fruity bittersweet chocolate that we both love to eat. I made one sauce with cream, one with milk, and one with water. We dipped slices of fruit into each as though sampling olive oil with chunks of good bread. The fruit, with its big tart juicy sweetness, made all of the sauces taste bitter, even sour, in comparison. "Ugh," we said.

The least offensive was the sauce made with cream. It was softer and lusher, and the cream buffered the natural tannins and the acidity in the chocolate slightly, so it tasted less sour against the acidic but sweet fruit. I added a little sugar to the sauce hoping to tame it further, but it was only a small improvement. Lucy announced that it was simply the wrong chocolate to go with a nectarine.

So I switched to a bittersweet Belgian chocolate, which is mellower and has less acidity to start with. I made the sauce with cream. Lucy decided it was a better match with the nectarine, but really boring. I thought the nectarine made the chocolate taste dull and flat. To wake up the chocolate flavor, I would have to back away from the cream. I made the Belgian chocolate sauce twice more, once with milk and once with water. The sauce with milk tasted brighter and the nectarine tasted better too. But the sauce made with water was better still! Now the nectarine and chocolate both finally tasted delicious. We "sampled" the combination repeatedly, which is always a good sign. I wondered if nectarine juice would be even better than water, but didn't get around to trying it that day.

Later that afternoon, one of my food magazines arrived in the mail. It's a magazine I enjoy and sometimes write for. It's the one that obsessively tests recipes to the point of exhaustion in search of superlatives: the ultimate roast chicken, the most exquisite chocolate brownie, the best lemon bar. The cover of the new issue proclaimed "The Perfect Bittersweet Chocolate Sauce!" Lucy was amused. "Perfect for what?" she wanted to know, speaking from experience.

Today, my daughter knows that chocolate is a magically complex ingredient, rather than just one single flavor. She knows there is no single best chocolate. For me the joy of this exquisite ingredient will always lie in the continuous rediscovery, the endless play, and the ongoing pleasure of tasting it.

This book is my journey with chocolate, from the time I was very young until the day of the nectarines.

2

Growing Up with Chocolate

Ice Cream and Brownies

I grew up in the suburban sprawl of Los Angeles in the fifties, an unpretentious place and time, on chocolate American style. Chocolate then was a treat, not junk food. I liked the shiny dark layer of skin— slightly chewy—on top of the Royal chocolate pudding. We ate Milky Ways directly from the freezer.

When we went to drive-in movies, my dad would buy Hershey bars from the concession stand and toss them in our laps as he climbed back into the car. We each unveiled and nibbled, with a particular private

IN PRAISE OF CHOCOLATE ICE CREAM

ritual—either breaking off and rationing individual squares or biting right across the divisions. Even today, tearing a wrapper and breathing the mingled smells of foil and chocolate transports me back in time.

On summer evenings, we drove for twenty minutes to get a chocolate ice cream cone or a soda—not because the best or only chocolate ice cream was twenty minutes away, but because a drive was a family outing. From our parents' point of view, it was a bonus that we could sustain good behavior long enough to reach that chocolate ice cream. And we enjoyed that time we spent together. We were partial to Baskin-Robbins and we preferred the crunchy brown sugar cones to the pale waffled ones that tasted like pleated sweet paper. We didn't care that the ice cream usually melted and leaked from the tip of the cone onto bare legs and car seats. We also ate dainty sundaes, served with macaroons, using tiny long-handled spoons at Will Wright's Ice Cream Parlor in Pasadena. The parlor was as feminine and frilly as a valentine, and we sat at round marble-topped tables with curvy iron chairs. My mother taught us how to order a chocolate soda properly, that is, with chocolate ice cream. I still do it that way.

At home, we ate gallons of chocolate ice cream. If pints of expensive brands existed then, my mother didn't buy them. We were a family of six, including my grandmother, and ice cream came into our house in multiple half-gallon containers from the supermarket. It was creamy and cold, sweet and satisfying, if not particularly dense or rich. There were other fanciful flavors loaded with chips and chunks, flecks, ribbons, and ripples and we tried many of them, in between the big cartons of chocolate. We had enormous servings from oversized cereal bowls. I thought everyone ate ice cream this way until I was fifteen and watched my boyfriend's eyes widen as I dished up a bowl for him.

During TV commercials, there was always some maneuvering about who would be the one to get up to spoon out the ice cream for all. Neither my brother nor I wanted to empty the carton and inherit the additional responsibility of having to throw it away. (Today I can't remember why that job was considered so onerous.) My mother used to complain about containers with only a spoonful of ice cream left in them.

And I loved to eat ice cream in movie theaters. You got a "chocolate sundae" with either vanilla or strawberry ice cream. I chose vanilla because I thought it made the chocolate taste stronger—which I believe to this day. The sundae came in a short paper cup covered by a white waxed cardboard circle with a little pull tab folded up against the rim of the cup. Once the cover was removed, there was vanilla ice cream with a well of fudgy sweet chocolate syrup hidden beneath the ice cream. The whole thing was eaten in the dark with a small flat wooden paddle. I did this strategically, and with enormous satisfaction, scraping the paddle around the edge of the cup as the ice cream softened and melted there first, taking a detour into the center for a little fudge now and then. The idea was to make the chocolate last as long as the ice cream. The chocolate had an icy texture that made the ice cream seem very smooth by comparison. The whole experience had that unmistakable delicate hint of Popsicle-stick flavor associated with childhood ice cream.

The ice cream I discovered in Paris at eighteen wasn't what we consumed by the bathtubful in my earliest days. It was a costly delicacy. We took our time and made low quiet noises over the tiny scoops from Berthillon on the Ile St.-Louis, only a few doors away from its current location. Its sublime flavors (crème caramel, espresso, coconut, prunes with Armagnac, and chocolate, of course) were worth every franc then (and now).

Married and living in Paris a couple of years later, I was astonished and captivated by the ritual and the cost of buying *glace à l'emporter,* "ice cream to take home." Fancy pastry shops, not grocery stores, sold ice cream. A typical container held little more than a half pint. The salesperson who rang up your purchase carefully locked the miniature block of ice cream into a thick Styrofoam box, like placing a frozen gem in a jewel box. I'd always assumed that this was because shopping was done on foot; one could not race home in the car to put the ice cream in the freezer before it melted. Thinking back, I realize that French households in the early seventies did not necessarily have freezers, certainly not large ones. Ice cream was purchased at the very last minute and the container was meant to keep it from melting until that evening when it would be served. What took our breath away was the cost; we paid around $6 for the equivalent of two normal American-sized scoops in 1972!

The cherry on top of that French year was a little trip to Italy and Yugoslavia. The whole time we were in Italy, I ate gelato three or four times a day, from a different cart every time. Under the certain impression that each purveyor made his own ice cream and no two were alike, I ate nothing but chocolate for several days running. I must surely have tasted over a dozen different chocolate ice creams before I was ready to flirt with strawberry or hazelnut or coffee. My regret in crossing into Yugoslavia was that I had not yet tasted all possible flavors even once.

Years later, I decided to experiment with ice creams that please my palate today. Just as I did in Italy a lifetime ago, I focused first on chocolate and then on more chocolate, the white, the milk, and the bittersweet of it.

Seriously Chocolate Ice Cream

Chocolate ice cream should be a natural to make, but in fact, it is tricky to get the flavors and textures right. This is partly because cocoa butter freezes harder than butterfat and can become grainy in ice cream. Also, ice cream has to be rich (from butterfat and/or egg yolks) and sweet (from sugar) to have the best texture. But fat and sugar also lessen the impact of the chocolate flavor. It was a challenge, and quite fun to play with ice cream formulas to get the taste and texture right for recipes using white, milk, and dark chocolate, not to mention cocoa.

Use your favorite chocolates and cocoas and the best natural cream you can find. Organic milks and creams can be especially flavorful. These recipes are simple to make, and they invite variations and flights of fancy. Please do play. I use a simple hand-crank machine with an insert that goes into the freezer for several hours, so no ice or salt is necessary. These ice creams are far from the giant scoops of my childhood. Instead they are the essence of my decades of eating ice cream and my passion for chocolate.

A LESSON FROM ICE CREAM

The ice cream recipes in this chapter were developed and tested using a Donvier Ice Cream Maker. I chose it because it was the smallest, simplest, and least expensive machine (if you can call such a simple device a machine) I could find. I wanted anyone to be able to make ice cream without a big investment in equipment, but I also assumed that if the ice cream came out great using a simple machine, it could only get better with a more sophisticated appliance. How wrong I was. Preparing ice cream for photographs, I borrowed a big serious ice cream maker. Rather than having to freeze a canister overnight in order to make a scant quart of ice cream, the big machine produced large batches in quick succession because it had a self-contained refrigeration unit. It was thrilling at first. But the ice cream was less flavorful and creamy than the smaller batches from the Donvier! The big machine stirred the ice cream continuously where the Donvier required the paddle to be turned by hand with three-minute rests. Continuous stirring made the ice cream airier, less flavorful, and even lighter in color. The simplest little machine made the best ice cream of all.

BITTERSWEET CHOCOLATE ICE CREAM photograph on page 17

MAKES ABOUT 3½ CUPS

Different kinds of chocolate affect the taste and texture of ice cream. Ice creams made with unsweetened chocolate cocoa powder melt more quickly, feel colder and more refreshing, and taste more distinctly of fresh cream than those made with bittersweet or semisweet chocolate. Because the latter two add extra cocoa butter to the recipe, the ice cream freezes harder. But, if you eat such ice cream soft from the ice cream maker, or after softening slightly in the microwave, you will find it exquisitely thick, rich, and voluptuous on the tongue. Each has its merits. All are divine.

3½ ounces unsweetened chocolate, coarsely chopped

1½ cups heavy cream

1½ cups milk

¾ cup sugar

⅛ teaspoon salt

4 large egg yolks

1 teaspoon pure vanilla extract

SPECIAL EQUIPMENT

Instant-read thermometer

Ice cream maker

Set a strainer over a medium bowl near the stove. Put the chocolate in a medium bowl next to it. In a 1½- to 2-quart saucepan, bring the cream, milk, sugar and salt to a simmer over medium heat.

Meanwhile, in a third medium bowl, whisk the egg yolks just to combine them. Whisking constantly, pour the hot cream mixture slowly over the egg yolks. Scrape the mixture back into the saucepan and cook over medium heat, stirring constantly with a silicone spatula or a wooden spoon, until the mixture thickens slightly and registers between 175° and 180°F. Strain the mixture into the waiting bowl to remove any bits of cooked egg. Stir in the vanilla. Pour just enough of the hot cream mixture over the chocolate to cover it. Stir until the chocolate is melted and the mixture is thick and smooth. Gradually add the rest of the cream mixture, stirring until perfectly blended and smooth. Cover and refrigerate until chilled.

Freeze according to the instructions for your ice cream maker.

continued

BITTERSWEET CHOCOLATE MINT ICE CREAM Start early in the day or a day ahead to allow the mint to infuse in the cream and milk. Increase the milk to 1¾ cups. In a bowl, combine the cream and milk with 1½ cups packed coarsely chopped fresh mint; cover and refrigerate for 8 to 12 hours or overnight.

Strain the cream mixture into a saucepan, pressing gently on the mint with a spoon to extract all of the liquid. Discard the mint. Add the sugar and salt, and bring to a simmer. Proceed as directed.

CHOCOLATE VANILLA BEAN ICE CREAM Normally a nuance in the background, here the vanilla steps forward to become a fragrant partner with the chocolate. Try Bourbon vanilla from Madagascar or the more floral Tahitian bean.

Use a sharp paring knife to split 3 moist vanilla beans lengthwise. Use the knife point to scrape the seeds out of each half into the pan with the milk and cream. Add the scraped bean to the pan, and bring to a simmer. Remove from the heat, cover, and let the vanilla infuse for 10 minutes. Fish out and discard the bean. Add the sugar and salt to the cream, bring to a simmer, and proceed as directed.

chocolate notes You can use any unsweetened baking chocolate or chocolate marked 99%. Branch out from the traditional individually wrapped baking squares if you can, and you will see that all chocolates do not taste the same!

To use cocoa instead of unsweetened: Substitute ¾ cup unsweetened natural or Dutch-process cocoa powder for the chocolate. Put the cocoa in the saucepan and stir in just enough cream to make a smooth paste, then add the rest of the cream and milk.

To use standard bittersweet or semisweet chocolate (without a percentage on the label) or any marked 50% to 62% instead of unsweetened: Increase the chocolate to 8 ounces and reduce the sugar to ¼ cup.

To use chocolate marked 64% to 66% instead of unsweetened: Increase the chocolate to 6½ ounces and reduce the sugar to ¼ cup plus 3 tablespoons.

To use chocolate marked 70% to 72% instead of unsweetened: Increase the chocolate to 6 ounces and reduce the sugar to ½ cup.

MINT CHOCOLATE CHIP ICE CREAM

MAKES ABOUT 3½ CUPS

Don't expect something green with gritty chips. Fresh mint–infused ice cream with homemade chocolate chunks redefines the genre.

2 cups heavy cream

¼ cup coarsely chopped fresh peppermint

1 cup milk

¼ cup plus 2 tablespoons sugar

⅛ teaspoon salt

4 large egg yolks

Homemade Chocolate Chunks (page 80)

SPECIAL EQUIPMENT

Instant-read thermometer

Ice cream maker

Combine the cream and mint in a bowl, cover, and refrigerate overnight.

Set a strainer over a medium bowl near the stove, for the finished ice cream base. Strain the cream into a medium bowl, pressing on the mint to extract all the liquid; discard the mint. Combine the cream, milk, sugar, and salt in a saucepan and bring to a simmer over medium heat.

Meanwhile, in another bowl, whisk the egg yolks just to combine them. Add the hot cream in a thin stream, whisking constantly. Return the mixture to the pan and cook, stirring constantly, until the mixture thickens slightly and registers between 175° and 180°F. Strain the mixture into the clean bowl. Let cool, then refrigerate, covered, until thoroughly chilled.

Freeze according to the instructions for your ice cream maker. Add the chocolate chunks at the end.

HOMEMADE CHOCOLATE CHUNKS

MAKES ENOUGH FOR 1 QUART OF ICE CREAM

A chopped-up bar of chocolate, even the best brand, feels hard and gritty in your mouth when it's frozen. Manufacturers of chocolate chips for ice cream solve that problem by adding coconut oil to the chocolate to make it melt faster after the initial crunch. But the oil dilutes the flavor of the chocolate. If you want crunchy chocolate shards that shatter and then melt with a big burst of bittersweet flavor even in rich chocolate ice cream, just melt the chocolate, chill it, and chop it. Melting destroys the chocolate's temper and diminishes its ability to harden *except when chilled*. In ice cream, the chocolate is brittle because it is cold, but in the warmth of your mouth it softens and releases flavor more quickly than frozen chunks from a brand-new bar of tempered chocolate. Alternatively, you can make fudgy chunks by adding water—either way, you can't beat homemade chocolate chunks.

4 ounces bittersweet or semisweet chocolate, coarsely chopped

2 tablespoons water (optional)

Melt the chocolate, with the optional water if you want fudgy chunks, in a medium heatproof bowl set in a skillet of barely simmering water, stirring frequently. Remove from the heat and pour the mixture onto a piece of parchment paper. Slide the paper onto a small baking sheet and freeze until firm.

Chop the chocolate into whatever size chunks you desire. Return the chunks to the freezer until needed.

chocolate note You can use any bittersweet or semisweet chocolate, regardless of percentage. Of course, the results will be more bittersweet with higher-percentage chocolates. If making fudgy chunks with the optional water, you must increase the water to prevent the chocolate from seizing when you use chocolate with more than 60% chocolate liquor. You can do this by eye. Just stir in a few extra drops, as necessary, to make a perfectly smooth mixture. Chocolate marked 66% to 72%, for example, will require at least 1 additional tablespoon of water, if not more.

COCOA NIB ICE CREAM photograph on page 17

MAKES ABOUT 3½ CUPS

This innocent-looking pale-mocha-hued "chocolate" ice cream is my most exciting new recipe. The base is exquisitely simple: cream infused with bits of roasted cocoa beans called nibs—an ingredient only recently available to home cooks—just lightly sweetened, and balanced with milk. Its rich, clean chocolate flavor is somehow both subtle and dramatic. It is unique—you will not have tasted anything like it ever. (For more information about and recipes using cocoa nibs, see pages 299–335).

1½ cups heavy cream

1½ cups whole milk

¼ cup cocoa nibs, finely chopped

½ cup sugar

⅛ teaspoon salt

SPECIAL EQUIPMENT

Ice cream maker

Fine strainer

Bring the cream, milk, nibs, sugar, and salt to a boil in a medium saucepan over medium heat. Remove from the heat, cover, and let steep for 20 minutes.

Pour the cream mixture through a fine strainer into a bowl, pressing on the nibs to extract all the liquid. Discard the nibs. Refrigerate, covered, until thoroughly chilled.

Freeze the mixture according to the instructions for your ice cream maker.

DOUBLE COCOA NIB ICE CREAM Chocolate chip ice cream was never this good. Stir 2 tablespoons of fresh nibs (not those used to infuse the cream) into the ice cream in the last stages of freezing. Or, serve the Cocoa Nib Ice Cream with nibs sprinkled over the top.

MILK CHOCOLATE LOVER'S ICE CREAM

MAKES ABOUT 3½ CUPS

Milk chocolate lovers, this is your ice cream. Make it with the milk chocolate that you love most. Then go on to try the variations that follow.

Milk chocolate behaves like white chocolate in ice cream: It can be tricky unless you follow the instructions to the letter and aren't tempted to try shortcuts. The results should be smooth and sensuous.

1½ cups heavy cream

1½ cups milk

½ cup sugar

4 large egg yolks

½ teaspoon pure vanilla extract

8 ounces milk chocolate,
very finely chopped

SPECIAL EQUIPMENT

Instant-read thermometer

Ice cream maker

Place a strainer over a medium bowl and set near the stove for the finished ice cream base. In a medium saucepan, bring the cream, milk, and sugar to a simmer over medium heat.

Meanwhile, in a medium bowl, whisk the egg yolks together just to combine them. Whisking constantly, pour the hot cream mixture slowly over the egg yolks. Scrape the mixture back into the saucepan and cook over medium heat, stirring constantly, until the mixture thickens slightly and registers between 175° and 180°F. Strain the mixture into the clean bowl. Stir in the vanilla and set aside to cool slightly.

Meanwhile, place the chocolate in a medium stainless steel bowl and set in a pan of hot tap water for several minutes to melt it gently. Stir with a clean dry spatula until smooth. Pour the warm cream mixture over the chocolate and stir until completely blended. Let cool, then refrigerate, covered, until chilled.

Freeze according to the instructions for your ice cream maker.

MILK CHOCOLATE LOVER'S HAZELNUT ICE CREAM Substitute 8 ounces gianduja (milk chocolate to which toasted hazelnut paste has been added; see Sources, page 366) for the milk chocolate.

MOCHA LATTE ICE CREAM Milk chocolate supplies a rich creamy background for ice cream with a clear, bright coffee flavor attainable only from freshly roasted coffee beans. Serve this ice cream on its own, or scoop it over hot Budini (page 120), with some caramelized nuts.

Increase the milk to 1¾ cups. Add 3 tablespoons regular (not French- or Italian-roast) coffee beans, coarsely chopped, to the cream, milk, and sugar and bring to a simmer over medium heat. Remove the pan from the stove, cover, and let the coffee infuse for 5 minutes. Strain the cream and return it to the saucepan (discard the coffee beans). Reheat the cream to a simmer, then, whisking constantly, pour it slowly over the egg yolks as directed and continue with the recipe.

MILK CHOCOLATE LOVER'S CINNAMON ICE CREAM The notes from testing and tasting sometimes makes the very best introduction to a recipe. Thus, from Maya Klein via E-mail, "Very cinnamony, very velvety, very good. I don't think anyone is going to make this unless they do like cinnamon, so I think it is OK that the cinnamon level is this high. The slight bitterness of the cinnamon balances out the sweet milk chocolate nicely." Enough said?

Increase the milk to 1¾ cups. Add 1 tablespoon crushed cinnamon stick, preferably *canela* (Ceylon or Mexican) cinnamon, to the cream, milk, and sugar and bring to a simmer over medium heat. Remove the pan from the stove, cover, and let the mixture infuse for 5 minutes. Strain the cream and return it to the saucepan (discard the cinnamon). Reheat the cream to a simmer, then, whisking constantly, pour the hot cream mixture slowly over the egg yolks as directed and continue with the recipe.

WHITE CHOCOLATE ICE CREAM

MAKES A SCANT QUART

White chocolate is a tricky ingredient in ice cream. If you've ever produced grainy results in the past (as I have), this recipe is especially for you. One caveat: Experienced cooks may be tempted to streamline the recipe by pouring the hot custard directly over the chopped chocolate to eliminate the melting step. Resist that urge! The result will be a superbly smooth white chocolate custard ice cream.

Rich and sweet, this ice cream is spectacular and elegant in small servings. When I scoop white chocolate ice cream, I think of the tiny servings at Berthillon in Paris. One might expect tart and tangy fruit, fresh or cooked, to be a perfect accompaniment. Surprisingly, the most sublime partners are themselves rich in flavor and rather sweet as well. The trick is to find intense flavors with a gentle rather than dramatic contrast of sweetness: rum-soaked raisins, dates, walnut praline topping (see page 245), candied chestnuts, or Blackberry-Raspberry Sauce (page 89).

1 1/2 cups heavy cream	SPECIAL EQUIPMENT
1 1/2 cups milk	Instant-read thermometer
1/2 cup sugar	Ice cream maker
4 large egg yolks	
8 ounces white chocolate, very finely chopped	
1/2 teaspoon pure vanilla extract	

Place a strainer over a medium bowl and set aside near the stove. In a medium saucepan, bring the cream, milk, and sugar to a simmer over medium heat.

Meanwhile, in another bowl, whisk the egg yolks just to combine them. Whisking constantly, pour the hot cream mixture slowly over the egg yolks. Scrape the mixture back into the saucepan and cook over medium heat, stirring constantly, until the mixture thickens slightly and registers between 175° and 180°F. Strain the mixture into the waiting bowl and set aside to cool slightly.

Meanwhile, place the chocolate in a medium stainless steel bowl in a pan of hot tap water for several minutes to melt it gently. Stir with a clean dry spatula until smooth. Pour the warm cream mixture over the chocolate and stir until completely blended. Stir in the vanilla. Let cool, then refrigerate, covered, until chilled.

Freeze according to the instructions for your ice cream maker.

RUM RAISIN–WHITE CHOCOLATE ICE CREAM Start at least several hours, or even a day, before you plan to freeze the ice cream.

While the White Chocolate Ice Cream base is chilling, combine $1/2$ cup raisins, $1/2$ cup water, and 2 tablespoons sugar in a small saucepan and bring to a simmer over medium heat. Cover the pan and simmer for 5 minutes. Remove from the heat and chill for at least 2 hours, or preferably, overnight.

When you are ready to freeze the ice cream, drain the raisins, discarding the liquid, and add them to the ice cream base.

WHITE CHOCOLATE ICE CREAM WITH DATES Prepare Rum Raisin–White Chocolate Ice Cream but decrease the sugar to 4 teaspoons and substitute coarsely chopped dates for the raisins.

WHITE CHOCOLATE ICE CREAM WITH PRUNES AND ARMAGNAC You can use brandy rather than Armagnac, although it doesn't sound quite so magnificent. The prunes are soft and boozy and fantastic. Start the day before you plan to freeze the ice cream.

While the White Chocolate Ice Cream base is chilling, chop $1\,1/3$ cups (8 ounces) pitted prunes into pieces the size of almonds. Place them in a bowl with $1/2$ cup Armagnac, $1/4$ cup sugar, and $1/2$ cup water and refrigerate overnight.

When you are ready to freeze the ice cream, drain the prunes, discarding the liquid, and add the prunes to the ice cream base.

TOASTED COCONUT–WHITE CHOCOLATE ICE CREAM

MAKES ABOUT 3½ CUPS

Toasted coconut is infused in cream and milk and then discarded. The flavored liquid is transformed into the custard base for the ice cream, which is served with more freshly toasted coconut.

The recipe is simple, although it seems to require lots of bowls, straining, and pouring back and forth—just treat it like a little dance with delicious results. The second time you make it, it's much easier.

½ cup sweetened shredded coconut	½ teaspoon pure vanilla extract
1 cup unsweetened dried shredded coconut	8 ounces white chocolate, very finely chopped
1¾ cups milk	
1½ cups heavy cream	
4 large egg yolks	SPECIAL EQUIPMENT
3 tablespoons sugar	Instant-read thermometer
	Ice cream maker

Position a rack in the center of the oven and preheat the oven to 350°F.

Spread the sweetened shredded coconut on a baking sheet and toast in the oven, stirring once or twice, until golden, 5 to 8 minutes; set aside to garnish the ice cream. Toast the unsweetened coconut the same way.

Set a medium bowl near the stove for the finished ice cream base. Combine the unsweetened coconut, milk, and cream in a medium saucepan and bring to a simmer over medium heat. Remove from the heat, cover, and let steep for 15 minutes.

Strain the mixture into another bowl, pressing on the coconut to extract all the cream. Discard the coconut and set the strainer over the clean bowl near the stove. Return the cream to the saucepan (keeping the used bowl handy) and bring to a simmer.

Meanwhile, briefly whisk the egg yolks together in the cream bowl. Whisking constantly, pour the hot cream slowly over the egg yolks. Stir in the sugar. Return the mixture to the saucepan and cook over medium heat, stirring constantly, until it thickens slightly and registers between 175° and 180°F. Strain the mixture into the clean bowl. Add the vanilla and set aside to cool slightly.

Place the chocolate in a medium stainless steel bowl set in a pan of hot tap water for several minutes to melt it gently. Stir with a clean dry spatula until smooth. Pour the warm cream mixture into it and stir until completely blended. Refrigerate, covered, until chilled.

Freeze according to instructions for your ice cream maker. Serve topped with the reserved toasted coconut.

SICILIAN CHOCOLATE GELATO Adapted from Mary Taylor Simeti

MAKES ABOUT 1 QUART

Sicilian ice cream! What luck to find something rich and delicious that is also relatively low in fat, at least compared with the ice cream we are accustomed to. Sicilian gelato is made with neither eggs nor cream, only milk with a little cornstarch to provide a satisfying puddinglike thickness. The chocolate flavor will reflect the type and quality of the cocoa that you use; a high-quality natural cocoa has much more complexity and liveliness than Dutch-process, but you can use either.

If you have ice pop or Popsicle molds, Sicilian gelato makes a better Fudgsicle than any you may remember.

3 cups whole milk

2/3 cup sugar

3/4 cup premium unsweetened cocoa powder (natural or Dutch-process)

1 1/2 tablespoons cornstarch

SPECIAL EQUIPMENT

Ice cream maker

In a medium saucepan, bring 2 cups of the milk to a simmer over medium heat.

Meanwhile, whisk the remaining 1 cup milk with the sugar, cocoa, and cornstarch in a small bowl. Scrape the cocoa mixture into the hot milk. Cook, stirring constantly, until the mixture thickens and bubbles a little at the edges. Then boil gently, stirring, for 2 minutes longer. Scrape into a bowl and let cool. Cover the mixture with plastic wrap placed directly against the surface and chill overnight.

Freeze according to the instructions for your ice cream maker. Because the mixture is slightly thick to begin with, it may take less time than usual to freeze and thicken to the desired consistency.

chocolate note Use the best cocoa, natural or Dutch-process; as usual, I find the flavor of natural cocoa to be more dynamic.

WALNUT PRALINE AND BLACKBERRY SUNDAE

SERVES 6 TO 8

This elegant, sensuous sundae—a scoop of white chocolate ice cream with blackberry-raspberry sauce, topped with chopped caramelized walnuts—entices you with the contrasting temperatures, textures, and sweetnesses. It's a long way from those cardboard cups of ice cream I loved at the movies.

Look for jam or preserves labeled "100% fruit." These have a particularly intense flavor because they are sweetened with fruit syrup instead of sugar.

BLACKBERRY-RASPBERRY SAUCE

2 cups (12 ounces) fresh or frozen (measured before thawing) blackberries

1/4 cup flavorful black raspberry jam or preserves, or more if needed

White Chocolate Ice Cream (page 84)

Praline topping (see page 245) made with walnuts, coarsely chopped

To make the sauce, puree the berries in a food processor or blender. Strain out the seeds. Stir in the jam. Taste a little of the sauce with a spoonful of ice cream and adjust the sweetness by adding more jam if necessary.

To serve, scoop the ice cream into bowls. Top with the sauce and sprinkle with the chopped praline.

I can close my eyes and still see the stained recipe in my mother's old edition of *Joy of Cooking*. I started making brownies as a child, unwrapping squares of unsweetened baking chocolate and taking seriously the

admonition that the melted chocolate must be cooled before the other ingredients are added, lest the brownies turn out tough and dry. I continue to make brownies, and every few years I go on a brownie baking binge, a flurry of research and recipe testing focused on flavor, texture, sweetness, denseness, crustiness, chewiness, softness.

My brownie binges are not about uncontrolled eating, but a several-week orgy of recipe testing and detailed note taking, which ends with the inevitable cajoling of friends and neighbors to stop by and taste or take brownies home (please!).

These binges first started when I was in search of the "best" brownie for my chocolate dessert shop in the mid-seventies. A few years later I was in search of a *new* "best" brownie for an article, or at the request of a chocolate manufacturer or another now-forgotten reason. When I'm testing, I compare oven temperatures, mixing methods, types of chocolate, etc.: I like details.

More recently, to solve a mystery: Whatever happenend to the elusive shiny crackled crust that some of us old-timers are sure we saw (touched and tasted) many years ago on the tops of brownies? Like Watson and Crick, a colleague and I have been in a friendly race to see who can crack the crackle-topped brownie first. I've also been trying to figure out how to make a really bittersweet brownie that is also chewy.

When I reviewed my notes from years of brownie research bingeing, I noticed the following: In two generations, brownies have gotten denser, more chocolatey, and less sweet, and they now contain less flour. Most people say they like chewy rather than cakey brownies. I suspect that "chewy" is sometimes confused with "moist, dense, and gooey." You can't tell unless you ask about sweetness. If they say they like especially bittersweet brownies, then what they really mean when they say "chewy" is moist, dense, and gooey. Brownies that are truly chewy in the old-fashioned way require far too much sugar to be really "bittersweet." Moist, dense, and gooey, on the other hand, are qualities achieved by using maximum chocolate, minimum flour, limited beating, and slight underbaking. And these techniques are perfectly compatible with bittersweet. What had eluded me was chewy and gooey *and* very bittersweet, the best of all worlds.

If I can't have chewy in the old-fashioned sense, I still want a little textural excitement, a little contrast: a crusty or chewy top surface that yields to the melting rich interior of an otherwise soft, not-too-sweet brownie, for example. I don't ask for much.

Two tricks dramatically affect the gloss and/or crackle of the top surface, and one of them seems also to magically provide chewiness, without extra sugar! The first flies right in the face of the brownie-recipe wisdom I grew up with, which warned the cook to let the melted chocolate cool completely before adding the sugar and eggs. Maya Klein, testing the umpteenth version of brownie variations for me, observed that a more beautiful, glossier, and crunchier top resulted from letting the chocolate and butter mixture get relatively hot when you melt it (about 150°F, which feels hot enough that you want to take your finger out of it pretty quickly after dipping) and then carrying on with the recipe without cooling. Indeed, sugar and *cold eggs*, right from the refrigerator, are added immediately, and the batter is beaten vigorously with a wooden spoon (or carefully with a mixer) until it cools, thickens, and pulls away from the sides of the bowl. (In the days when brownies had more flour in them, we cautioned against overbeating for fear of deadly dry brownies. With significantly less flour, it is now important to beat enough!) In addition, refrigerating the brownie batter in the pan for several hours, or as long as two days before baking, wreaks enormous transformations: It improves the top gloss and crustiness, and it also blends the flavors so that the brownies taste much richer—and the texture is chewier too. One taster said it made the brownies almost too rich! Such a notion led to the intriguing possibility that a not-rich-enough brownie recipe can be made richer simply by refrigerating the batter overnight before baking—an excellent idea for improving low-fat brownie recipes too. And it works!

My latest binge also focused on the differences among brownies made with cocoa, unsweetened chocolate, semisweet chocolate, and bittersweet 70 percent chocolate. This occurred because my friends call late at night: "I'm in my bathrobe making brownies, and the recipe calls for four ounces of unsweetened chocolate; I've got bittersweet and I've got cocoa in the pantry. Do I have to get dressed?" In response, I came up with a single master recipe turned into a quartet of variations compatible with any one of those ingredients.

Different forms of chocolate and cocoa offer different convenience, quality, and flavor choices (and prices). I love choices. Traditional brownie recipes call for unsweetened chocolate, of which there are a limited number of brands widely available. However, there are myriad bittersweet and semisweet chocolates with a wide range of flavors, including those bittersweets with ever higher percentages of chocolate liquor. These chocolates produce fascinating differences in flavor and texture even when I've made the sugar, fat, and nonfat cocoa solids roughly equal from one version to the next. Who would want to miss the experience of tasting all of the differences?

In the meantime, I've noticed that cocoa makes brownies with a crusty, almost candylike crust and the softest interior. This is because the recipe requires more butter to compensate for the small amount of fat in the cocoa (compared with the cocoa butter in unsweetened or bittersweet and semisweet chocolate). Butter is a softer fat and melts at a lower temperature than cocoa butter; therefore, recipes with more butter and less cocoa butter are softer. The top of a cocoa brownie is crusty because the sugar in the brownies is all added granulated sugar rather than the imperceptible ultrafine particles of sugar in bittersweet and semisweet chocolate. I am not quite sure why granulated sugar particles make more of a crust than finely milled particles, but they do. So, if you use superb cocoa, you will get an all-around superb brownie.

Unsweetened chocolate, the classic brownie ingredient, also results in some crust, but the interior is a little firmer, so the difference between the two is not so dramatic. However, you can increase the crust-to-interior texture contrast if you employ the ice bath ritual described on page 93.

Finally, bittersweet and semisweet chocolate make a firm but good brownie with, relative to the other recipes, a glossier crackled crust. And, as mentioned above, for an even crustier surface on any brownie (not to mention a great way to have just-baked brownies at the last minute), make the batter in advance, spread it in the pan, cover, and refrigerate for up to two days before baking.

CLASSIC UNSWEETENED-CHOCOLATE BROWNIES

MAKES 16 LARGE OR 25 SMALLER BROWNIES

This recipe makes brownies that are crusty on top and wonderfully gooey within. They are baked at a high temperature for a short period of time, then cooled in an ice bath. For brownies with a cakier texture, or to use the same basic ingredients but different chocolates, see the variations on page 94.

4 ounces unsweetened chocolate, chopped

8 tablespoons (1 stick) unsalted butter

1$1/4$ cups sugar

1 teaspoon pure vanilla extract

$1/4$ teaspoon salt

2 cold large eggs

$1/2$ cup all-purpose flour

$2/3$ cup walnut or pecan pieces (optional)

SPECIAL EQUIPMENT

An 8-inch square baking pan

Position a rack in the lower third of the oven and preheat the oven to 400°F. Line the bottom and sides of the baking pan with parchment paper or foil, leaving an overhang on two opposite sides.

Place the chocolate and butter in a medium heatproof bowl set in a wide skillet of barely simmering water. Stir frequently until the chocolate is melted and the mixture is smooth and hot enough that you want to remove your finger fairly quickly after dipping it in to test.

Remove the bowl from the skillet. Stir in the sugar, vanilla, and salt with a wooden spoon. Add the eggs one at a time, stirring until the first one is incorporated before adding the next. Stir in the flour and beat with a wooden spoon or rubber spatula until the batter is smooth, glossy, and beginning to come away from the sides of the bowl, 1 to 2 minutes. Stir in the nuts, if using. Scrape the batter into the lined pan and smooth to even it.

Bake for 20 minutes, or until the brownies just begin to pull away from the sides of the pan. The surface of the brownies will look dry but a toothpick inserted in the center will come out quite gooey.

continued

Meanwhile, prepare an ice bath: Fill a roasting pan or large baking pan with ice cubes and about ¾ inch of water.

When the brownies are ready, remove the pan from the oven and immediately set it in the ice bath. Take care not to splash water on the brownies. Let the brownies cool.

Remove the pan from the ice bath, lift up the ends of the parchment or foil liner, and transfer the brownies to a cutting board. Cut into 16 or 25 squares. (The brownies can be stored, airtight, for 2 to 3 days.)

CAKIER CLASSIC UNSWEETENED-CHOCOLATE BROWNIES For cakier brownies, bake at 350°F for 30 to 35 minutes, until a toothpick inserted in the center comes out with some thick, gooey batter still clinging to it. Omit the ice bath; cool on a rack.

CLASSIC BITTERSWEET BROWNIES Use your favorite imported or American bittersweet chocolate that contains 66 to 72 percent chocolate liquor.

Position a rack in the lower third of the oven and preheat the oven to 350°F.

Combine 6½ ounces chocolate labeled 66% to 72%, 7 tablespoons butter, and 1 cup sugar in a medium heatproof bowl. Proceed as directed.

After baking, omit the water bath and let cool completely on a rack.

CLASSIC SEMISWEET BROWNIES This recipe produces brownies with a beautifully glossy, crackled crust. The batter will probably be stiffer than you are used to because most of the fat is cocoa butter (from the chocolate) rather than dairy butter, which is softer.

Position a rack in the lower third of the oven and preheat the oven to 350°F.

Combine 10 ounces semisweet chocolate (without a percentage on the label) or any labeled 50% to 62%, 5 tablespoons butter, and ⅔ cup sugar in a medium heatproof bowl. Proceed as directed.

After baking, omit the water bath and let cool completely on a rack.

chocolate note You can use any unsweetened baking chocolate including any chocolate marked 99%. Branch out from the standard American brands if you can, and you will see that even in brownies, all chocolates do not taste the same!

BEST COCOA BROWNIES

MAKES 16 LARGE OR 25 SMALLER BROWNIES

Cocoa brownies have the softest center and chewiest candylike top "crust" of all because all of the fat in the recipe (except for a small amount of cocoa butter in the cocoa) is butter, and all of the sugar is granulated sugar rather than the finely milled sugar used in chocolate. Use the best cocoa you know for these fabulous brownies.

10 tablespoons (1 1/4 sticks) unsalted butter	2 cold large eggs
1 1/4 cups sugar	1/2 cup all-purpose flour
3/4 cup plus 2 tablespoons unsweetened cocoa powder (natural or Dutch-process)	2/3 cup walnut or pecan pieces (optional)
1/4 teaspoon salt	SPECIAL EQUIPMENT
1/2 teaspoon pure vanilla extract	An 8-inch square baking pan

Position a rack in the lower third of the oven and preheat the oven to 325°F. Line the bottom and sides of the baking pan with parchment paper or foil, leaving an overhang on two opposite sides.

Combine the butter, sugar, cocoa, and salt in a medium heatproof bowl and set the bowl in a wide skillet of barely simmering water. Stir from time to time until the butter is melted and the mixture is smooth and hot enough that you want to remove your finger fairly quickly after dipping it in to test. Remove the bowl from the skillet and set aside briefly until the mixture is only warm, not hot.

Stir in the vanilla with a wooden spoon. Add the eggs one at a time, stirring vigorously after each one. When the batter looks thick, shiny, and well blended, add the flour and stir until you cannot see it any longer, then beat vigorously for 40 strokes with the wooden spoon or a rubber spatula. Stir in the nuts, if using. Spread evenly in the lined pan.

continued

Bake until a toothpick plunged into the center emerges slightly moist with batter, 20 to 25 minutes. Let cool completely on a rack.

Lift up the ends of the parchment or foil liner, and transfer the brownies to a cutting board. Cut into 16 or 25 squares.

chocolate note Any unsweetened natural or Dutch-process cocoa powder works well here. Natural cocoa produces brownies with more flavor complexity and lots of tart, fruity notes. I think it's more exciting. Dutch-process cocoa results in a darker brownie with a mellower, old-fashioned chocolate pudding flavor, pleasantly reminiscent of childhood.

MACADAMIA SHORTBREAD BROWNIES photograph on page 16

MAKES 25 BROWNIES

Nuts underneath shortbread batter rather than mixed into it save a toasting step and make an especially crunchy layer. This technique transforms macadamias (which most people love but I find rich and boring) into a quite fantastic, rich and nutty contrast to the brownies. Try these whether you love macs or not. Or substitute hazelnuts or almonds.

1 recipe of any brownie batter on pages 93–95 (without nuts)

6 tablespoons unsalted butter, melted

2 tablespoons sugar

1/4 teaspoon pure vanilla extract

Pinch of salt

3/4 cup all-purpose flour

1/2 cup untoasted unsalted macadamia nuts, chopped medium-fine

SPECIAL EQUIPMENT

A 9-inch square baking pan

Position a rack in the lower third of the oven and preheat the oven to 350°F.

To make the crust, combine the melted butter, sugar, vanilla, and salt in a bowl. Stir in the flour to make the dough.

On a square of foil or wax paper, pat or roll out the dough to a square slightly smaller than the bottom of the baking pan. Sprinkle the dough evenly with the nuts and press them in. Cover with a 12-inch square of foil and then a tray or piece of cardboard. Slide your hand under the bottom piece of foil or paper and invert the dough onto the tray. Remove the top sheet of foil or paper. Lift the foil and dough off the tray and into the pan. Press the dough, on the foil, evenly into the bottom, and press the foil up the sides of the pan.

Bake until the crust is nicely brown all over, 15 to 20 minutes.

Spread the brownie batter evenly over the hot crust and bake until the edges puff and begin to show fine cracks, 20 to 25 minutes. Let cool completely in the pan on a rack.

Remove the brownies from the pan by lifting up the ends of the foil, and transfer to a cutting board. Cut into 25 squares with a heavy knife.

BLACK-BOTTOM PECAN PRALINE BARS photograph on page 16

MAKES 25 BARS

Bittersweet chocolate brownies with a buttery, chewy brown sugar–pecan layer baked on top. . . . The perfect marriage?

1/2 recipe of any brownie batter on pages 93–95 (without nuts), made with 1 tablespoon less sugar

1/4 cup all-purpose flour

1/4 teaspoon baking soda

4 tablespoons unsalted butter, melted

1/4 cup plus 2 tablespoons packed brown sugar

1/4 teaspoon salt

1 large egg yolk

1/2 teaspoon pure vanilla extract

1 1/4 cups coarsely chopped pecans or walnuts

SPECIAL EQUIPMENT

A 9-inch square baking pan

Position a rack in the lower third of the oven and preheat the oven to 350°F. Line the bottom and sides of the baking pan with parchment paper or foil, leaving an overhang on two opposite sides.

Spread the brownie batter in a thin even layer in the bottom of the lined pan. Set aside.

Mix the flour and baking soda together thoroughly and set aside.

Combine the melted butter, sugar, and salt in a medium bowl. Stir in the egg yolk and vanilla, then the flour mixture, and finally the nuts. Drop spoonfuls all over the top of the brownie batter (they will spread and cover the brownies entirely during baking).

Bake until the edges of the topping are well browned and cracked, 20 to 25 minutes. Let cool completely in the pan on a rack.

Lift up the ends of the parchment or foil liner, and transfer the brownies to a cutting board. Cut into 25 squares.

LACY COCONUT-TOPPED BROWNIES photograph on page 16

MAKES 25 BROWNIES

These extra-bittersweet brownies with a chewy golden-brown coconut macaroon topping put a certain popular candy bar to shame.

1 recipe of any brownie batter on pages 93–95 (without nuts), made with 2 tablespoons less sugar

1 large egg white

1 cup (3 ounces) sweetened shredded coconut

¼ cup sugar

A pinch of salt

¾ teaspoon pure vanilla extract

SPECIAL EQUIPMENT

A 9-inch square baking pan

Position a rack in the lower third of the oven and preheat the oven to 350°F. Line the bottom and sides of the baking pan with parchment paper or foil, leaving an overhang on two opposite sides.

Spread the brownie batter in the lined pan and set aside.

Combine the egg white, coconut, sugar, salt, and vanilla in a medium heatproof bowl, preferably stainless steel, and set the bowl in a wide skillet of barely simmering water. Stir the mixture, scraping the bottom to prevent burning, until it is very hot to the touch and the egg whites have thickened slightly and turned from translucent to opaque, 3 to 4 minutes; a spoonful on a plate will hold a soft shape with no puddle of syrup forming around it.

Use your fingers to drop lacy clumps of coconut topping over the brownie batter. Bake until the brownies puff at the edges and the shreds of coconut look deep golden brown and crusty, about 25 minutes. Let cool completely in the pan on a rack.

Lift up the ends of the parchment or foil liner, and transfer the brownies to a cutting board. Cut into 25 squares.

I've always loved to eat. I grew up with very simple food: lots of fresh produce and not much in the way of sauces or fussiness. Yet we cared about how things tasted. Even today, with my parents on either side of eighty, family gatherings always involve tasting and comparing foods. It happens spontaneously. We might sample new-crop apples in the fall, taste several kinds of smoked fish at breakfast, or sip a trio of single malt scotches when all three of us show up for Dad's birthday with a different bottle. We taste, argue, and exchange insults, and a good time is had. I only recently realized that we have been doing this for as long as I can remember.

THE BLUE PIE

My maternal grandmother hated to cook but, as I think back, knew a lot about food. When I was growing up, she was full of opinions about the way things should be done, suggestions, taste memories. Although I rarely saw her do more in the kitchen than boil water for tea, she had a great influence on my cooking because she was so explicit in her understanding of the relationship between quality and simplicity. "Plain is best" was how she put it. But it meant a lot more than that. Her sister Martha was an enthusiastic and accomplished baker and cook, and they both remember their mother as an extraordinary talent in the kitchen

My father is an engineer. He was always designing something or figuring something out, so we also learned to enjoy activities that involved "making" some-thing—which, for me, included making food. There was no feeling in our house that you had to be taught things—rather, it was that you could learn on your own. My early experiments with baking were untutored explorations. When I was a young teenager, my best friend, Linda, and I used food color to tint (a delicate word considering the unpleasant results) the filling of an apple pie very blue. It tasted good if you closed your eyes, which we did.

By fourteen, we were far more sophisticated. We undertook to entertain our boyfriends with an ambitious dinner for four. The grand finale was to be a flaming baked Alaska. We assembled the dessert beforehand, complete with plenty of swirly meringue, and stashed it in the freezer. The plan was to pop it casually into a hot oven to brown just before serving. We had such a great time that evening that we forgot all about dessert, and the Alaska didn't see a hot oven until the next night. But it held up perfectly and impressed our families so much that they forgot to tease us about anything. I still love baked Alaska, but when I married and moved to Paris about ten years later, I was ready for the next culinary step.

I was twenty-three when I took cooking classes in Suzanne Bergeaud's cramped and unglamorous kitchen in the 7th arrondissement, in a solidly middle-class apartment not far from the venerable Left Bank department store Au Bon Marché. Friendly yet formidable, Mme. Bergeaud had been teaching for twenty years, and her recipes were collected in a slim limited-edition volume with a red cover, into which I wrote my own notes, mostly in French. (When I visited Madame a few years later, the slim red volume had been replaced by a revised and expanded edition published by Flammarion, touted, right on the cover, as *Le livre le plus clair et le plus simple qui ait jamais été ecrit,* "The clearest, simplest book ever written!") Her little chocolate cake called Cocolat eventually lent its whimsical name to my dessert shop, although I never used that particular recipe.

There in my time with Madame, classes were filled by word of mouth with the wives of OECD staffers and diplomats, some of whom brought their cooks along. We came to learn French cooking from an accomplished home cook who wore a patterned apron, no toque in sight. Everything from *les recettes de famille* to *la grande cuisine* could be learned at Madame's (tiny) stove. My four classmates, none French, and I barely fit into the kitchen. I was surely the youngest. Within the framework of teaching us about food, Madame was giving us a peep at French culture. She handed a plate of dinner to her husband in the dining room just before class, along with a bowl containing a nice green salad with mustard vinaigrette at the bottom. This was to be tossed and eaten after the main course, naturally. An academic or a writer, he could be glimpsed in his study from time to time. I once heard him described as an *homme de lettres,* which left me with a lasting impression of a mild-mannered, somewhat unworldly scholar. In any case, there in Madame's kitchen I learned to make the simple, rich, low-lying *gâteau au chocolat* that, along with my landlady's recipe for homemade chocolate truffles, changed my future.

The gâteau was different from any cake I had ever eaten or baked. It was richer and denser, and it tasted more of chocolate than sugar. And it had less flour in it than I was accustomed to. It was made with a bittersweet chocolate that was fine enough to eat on its own, rather than what I was used to: cocoa powder or squares of harsh, gritty unsweetened American baking chocolate (which couldn't be found in the neighborhood *épicerie* anyhow). And it was leavened not with baking powder or baking soda, but with folded-in egg whites beaten by hand in a copper bowl.

I went home and made the cake in our tiny flat, on the third floor of a *maison particulière* near the Place Victor Hugo. The oven had no thermostat, so I stuck my hand in to gauge the heat, as though I knew what I was doing, extending my fingers the way I knew generations of cooks had done. I still remember serving that cake to friends: the first taste, and the gooey smudge on my plate. That cake was a beginning.

Mme. Bergeaud's cake was not supposed to be light and fluffy. It was not a multilayered creation from the Viennese school or a fancy "opéra" from the pâtisserie. It was a simple thing, my introduction to a family of cakey-yet-gooey chocolate tortes consisting mostly of excellent chocolate and butter, bound by eggs and given texture with perhaps a little flour (or perhaps not) and a handful or three of ground nuts. *C'est tout.* But from there a whole world of chocolate tortes opened. I found recipes for them in homey French cookbooks, and in the work of Julia Child and Simone Beck, and I got them from friends. The best of the best was surely the luxuriously moist torte with a nuance of almond, regally named *La Reine de Saba,* or "Queen of Sheba." A few years later, in Berkeley, I built a business around it.

Queen of Sheba

Chocolate Tortes and Variations

A t twenty-seven, I was working too many hours, overwhelmed by the response to my little chocolate truffle and dessert shop. Newspaper food editors were calling regularly, especially at holiday time, asking for recipes to go along with articles they had written about the shop. I didn't have time to create and test new recipes for every newspaper.

In desperation, I typed out my Queen of Sheba recipe, substituting walnuts for almonds, rum for brandy and adding minced dried apricots. In effect, I merged it with Simone Beck's chocolate whiskey-and-raisin torte. Voilà, my own Queen of California Torte!

After that I was hooked. I developed a series of new chocolate tortes just sitting at the typewriter, knowing they would work. My beloved *Reine de Saba* was saving my life; it became a dessert for all seasons and all reasons. To meet a deadline, I created an October Torte for a seasonal newspaper article, then a November Torte and a December Torte. After each, I promised myself I would stop and branch out. When I eventually got around to baking these "new" tortes (long after publication, I admit), I found them delicious, thank goodness.

Close to thirty years later, I continue to use the Queen of Sheba more as a concept than as a recipe. I use it as a teaching tool, as a way to taste flavors and learn how different ingredients work. To show off the flavor and intensity of a particular chocolate, I make the torte with less butter. To accommodate the reduced sugar and higher levels of cocoa and carbohydrates in chocolates that contain 70 percent chocolate liquor, I decrease the flour a little and/or bake the torte for a shorter period so it remains moist. Sometimes I select fruit and liquor combinations specifically to complement, or contrast with, the flavor of the chocolate that I am using. I might use chestnut flour or semolina or matzoh meal in place of flour. Or I might use nut pastes—peanut butter, almond butter, even tahini—instead of ground nuts. Sometimes I grind the chocolate instead of melting it. Each change produces a different torte.

I have this glorious latitude because this chocolate torte is nothing like most other cakes, and unlike most baking in general. One version may be denser or lighter, creamier or "nubblier," sweeter or more bitter, but there is no precisely correct texture, and the thing almost always looks like a fallen soufflé anyhow. The classic Anglo-American butter cake requires precise measurement, ingredients at the right temperature, patience in creaming the butter and sugar, and an exact choreography of alternately adding wet and dry ingredients thoroughly but carefully so as not to overmix. The sponge cake and finicky génoise are demanding and require technique. By comparison, the chocolate torte is endlessly flexible, wildly forgiving. The sheer abundance of rich and luxurious ingredients (chocolate, butter, eggs, nuts) seems enough to ensure a pleasurable result.

As a baker, I love the measured exactness, the precarious play of details required for the more formidable classic cakes, but the cook in me loves the torte for its utter lack of rigor, its generous invitation to play. Even the method of mixing used can change the flavor and texture of the exact same ingredients.

Because the torte is more a general idea than a precise recipe, it is a boon to novice bakers and cooks who resist precision. It tolerates both inexperience and uncertain technique, and it thrives on creative impulse and whimsy (which is not to say that good technique and experience cannot raise the dessert to greater heights). If your newest bright idea doesn't taste exactly the way you imagined, a generous dollop of whipped cream usually helps. Then simply try again.

The chocolate tortes that follow are my latest riffs on the Queen of Sheba. Each takes the flavor and texture in a different direction. Each has the ingredients in different proportions. Each cake is mixed differently. But do not feel bound by the recipes or the methods. Vary the ingredients and interchange the methods, a wonderful way to learn to feel the freedom this cake allows, and develop your own virtuosity.

A FEW WORDS ABOUT VERSATILITY AND
THE ROLE OF INGREDIENTS

This type of torte is essentially an extremely buttery chocolate egg custard given texture with ground nuts and maybe a little flour. The basic ingredients are standard, but the quantity of each is almost infinitely flexible.

- Eggs, whether whole or separated, bind the rest of the ingredients lightly and hold them in suspension. Four eggs is the average for an 8-inch torte, but I sometimes use five or three.

- Flour, which is used very sparingly, also helps bind the ingredients by affecting the way the eggs cook. Even a small quantity of flour adds a creamy smoothness to otherwise nutty-textured tortes.

- Nuts contribute flavor and a pleasantly coarse texture. I have used as little as 3 tablespoons of ground nuts for an 8-inch torte and as much as 1 cup. Nuts may be skinned or not, toasted or raw. The more you use, the heavier and more substantial the torte will be and the nubblier its texture. A torte with a minimal measure of nuts—and flour—has a less cakey texture and is more like a baked mousse or textured custard.

- Liqueurs add flavor. Most of the alcohol is eliminated in the baking. You may omit the liquor if you like; if you do, there is no need to substitute another liquid in its place.

- Butter adds richness to both flavor and texture and helps the torte stay moist as well. Butter also softens or mutes the flavor of the chocolate. To make a torte that tastes more chocolatey without adding more chocolate, just reduce the quantity of butter. The classic Queen of Sheba calls for 12 tablespoons of butter. Over the years, I have cut back to 10 or even 8 tablespoons to heighten the chocolate flavor.

In Claudia Roden's magnificent *Book of Jewish Food,* she presents a beloved family recipe for a Passover chocolate torte. The recipe had been given to her mother by an old friend who realized many years later that she had accidentally left the butter out. Claudia's family had enjoyed the torte without butter for so long that they never corrected the omission. The chocolate torte is nothing if not versatile!

FORMS AND FUNCTIONS

Not only can this one torte be prepared in 1,001 variations, it can also be served in myriad ways. In my bakery, we transformed the shaggy-looking torte into something extremely chic by leveling the uneven edges, inverting it, and applying a sleek and shiny chocolate glaze. More recently, I have rarely bothered to level and glaze, preferring to serve the torte looking like a fallen soufflé. From the perspective of flavor alone, chocolate glaze or frosting, though dressy, is really just too much.

To the uninitiated, a baked and cooled torte, still in its pan, looks suspiciously like a baking disaster. How many times have I answered the innocent question, "What happened to your cake?" Thank heavens a light dusting of powdered sugar adds a purposeful look of "rustic elegance." I reassure the home cook who might be nervous about offering such a homely creation to guests for the first time that after one taste everyone will be captivated. And you will be able to take pleasure in serving something that looks so humble and elicits such happiness.

Because the torte itself is exquisitely rich and so delicious, it really needs no accompaniment. But if the lily must be gilded, a little whipped cream, only lightly sweetened, is the finest partner of all. It sets off the flavor of the torte by providing a dramatic contrast, and it looks terrific on the plate.

QUEEN OF SHEBA photograph on page 22

SERVES 12 TO 14

If I had not jotted down a few notes occasionally over the thirty years or so that I have been making this cake, I might not recognize quite how much it has evolved. My latest scribble reminds me that I now like the cake best with stronger chocolate: I often use 66 or 70 percent chocolate and a little less butter and flour than before. Instead of the original blanched almonds, I now use whole almonds with skins because they have more flavor. Mission almonds, although small and homely to look at, are especially flavorful if you can get them.

Making this cake so often, I noticed that this type of batter sometimes cools and stiffens (like cement!), making it difficult to fold in the egg whites. So I changed the mixing procedure to avoid that problem: I beat the egg whites, then fold the flour and nuts into the batter along with the first addition of egg whites.

The cake is rich and magnificent unadorned, although it can be dressed up with chocolate glaze (see pages 234–237). However, I love it best "naked" with a little whipped cream or Cocoa Bean Cream. The former is a dramatic counterpoint that heightens the impact of the bittersweet chocolate; the latter is subtler, more complex, and very sophisticated.

6 ounces bittersweet 66% to 70% chocolate, coarsely chopped

10 tablespoons (1 1/4 sticks) unsalted butter, cut into pieces

3 tablespoons brandy

1/8 teaspoon pure almond extract (optional)

1/8 teaspoon salt

1/2 cup (2 1/2 ounces) unblanched whole almonds

2 tablespoons all-purpose flour

4 large eggs, separated, at room temperature

3/4 cup sugar

1/8 teaspoon cream of tartar

Powdered sugar for dusting (optional)

Lightly sweetened whipped cream or Cocoa Bean Cream (page 304)

SPECIAL EQUIPMENT

An 8-by-3-inch springform pan or cheesecake pan with a removable bottom

continued

Position a rack in the lower third of the oven and preheat the oven to 375°F. Unless you are planning to serve the cake on the pan bottom, line the cake pan with a circle of parchment paper.

Place the chocolate and butter in a medium heatproof bowl in a wide skillet of barely simmering water. Stir occasionally until nearly melted. Remove from the heat and stir until melted and smooth. Or microwave on Medium (50%) power for about 2 minutes, then stir until completely melted and smooth. Stir in the brandy, almond extract, if using, and salt. Set aside.

Meanwhile, pulse the nuts and flour in a food processor until the mixture has the texture of cornmeal. Set aside.

In a large bowl, whisk the egg yolks with $1/2$ cup of the sugar until well blended. Stir in the chocolate mixture. Set aside.

In a clean dry bowl, with an electric mixer, beat the egg whites and cream of tartar at medium speed until soft peaks form when the beaters are lifted. Gradually sprinkle in the remaining $1/4$ cup sugar and beat at high speed (or medium-high speed in a heavy-duty mixer) until the peaks are stiff but not dry. Scoop one-quarter of the egg whites and all of the nut mixture on top of the chocolate batter, and, using a large rubber spatula, fold them in. Scrape the remaining egg whites onto the batter and fold together. Turn the batter into the prepared pan, spreading it level if necessary.

Bake for 25 to 30 minutes, or until a toothpick inserted about $1\frac{1}{2}$ inches from the edge emerges almost clean but a toothpick inserted in the center is still moist and gooey. Set the pan on a rack to cool. (The cooled torte can be covered tightly with plastic wrap, or removed from the pan and wrapped well, and stored at room temperature up to 3 days or frozen for up to 3 months.

To serve, slide a slim knife around the inside of the pan to loosen the cake. Remove the pan sides and transfer the cake, on the pan bottom, to a platter, or invert the cake onto a rack or tray, remove the paper liner, and invert onto a platter. Using a fine-mesh sieve, sift a little powdered sugar over the top of the cake before serving, if desired. Serve each slice with a little whipped cream.

chocolate note I like this torte best with bittersweet 70% chocolate. You can get a somewhat similar effect with a standard bittersweet or semisweet chocolate (without a percentage on the label) by adding $2\frac{1}{2}$ tablespoons unsweetened cocoa powder to the recipe. Or select chocolates with lower percentages and let the chocolate determine the sweetness and intensity of the torte. No recipe adjustments are necessary other than baking from 5 to 10 minutes longer, if necessary, with lower-percentage chocolates.

❋ FALLEN CHOCOLATE SOUFFLÉ CAKE photograph on pages 254–255

SERVES 10

This is the slimmer reincarnation of the ever-reliable Queen of Sheba (page 109) and remarkable proof, if any were needed, that "the Queen" really can be varied infinitely. Most people cannot tell that I cut all 6 ounces of butter, 2 of the 4 egg yolks, and traded half of the bittersweet chocolate for a little cocoa. Good bittersweet chocolate with 70 percent chocolate liquor adds extra chocolate flavor with only a tad more fat. You can emphasize the intensity of the chocolate flavor by topping the dessert with a small dollop of whipped cream, but it is not essential for enjoying this splendid cake.

$^{1}\!/_{4}$ cup (1 ounce) blanched almonds

3 tablespoons all-purpose flour

3 ounces bittersweet or semisweet chocolate, finely chopped

$^{1}\!/_{2}$ cup unsweetened cocoa powder (natural or Dutch-process)

1 cup sugar

$^{1}\!/_{2}$ cup boiling water

2 large eggs, separated, at room temperature

1 tablespoon brandy

2 large egg whites, at room temperature

Scant $^{1}\!/_{4}$ teaspoon cream of tartar

2 to 3 teaspoons powdered sugar

Lightly sweetened whipped cream for topping (optional)

SPECIAL EQUIPMENT

An 8-by-3-inch springform pan or cheesecake pan with a removable bottom

Position a rack in the lower third of the oven and preheat the oven to 375°F. Place a round of parchment paper in the bottom of the cake pan and spray the sides with vegetable oil spray.

In a food processor or blender, grind the almonds with the flour until very fine. Set aside.

Combine the chocolate, cocoa, and ¾ cup of the sugar in a large bowl. Pour in the boiling water and whisk until mixture is smooth and the chocolate is completely melted. Whisk in the egg yolks and brandy; set aside.

Combine the egg whites and cream of tartar in a medium bowl. Beat with an electric mixer on medium speed until soft peaks form. Gradually sprinkle in the remaining ¼ cup sugar and beat on high speed until stiff but not dry.

Whisk the flour and almond mixture into the chocolate. Fold about a quarter of the egg whites into the chocolate mixture to lighten it, then fold in the remaining egg whites. Scrape the batter into the pan and level the top if necessary.

Bake for 30 to 35 minutes (a little less if you have used a 66% to 72% chocolate), until a toothpick or wooden skewer inserted into the center comes out with a few moist crumbs clinging to it. Cool in the pan on a wire rack. The torte will sink like a soufflé.

Taking care not to crack the edges of the torte, run a knife between the torte and the sides of the pan to release the cake. Remove the sides of the pan and invert the cake onto a plate. Remove the pan bottom and paper liner. Turn right side up on a platter. Using a fine-mesh sieve, sift a little powdered sugar over the top. Serve with a little whipped cream, if you like.

chocolate note I prefer a bittersweet 70% chocolate in this recipe, as it delivers the most flavor, but you will have good results with standard bittersweet or semisweet chocolates (without a percentage on the label), or any marked from 50% to 72%. No adjustments are needed.

PEANUT BUTTER–CHOCOLATE TORTE WITH STRAWBERRY SAUCE

SERVES 12 TO 14

If you think you are too sophisticated for a French twist on PB&J, you can substitute another nut paste, such as cashew butter or almond butter or even tahini (sesame paste), or any others you can think of. I discovered this variation when I tried making a chocolate torte using nut butter instead of the usual ground nuts. While I was at it, I tried a new mixing method, now dubbed the "frosting method," to eliminate the steps of separating the eggs and beating the egg whites. Essentially everything goes into the bowl at once, and you beat like mad. Child's play. And the ingredients are probably in your pantry.

4 ounces bittersweet or semisweet chocolate, coarsely chopped

1/2 cup sugar

2 tablespoons natural peanut butter

1/8 teaspoon salt

6 tablespoons unsalted butter, cut into chunks, slightly softened

4 cold large eggs

1 tablespoon bourbon or other whiskey

1 teaspoon pure vanilla extract

Powdered sugar for dusting (optional)

Mashed or pureed strawberries, sweetened to taste with strawberry jam

White Chocolate Ice Cream (page 84) or vanilla ice cream (optional)

SPECIAL EQUIPMENT

An 8-by-3-inch springform pan or cheesecake pan with a removable bottom

Position a rack in the lower third of the oven and preheat the oven to 350°F. Unless you are planning to serve the cake on the pan bottom, line the bottom of the cake pan with a circle of parchment paper.

Place the chocolate in a large heatproof bowl in a wide skillet of barely simmering water and stir occasionally until nearly melted. Remove from the heat and stir until melted and smooth. Or microwave on Medium (50%) power for about 1 1/2 minutes, then stir until completely melted and smooth.

Whisk the sugar, peanut butter, and salt into the chocolate. Add the butter and beat with an electric mixer at medium speed until smooth and creamy. Beat in the eggs one by one, followed by the bourbon and vanilla. Continue beating at high speed (or medium-high speed in a heavy-duty mixer) for 2 to 3 minutes, or until the batter is fluffy, lightened in color, and the consistency of frosting.

Turn the batter into the prepared pan, spreading it level if necessary. Bake for 25 to 30 minutes, or until a toothpick inserted about 2 inches from the edge comes out clean but one inserted in the center comes out with moist crumbs clinging to it. Set the pan on a rack to cool. (The cooled torte can be covered tightly with plastic wrap, or removed from the pan and wrapped well, and stored at room temperature for up to 3 days or frozen for up to 3 months. Bring to room temperature before serving.)

To serve, slide a slim knife around the inside of the pan to loosen the cake. Remove the pan sides and transfer the cake, on the pan bottom, to a platter, or invert the cake onto a rack or tray, remove the bottom and paper liner, and invert onto a platter. Using a fine-mesh sieve, sift a little powdered sugar over the top of the cake before serving, if desired. Serve each slice with sweetened strawberry puree and a little ice cream, if you like.

chocolate notes You can use standard bittersweet or semisweet chocolate (without a percentage on the label) or any marked 50% to 62%. To keep the flavors in balance, I compensate for the intensity of the higher-percentage chocolates as follows.

To use chocolate marked 64% to 66% instead of standard bitterweet: Use 3½ ounces chocolate.

To use chocolate marked 70% to 72%: Use 3 ounces chocolate, and increase the sugar to ½ cup plus 1 tablespoon.

CHESTNUT TORTE

SERVES 12 TO 14

Chestnuts have such a starchy consistency that you don't have to add any flour to this cake batter. I use less chocolate than in other variations to balance the subtle chestnut flavor. In season, roast or steam the chestnuts yourself; otherwise use canned unsweetened chestnut puree or puree the steamed whole chestnuts that come in jars or plastic packages.

4 ounces bittersweet or semisweet chocolate, coarsely chopped

8 tablespoons (1 stick) unsalted butter, cut into pieces

3/4 cup (about 6 ounces) mashed, steamed, or roasted chestnuts or canned unsweetened chestnut puree (see page 38)

1 tablespoon rum or brandy

1 teaspoon pure vanilla extract

Pinch of salt

4 large eggs, separated, at room temperature

1/2 cup sugar

1/8 teaspoon cream of tartar

Powdered sugar for dusting (optional)

Rum- or brandy-flavored whipped cream

SPECIAL EQUIPMENT

An 8-by-3-inch springform pan or cheesecake pan with a removable bottom

Position a rack in the lower third of the oven and preheat the oven to 375°F. Unless you are planning to serve the cake on the pan bottom, line the bottom of the cake pan with a circle of parchment paper.

Place the chocolate and butter in a large heatproof bowl in a wide skillet of barely simmering water and stir occasionally until nearly melted. Remove from the heat and stir until melted and smooth. Or microwave on Medium (50%) power for about 1 1/2 minutes. Stir until completely melted and smooth.

Stir the chestnuts, rum, vanilla, and salt into the chocolate. Whisk in the egg yolks, along with 6 tablespoons of the sugar. Set aside.

In a clean, dry bowl, beat the egg whites and cream of tartar with an electric mixer at medium speed until soft peaks form when the beaters are lifted. Gradually sprinkle in the remaining 2 tablespoons sugar and beat at high speed (or medium-high speed in a heavy-duty mixer) until the peaks are stiff but not dry. Scoop one-quarter of the egg whites onto the chocolate batter. Using a large rubber spatula, fold them in. Scrape the remaining egg whites onto the batter and fold together.

Turn the batter into the prepared pan, spreading it level if necessary. Bake for 25 to 30 minutes, or until a toothpick inserted in the center of the pan still has moist crumbs clinging to it.

Set the pan on a rack to cool. (The cooled torte can be covered tightly with plastic wrap, or removed from the pan and wrapped well, and stored at room temperature for up to 3 days or frozen for up to 3 months. Bring to room temperature before serving.)

To serve, slide a slim knife around the inside of the pan to loosen the cake. Remove the pan sides and transfer the cake, on the pan bottom, to a platter, or invert the cake onto a rack or tray, remove the bottom and the paper liner, and invert again onto a platter. Using a fine-mesh sieve, sift a little powdered sugar over the top of the cake before serving, if desired. Serve each slice with a little whipped cream.

chocolate notes You can use standard bittersweet or semisweet chocolate (without a percentage on the label), or any marked 50% to 62%. I don't like to overwhelm the flavor of the chestnuts. To keep the flavors in balance, I compensate for the intensity of the higher-percentage chocolates as follows.

To use chocolate marked 64% to 66% instead of standard bittersweet: Use 3½ ounces chocolate.

For chocolate marked 70% to 72% instead of standard bittersweet: Use 3 ounces chocolate, and increase the sugar to ½ cup plus 1 tablespoon.

GRAPPA, CURRANT, AND PINE NUT TORTE photograph on page 12
SERVES 16 TO 18

Grappa is an unaged Italian brandy. Traditionally distilled from the leftover (and not necessarily fresh or first-quality) juice left on the skins after pressing grapes to make wine, grappa bore some resemblance to our moonshine. Today, fine sipping-quality grappas are made from fresh grape skins reserved for the purpose. Some producers even make varietal grappas. The fragrant grappas of zinfandel and of muscat made by the artisan distiller St. George Spirits in California inspired this cake.

For the most chocolate flavor, make the cake one day ahead. At Passover, substitute matzoh cake meal for the semolina flour and margarine for the butter. Voilà!

1/4 cup grappa	1 cup sugar
1/3 cup dried currants	1/8 teaspoon salt
1/4 cup blanched or unblanched whole almonds	1/4 teaspoon cream of tartar
1/4 cup semolina flour	3 tablespoons pine nuts
9 ounces bittersweet or semisweet chocolate (preferably 70%), coarsely chopped	Powdered sugar for dusting (optional)
14 tablespoons (1 3/4 sticks) unsalted butter, cut into pieces	SPECIAL EQUIPMENT
6 large eggs, separated	A 9-by-3-inch springform pan or cheesecake pan with a removable bottom

Position a rack in the lower third of the oven and preheat the oven to 375°F. Unless you are planning to serve the cake on the pan bottom, line the bottom of the cake pan with a circle of parchment paper.

In a small bowl, combine the grappa and currants. Set aside.

In a food processor, pulse the almonds and semolina flour until the almonds are very finely ground. Set aside.

Place the chocolate and butter in a large heatproof bowl in a wide skillet of barely simmering water and stir occasionally until nearly melted. Remove from the heat and stir until melted and smooth. Or microwave on Medium (50%) power for about 2 1/2 to 3 minutes. Stir until completely melted and smooth.

In a large bowl, whisk the egg yolks with ⅔ cup of the sugar and the salt until pale and thick. Stir in the warm chocolate mixture and the grappa and currants. Set aside.

In a large clean, dry bowl, beat the egg whites and cream of tartar with an electric mixer at medium speed until white and foamy. Gradually sprinkle in the remaining ⅓ cup sugar, beating at high speed until almost stiff. Scrape about one-quarter of the egg whites onto the chocolate mixture, sprinkle all of the almond mixture over the top, and fold together. Fold in the remaining whites. Scrape the batter into the prepared pan. Sprinkle the top with the pine nuts.

Bake for 20 to 25 minutes (or longer if you have used a less bittersweet chocolate; see Chocolate Notes), or until a toothpick inserted into the cake about 1½ inches from the edge comes out clean. The center of the cake should still jiggle slightly when the pan is jostled and still be gooey if tested. Set the cake on a rack to cool completely; the surface of the cake will crack and fall as it cools. (The cooled cake can be covered tightly, or removed from the pan and wrapped well, and stored at room temperature for 2 to 3 days or frozen for up to 3 months. Bring to room temperature before serving.)

To serve, slide a slim knife around the sides of the cake to release it. Remove the pan sides and transfer the cake to a serving platter. Sprinkle a little powdered sugar over the top before serving, if desired.

chocolate notes You can make this torte with any bittersweet or semisweet chocolate. I like it best with 70% chocolate, especially if the torte will be served warm, which tastes really voluptuous (although the grappa is very pronounced). The chocolate flavor gets more intense as the torte cools and ages and the liquor recedes. If you use chocolate marked less than 70% (or without a percentage on the label), I suggest that you make it a day ahead, and serve it at room temperature, for the richest chocolate flavor.

To use standard bittersweet or semisweet chocolate (without a percentage on the label), or any marked 50% to 66% instead of bittersweet 70%: Increase the baking time by up to 10 minutes as necessary.

BUDINI
SERVES 6

Budino is the Italian word for pudding; *budini,* the plural, are individual servings. This is an easy and luscious hot dessert. Order it in a trendy American restaurant and you get a to-die-for hot bittersweet dessert served in the dish it was baked in.

Recently I was testing a splendid budino recipe from a local pastry chef in order to write it for the home kitchen when I realized that it was none other than *the torte,* dead on, but without any flour or nuts. The batter was divided among big café au lait bowls, baked, and served hot . . . and, OK, it was also topped with ice cream, caramelized nuts, and caramel sauce. But under that delicious camouflage, it was none other than my beloved chocolate torte. Even in this form, the recipe is just as versatile. You can make the budini in advance, refrigerate them unbaked, and then bake them right before serving, or you can bake them in advance and then reheat.

In my version of budini, just to be perverse, I have added a little semolina flour, but it can be omitted. Feel free to add a handful of chopped or pulverized nuts, or cocoa nibs, or diced candied chestnuts (or drained chestnuts in syrup) to the batter, or just sprinkle any of those on the top of each budino before baking. Or add rum-soaked raisins or crumbled amaretti cookies to the batter. You too can invent new budini. By the way, the liquor is completely optional too.

6 ounces bittersweet chocolate, coarsely chopped

8 tablespoons (1 stick) unsalted butter

1 1/2 tablespoons brandy or rum (optional)

3 tablespoons semolina flour (optional)

3 large eggs

2/3 cup sugar

Pinch of salt

Whipped Cocoa Bean Cream (page 304) or Cocoa Nib Ice Cream (page 81) with a sprinkling of chopped cocoa nibs or Milk Chocolate Lover's Cinnamon Ice Cream (page 82) or whipped cream or store-bought vanilla ice cream

SPECIAL EQUIPMENT

Six 8- to 16-ounce ramekins or ovenproof bowls (use the larger size if you plan to top the budini with ice cream)

If you are going to bake the budini immediately, position a rack in the lower third of the oven and preheat the oven to 375°F.

Combine the chocolate and butter in a medium heatproof bowl set in a wide skillet of barely simmering water, and stir frequently until completely melted and smooth. Or microwave on Medium (50%) power for about 2 minutes, then stir until completely melted and smooth. Remove from the heat. Stir in the liquor and semolina flour, if using.

In a large bowl, beat the eggs, sugar, and salt with an electric mixer at high speed until light and fluffy and the consistency of softly whipped cream. Use a large rubber spatula to fold one-third of the eggs into the chocolate mixture, then scrape the chocolate batter over the remaining eggs and fold until blended. Divide the batter among the ramekins or bowls. You can bake the budini now or later in the day. Simply refrigerate, covered, until about 30 minutes before you want to serve them.

To bake the budini: Place them on a cookie sheet. Bake until puffed, crusted, and deeply cracked but still gooey inside when tested with a toothpick, about 20 minutes, or 25 minutes if they have been refrigerated. Serve hot or let cool, cover, and set aside at room temperature for up to 1 day. The budini will sink as they cool, but they will puff up again when reheated in a 375°F oven for about 10 minutes.

chocolate note These are as versatile as the Queen of Sheba. Choose your favorite bittersweet or semisweet chocolate, up to and including one with 72% chocolate liquor. Check for doneness about 5 minutes early when using higher-percentage chocolates.

ocolat, my chocolate dessert shop, emerged entirely out of my imagination. Nothing like it existed either in this country or in France, so there was no standard to measure it against. I was not presuming to copy a French pâtisserie, but rather to take what interested me and leave the rest. I wanted to evoke my own experience of eating chocolate in France.

Later I added selected American chocolate desserts, usually reinvented with lots more dark chocolate and less sugar. I was influenced, naturally, by both my American background and my love of France, but otherwise I made it all up as I went along. Even the name "Cocolat" is not a real French word. It is French baby talk, a word I came across in my teacher Suzanne Bergeaud's recipe collection. I liked the whimsy of it and the lack of pretension.

It seems hardly worth mentioning now, because the practice is commonplace today, but one of the most unusual things we did at Cocolat was to sell every dessert or cake by the slice as well as whole. Imagine! Customers could walk in and see a beautifully decorated cake piled high with chocolate ruffles and ask to buy one slice of it. Or they could buy just a single truffle. At the time, American bakery cakes didn't have chocolate ruffles, and almost no one knew what a chocolate truffle was. The impact was enormous. Our desserts were more expensive than others at the time, so selling slices was a way to introduce them to people who might never have dreamed of paying for a whole cake. And it was a way to make sure that devotees came in often rather than only on special occasions. Some customers even showed up daily, if only for a single truffle or cup of chocolate mousse or slice of cake. But they also showed up to shop for dinner parties, birthdays, weddings, and every other special occasion when desserts or gifts were needed.

If I wasn't presuming to copy a French pâtisserie, I certainly did not aspire to emulate American bakery desserts. At that time, commercial bakeries used commercial ingredients that were economical but often not as good as those a quality-conscious and knowledgeable home cook would buy. Some bakeries even used commercial mixes. The people I hoped to sell to, the people I knew who really cared about good desserts, made desserts at home with recipes from Julia Child or ate them in sophisticated restaurants like the newborn Chez Panisse. I wanted a shop that sold desserts otherwise available only in that sort of restaurant, or from the very best pastry shops in Paris. I wanted to make European-style desserts with homemade quality, but that looked and tasted better than homemade.

Ingredients were our top priority. So I spent hours, days, weeks, assembling ingredients. I couldn't find ground blanched almonds, a staple in European pastry kitchens (and available to home bakers there as well), so I decided we would grind our own. We burned out the grinder attachment on my (anniversary gift!) Braun mixer before I finally found a supplier.

But I knew what I wanted. We squeezed fresh oranges and lemons for juice and grated the zest by hand. We whipped fresh heavy cream, without stabilizers; folded in freshly beaten egg whites, these literally by hand; used unsalted butter exclusively; splashed sipping-quality liqueurs over cake layers or poured them into our mousses and fillings. Ingredient heaven!

But the foundation of our delicacies was chocolate, and that was our most important ingredient. What we melted and used in batters and glazes was hundreds (ultimately thousands) of pounds of chocolate good enough to eat; bittersweet chocolate instead of compound coatings or other substances scooped from bakery supply house buckets.

I did not know how to run a business and I had never even worked a day in a bakery. But I knew the cakes and truffles I wanted to make, and what I wanted my customers to experience, and how I wanted things to look in the store. Sometimes the more practical details had to smack me in the face—or my unfailingly practical husband had to intervene.

The memory of opening day in 1976 still makes me smile. Just before the store opened, I ran to the bank to get cash for the register (which the cash register salesman had just shown me how to use). I came back with a bunch of twenty-dollar bills. It didn't occur to me that I needed singles and fives and some change as well!

We had spent nearly a week making enough cakes and truffles to stock the store. We opened late, and then every thing we had was sold in three crazy hours. My husband snapped photos from the back wall of customers four deep in front of the showcase. Then he took my picture after the chocolate dust settled that day. I was wearing flared jeans and a pair of very comfortable (yet trendy, I thought) Pierre d'Alby "golf" shoes, with thick blue-and-red squishy soles . . . covered in chocolate glaze. Slumped in a director's chair in the kitchen with a can of beer in one hand and an expression that I cannot describe from looking at the picture, I remember feeling utter amazed satisfaction. Thank goodness the store would be closed on Sunday and Monday . . . we had two days to replenish the showcases and get ready for Tuesday.

At first, most of what I learned came from simply wading in and doing it. My first employee had worked briefly in the bakery down the block, and she was able to show me a few things about handling equipment and establishing routines. Later I was lucky enough to hire some culinary school graduates—I learned from them, and they learned from me. My first recipes were all for making one cake. Before I opened my shop, I'd been baking at home and selling a few cakes at a time to the local charcuterie, so I simply multiplied the recipes I had by four. It never occurred to me that now that I had a bakery I couldn't simply multiply the recipe for one cake up and up and up . . . so that is exactly what I did. Among my memorabilia from this period is a stack of stained and dog-eared handwritten recipe cards that include directions for Queen of Sheba and Gâteau au Chocolat Maison, among others. The earliest cards have recipes for making six cakes at a time, which was the first batch size we made in the Cocolat three-deck "pizza" ovens, purchased used from a local restaurant. Farther down in the stack I find recipes for twelve, and then twenty-four, and then thirty-six. Each multiplication was a learning experience, and so it made sense to scale up gradually. Customers and sales were multiplying at the same time, and by the time Cocolat was sold, more than twelve years later, the Queen of Sheba recipe had been neatly typed on the computer by the company secretary in the front office(!) and laminated in plastic for easy cleaning. The recipe made enough batter for 108 Qs of S.

The learning curve was steady. We went from one little bakery and shop to several, and we moved to a larger, separate baking facility. Recipes and procedures were translated to accommodate ever-larger mixers and convection ovens—big enough for two or more people to hide in. Throughout, however, the quality of the desserts and the level of artistry got better . . . one of the things I am the most proud of these many years later.

As the kitchen staff grew into a production team, we continued to learn by doing, even when the kitchen was supplying cakes to seven Cocolat stores, and then ten and fourteen after the business was sold, and I continued to work (briefly) with the new owners. We consulted in the industry when we needed to, and other bakers, thank goodness, were generous with their help. But our own experimentation was always critical, because we were still making desserts that no one else made, with ingredients that no one else used in quite the way we did, often using techniques that could have evolved only in our kitchen.

Only a few years ago, but long after Cocolat was sold and then closed, friends and volunteers were helping Flo Braker and me make Chuck Williams's birthday cake in a Boston hotel kitchen (see page 214). I watched as one of them spread the cake batter evenly in a sheet pan and, before sliding it into the oven, ran a finger neatly around the inside edge of the pan to make a tiny margin of space that would aid in unmolding the layer later. I told him that I had never seen anyone other than a Cocolat baker do that exact thing in that exact way. He grinned and informed me that several tricks he had subsequently made standard in his own San Francisco catering kitchen he'd learned from former Cocolat bakers.

Sometime in the first years, James Beard came into the store, escorted by Marion Cunningham. I was mortified because some of my staff were so young that they had no idea who he was! And Marion, of course, had not yet come into her own. A few years later (by this time the bakery was no longer behind the store, so I could finally sleep in on a rare Saturday morning), I got an excited call on the phone I kept for staff use only. It wasn't the usual truck breakdown or refrigeration crisis, it was charming Ivan Cousins, calling to say that his sister-in-law, Julia, was in town, and he was bringing her to see the bakery. Out of bed like a shot, I arrived just in time to escort Julia Child and her sister, Dorothy, (and Ivan) around the kitchen. Julia chatted with each of the bakers and decorators. I was gratified that when I then drove Julia to the Berkeley store to show her how all of the desserts were presented, even the youngest workers knew who she was!

The earliest years were intense, an exhausting time of living on the edge. But it was a period of extraordinary accomplishment. I would not have missed it, and I am immensely proud, although I also understand today what it cost. I know now that it was thrilling and satisfying, but I don't remember then feeling or enjoying that thrill or satisfaction often. To do what needed to be done required almost impossible tunnel vision—often euphemistically called dedication. And yet it was never possible to do only one thing at a time.

Every few years, cleaning out my office, I again come across my little notebooks and to-do lists from those years. I am somewhat amazed and aghast each time. What I had to accomplish in a day and a week makes me simultaneously awed and horrified by that other person I must have been. And no matter how focused I was, I could not have done a fraction of it without the staff, who, for very little money, worked with dedication and, I have to say, love for what we were doing. Many are good friends still. And in those years, when any other marriage I knew would have come apart, my husband provided the most critical support.

My daughter, Lucy, was born in 1989, when I was thirty-nine, shortly before the publication of my first book, *Cocolat*. These two events marked a beginning and an end. Lucy took her central place in our lives. A few months later, the book's reception, and then my first James Beard Award for Cookbook of the Year, coincided with the enormous sadness—yet greater relief—I felt at selling a business that had been devouring me alive. The great sense of loss I felt was ameliorated, unexpectedly, by the book *Cocolat*. In my mind, the book became a beautifully wrapped box tied with a silk ribbon. In it, perfectly preserved, were the best and most important aspects of the experience that had been my life's work and, until Lucy, my only child. To this day, when I think of that book, I see the box. At any moment I can open it and begin to read, picking up and savoring the precious pieces of experience and friendship and accomplishment. The box contains everything positive and radiant, everything that brings a smile to my face (even writing this), everything creative and cherished from my life before Lucy.

It all began with chocolate truffles.

Celebrating

*Spinning sugar, piping chocolate, making
ruffles, ribbons, and swirls will transform
a simple dessert into one that is grand.
There is pleasure in the very process itself.*

PRECEDING PAGE: Strawberry Celebration Cake (PAGE 211). **OPPOSITE:** Coconut Saras (PAGE 224). **ABOVE:** Tribute Cake (PAGE 214).

Carmen Meringay (PAGE 226).

Spun sugar (PAGE 244) atop Albert's Mousse (PAGE 166). **OPPOSITE:** Triple Mousses (PAGE 177).

4 Cocolat

Truffles, Mousses, and More

I was not a formally trained pastry chef or chocolatier when I started selling truffles in 1974. I had no preconceived notions about what was right and wrong. I went about things my own way rather than the "right" way. While I occasionally went to great trouble just to reinvent the wheel, I also made discoveries because I came to the profession with the innocence and questioning attitude of an outsider. **YOUTHFUL FOLLY**

The chocolate truffles are one good example of naive good fortune. In 1974, most Americans weren't familiar with these now-ubiquitous treats. My customers had no idea what chocolate truffles were. I made traditional bite-sized truffles rolled in cocoa, the ones I had learned from Madame Lestelle, and I also made oversized truffles dipped in chocolate. These, which we later called American Chocolate Truffles—exuberant and as big as Ping-Pong balls—were born in my home kitchen by accident. I had never intended to make big chocolate truffles. It was just that my earliest attempts at shaping and dipping treacherously soft ganache yielded some very large and exquisitely ugly truffles, which also happened to taste divine. They melted instantly in my mouth with a burst of big chocolate flavor. Shamelessly (in retrospect), I did not hesitate to sell those first results at the charcuterie where I was already selling chocolate tortes and the more traditional small truffles rolled in cocoa.

The response to the big truffles was immediate and ecstatic. They were big and vulgar by European standards, and, looking back, I regard them as something of a youthful folly. But they had an enormous impact. They created a national trend for giant chocolate truffles and encouraged scores (hundreds?) of small entrepreneurs across the country to start truffle businesses. Later, in order to distinguish among the more than twenty-five flavors in my shop, we decorated each kind of truffle with a little topping or streak or swirl of drizzled chocolate or some other distinctive visual treatment. Imagine my surprise, years later, to see large truffles like mine in Paris and London!

By the time I had mastered truffle forming and truffle dipping, so that they weren't ugly anymore and so I could make them any size I wanted, my audience was hooked on the big ones. Attempts to make them dainty met with the polite equivalent of hissing and booing.

My truffles did not depart from European tradition in size and décor only. Almost everything else about them (including the recipe and technique) was "wrong" as well. They were so highly unorthodox that, to make them as perfect as they could be, I had to keep on breaking the entire string of interrelated chocolatier rules (some of which I didn't even know). If I had done just one thing the "right" way, the whole house of cards would have tumbled, and the truffles wouldn't have worked!

Because my ganache (cream and chocolate) had too much cream in it, my truffle centers were too soft even to hold a shape, much less to be dipped into warm chocolate without melting into a puddle. Rather than reducing the amount of cream to make firmer centers (which, in retrospect, would have been so easy), I froze them to make them firm. And it's a good thing that I was dipping them in melted untempered chocolate (because I didn't know any better at first)— tempered chocolate (see page 357) would have cracked and lost its temper on frozen centers anyway. After dipping, I had to refrigerate the truffles because the untempered chocolate bloomed, turning gray and gritty and tasting less chocolatey, when I left them at room temperature for any length of time. Refrigeration prevented all of those bad things and also kept the truffles, with all that extra cream in them, from spoiling as well.

The result of such blissful ignorance? Incomparable chocolate truffles precisely because of all the broken rules. Extremely soft, creamy centers (because the frozen ganache thaws inside the chocolate coating) dipped in untempered chocolate ultimately set Cocolat truffles apart and kept our clientele coming back, even when chocolate truffles began to crop up everywhere.

Meanwhile, my untempered coating gave me a kind of inferiority complex whenever I met or mingled with professional pastry chefs or "real" European chocolatiers. I knew that I liked my results and so did my customers, but I didn't have the confidence to admit to anyone formally trained that I purposely didn't temper my chocolate, or to discuss it with those to whom it was obvious. It just wasn't done, yet I was doing it. I was also making chocolate ruffles with untempered chocolate and dipping strawberries in it too. Meanwhile, I was mixing cakes in unconventional ways and purposely combining water and chocolate.

Over the years I would occasionally call a local chocolate technologist for advice. No matter what I asked him, he almost always said, "Alice, you can't do that," to which I would almost always reply, "Terry, I *am already* doing that, I just want you to help me do it better!" And sometimes he did.

I gained such a reputation for not tempering chocolate that when I starting teaching tempering classes, people reacted as if I had renounced my faith. As if tempering were a religion.

Cocolat truffles were sensational, but I did not fully understand why. More than twenty years later, I do. Chilled untempered chocolate melts at a lower temperature than tempered chocolate because the fat is crystallized in a less stable form. This simply means that when you bite into the truffle, the coating melts and releases its flavor the moment it makes contact with the warmth of your mouth. Tempered chocolate requires more heat, thus more time to melt. The speed and temperature of the melting change our perception of flavors and textures. Similarly, ganache that is chilled (or frozen) immediately after it is mixed also becomes softer and melts faster in your mouth. Freezing was my naive solution to firming up the centers, but the bonus result was a soft, luxurious truffle center that felt and tasted like the richest chocolate ice cream. In addition, chilling the ganache ensured against fat separation and other technical flaws that plague classic genache makers. So my weird method is great for beginners too. How lucky was I, just an innocent young thing who wanted to make chocolate truffles in Berkeley?

TRUFFLES AU COCOLAT

MAKES 64 OR MORE TRUFFLES

These are the truffles my landlady on the rue Copernic made for my birthday in 1972. A year later, I asked for her recipe as a going-away gift and with it, I started my career, making truffles in my home kitchen in Berkeley and selling them to a local charcuterie. Without this very authentic yet virtually obsolete recipe, I would never have dreamed of my own chocolate shop. Bite-sized cocoa-dusted truffles made with butter and egg yolks rather than cream have a unique bittersweet intensity and a smooth, dense texture that is different from the cream-based ganache truffles most people know. Every few years I update the recipe for these, my first and still-favorite truffles.

I now use chocolate with more chocolate liquor than before and I have slightly reduced the amount of butter to create truffles with a heightened chocolate flavor. I have changed the way the egg yolks are handled too; now I heat them first for safety. The result is still an elegant and stunningly easy-to-make confection. No dipping is required; the truffles are rolled directly in good cocoa powder. Choose a fine distinctive chocolate. I like a fruity, not too austere chocolate, such as Scharffen Berger semisweet (62 percent) or Valrhona Le Noir Gastronomie (61 percent). These truffles are perfect after dinner with a little Cognac or espresso. The recipe is a treasure; an old idea now perfectly suited to the best contemporary chocolate.

1 pound bittersweet or semisweet chocolate, coarsely chopped

10 tablespoons (1¼ sticks) unsalted butter, cut into small pieces

2 large egg yolks, at room temperature

½ cup boiling water or freshly brewed espresso

½ cup premium unsweetened cocoa powder (natural or Dutch-process)

SPECIAL EQUIPMENT

An 8-inch square baking pan

Fine-mesh strainer

Instant-read thermometer

Line the bottom and sides of a baking pan with parchment paper or foil. Set aside.

Place the chocolate and butter in a medium heatproof bowl in a wide skillet of barely simmering water over low heat. Stir frequently until the chocolate and butter are almost completely melted and smooth. Remove the bowl and stir with a spatula to complete the melting. Set aside. Leave the heat under the skillet on low.

Place the egg yolks in a small heatproof (preferably stainless steel) bowl, and stir in the boiling water. Place the bowl in the skillet and stir constantly with a heatproof spatula, sweeping the bottom of the bowl to prevent the eggs from scrambling, until the mixture registers 160°F on an instant-read thermometer. (You will have to remove the bowl from the skillet to take the temperature unless you are agile enough to stir, hold, and read the thermometer at the same time.) For safety, rinse the thermometer stem in the simmering water to sterilize it after each reading. When the yolk mixture is ready, scrape it immediately over the melted chocolate. Stir gently (without whisking or beating) until completely blended and smooth. Pour the mixture through a fine-mesh strainer into the lined pan and spread it evenly. Cover and chill until firm, at least 2 hours.

Put the cocoa in a medium bowl. Remove the truffle pan from the refrigerator and use the liner to transfer the truffle sheet to a cutting board. Allow it to soften until you can cut it without it cracking, about 30 minutes if the mixture is very hard. Invert the sheet and peel off the liner. Cut the truffles into squares 1 inch or smaller and toss them in the bowl of cocoa powder. You can leave the truffles square or dust your hands with cocoa and roll them into balls. (Store the truffles tightly covered for up to 2 weeks in the refrigerator or freeze for up to 3 months.) Remove from the refrigerator about 20 minutes before serving to soften slightly.

chocolate notes You can use standard bittersweet or semisweet chocolate (without a percentage on the label), or any marked 50% to 62%.

To use chocolate marked 64% to 66% instead of standard bittersweet: Use 12 ounces chocolate, and increase the butter to 12 tablespoons (1½ sticks). Dissolve 1 tablespoon of sugar in the hot water before adding it to the egg yolks.

To use chocolate marked 66% to 72% instead of standard bittersweet: Use 11 ounces of chocolate, and increase the butter to 12 tablespoons (1½ sticks). Dissolve ¼ cup sugar in the boiling water before adding it to the egg yolks.

COLD CREAMY TRUFFLES

MAKES ABOUT 50 TRUFFLES

With a crisp chocolate shell and a meltingly soft center, these may be the easiest and most sensational chocolate-dipped truffles you will ever make. I've updated and fine-tuned this recipe and procedure so you can enjoy it with a variety of standard or high-percentage bittersweet or semisweet chocolates. For the ultimate experience with these truffles, consult the Chocolate Notes (page 144). After years of not making them, I was stunned again to find out how good they are, especially with the newest chocolates. At a glance the recipe looks similar to the classic ganache truffle recipes that follow (pages 151–154), but the ratio of ingredients and the way of handling them sidestep all the finicky steps for perfect classic ganache—with dramatic and wonderful results. A high ratio of cream to chocolate not only produces the softest center, it eliminates any danger that the ganache will separate or break. Unlike ganache for Classic Ganache Truffles (page 151), this one must be mixed gently with a spatula rather than vigorously with a whisk.

Because the chocolate coating is not tempered, you must keep these truffles in the refrigerator to prevent them from discoloring. If you give them as a gift, be sure the recipient knows to put them in the refrigerator. Enjoy them cold, right from the fridge, or let them warm up for half an hour or so, rather like a piece of cheese. But leftovers, if any, should always go back into the fridge.

8 ounces (9 ounces if using the rum) bittersweet or semisweet chocolate, cut into pieces no bigger than almonds

1 cup heavy cream

2 tablespoons rum or other liquor (optional)

12 to 16 ounces bittersweet, semisweet, milk, or white chocolate, cut into bits for dipping

About 2 tablespoons premium unsweetened cocoa powder (optional)

SPECIAL EQUIPMENT

Fine-mesh strainer

Tiny ice cream scoop (about 1 inch in diameter) or melon baller

Instant-read thermometer

To make the ganache: Place the 8 (or 9) ounces chocolate in a medium bowl. Set aside. In a small saucepan, bring the cream to a low boil. Pour over the chocolate. Stir gently with a rubber spatula until the chocolate is completely melted and the mixture is smooth; do not whisk or splash the mixture by stirring too briskly, or the texture of the truffles will be cakey and granular instead of smooth and creamy. Stir in the liquor, if using, and mix only enough to blend. To refine the texture, strain the mixture through a fine-mesh sieve into another bowl. Refrigerate, without stirring, until the ganache is firm enough to scoop into balls, at least 4 hours.

To form the centers: Line a baking pan or shallow plastic storage container with wax paper or foil. Scrape the ice cream scoop or melon baller across the cold ganache to form a scant 1-inch ball. Place the centers in the lined pan. Repeat with the remaining ganache. Cover the pan with foil or plastic wrap and freeze for several hours, or overnight, until very hard. Leave the centers in the freezer until the moment you are ready to dip them. (The centers can be sealed in an airtight container and kept frozen for up to 2 months.)

To dip the centers: Melt the 12 to 16 ounces chocolate in a medium bowl set in a pan of barely simmering water, stirring frequently. (Be sure that all your utensils are dry and that no moisture is introduced into the chocolate.) Or microwave on Medium (50%) power for about 5 minutes. Stir frequently to hasten the melting. When the chocolate is smooth, melted, and at 100° to 105°F, it is ready to use. Wipe the bottom of the bowl dry if you have used a water bath.

Place the bowl of chocolate in front of you. Remove one-third (if you are a beginner) or half of the truffle centers from the freezer and place them on a plate to the left of the chocolate (reverse all the instructions as appropriate if you are left-handed). Set a baking sheet, lined with wax paper, parchment, or foil, to the right of the chocolate. Use your left hand to place a frozen center in the chocolate. Use the middle and forefinger of your right hand to push the center around in the chocolate until it is thoroughly coated on all sides. Leaving the center in the chocolate, wipe excess chocolate from your fingers on the sides of the bowl, then pick up the truffle with the two wiped fingers and your thumb, shake off the excess chocolate, and place the truffle on the lined baking sheet. Continue to coat the truffles, setting them on the baking sheet so that they do not touch each other, and working as quickly as possible to prevent the centers from thawing and melting in the warm chocolate. Don't hold the dipped centers any longer than necessary, or the chocolate will harden and the truffles will stick to your fingers. Wiping your fingers on the bowl and shaking off the excess chocolate prevents the chocolate from forming the puddles called "feet" around the bottoms of the truffles. Practice makes perfect when it comes to dipping without feet!

When you have dipped all of the centers on the plate, remove more frozen centers from the freezer and dip them likewise; repeat as necessary until all of the centers are dipped. Sift a little cocoa over the dipped truffles, if you like. Refrigerate the sheet of dipped truffles for at least long enough to harden the coating. Once the coating is hard, peel the truffles from the paper and transfer them to a covered container. Store in the refrigerator for up to 2 weeks, or freeze for up to 3 months.

chocolate notes Perfection in this truffle is a center that tastes great *and* melts in your mouth like ultrarich ice cream. This requires the right balance of chocolate and cream. You can use standard bittersweet or semisweet chocolate (without a percentage on the label), or any marked 55% to 60% for these. But an even more bittersweet truffle can be made with higher-percentage chocolates—in smaller quantities to ensure that the texture remains dramatically soft.

To use chocolate marked 60% to 64% instead of standard bittersweet: Use 7 ounces chocolate (with or without the rum) for the centers.

To use chocolate marked 66% instead of standard bittersweet: Use 6 ounces chocolate (with or without the rum) for the centers. Stir 1 tablespoon sugar into the cream before heating it.

To use chocolate marked 70% to 72% instead of standard bittersweet: Use 5 1/2 ounces (6 if using the rum) chocolate for the centers. Stir 2 tablespoons sugar into the cream before heating it. Pour only half of the hot cream and sugar over the chocolate and stir until the chocolate is melted, then add the remaining cream and stir to blend thoroughly.

TROUBLESHOOTING COLD CREAMY TRUFFLES

Since no two chocolates are identical in composition and the fat content of cream varies from region to region, your ganache might not set up exactly as mine does. If it does not get firm enough to scoop and hold a shape after several hours in the refrigerator, freeze it for an hour or two. If that doesn't work, here's the fix: In a microwave on Medium (50%) power or in a wide skillet of almost simmering water, reheat the ganache gently, with minimal stirring, until it is around 110° or 115°F. Add 1 to 2 ounces of warm melted chocolate and stir gently but thoroughly to incorporate it into the ganache. Return the bowl to the refrigerator until the ganache is firm enough to scoop. (Make a note on the recipe to increase the amount of chocolate next time.)

On the other hand, if your finished truffles are firmer in the center than you would like them to be, reduce the amount of chocolate by $\frac{1}{2}$ ounce each time you make the recipe until you get the texture just the way you like it. Now you are learning about chocolate!

Classic Ganache Truffles

After such rave reviews for cold untempered truffles, why even think about classic truffles? Why worry about making a perfect ganache emulsion, then tempering the chocolate for the coating? Apart from the convenience of having sublime fresh chocolates that do not require refrigeration, I was personally attracted to the challenge, the Zen-like importance of each detail, and the virtuosity involved in mastering the classic techniques. Maybe it's all about overcoming my old complex about not tempering, a way of proving that I can if I want to!

Then there are the subtleties of flavor and texture. Done well, classic ganache truffles are exquisite in an entirely different way from the cold creamy untempered variety. Untempered truffles made with frozen centers are cold at first and the melting sensation on your palate is quite exciting. Because the centers are frozen before dipping, these truffles can be made with a higher proportion of cream (one part cream to one part chocolate is excellent), which produces an especially soft creamy center. And because they are dipped frozen, these truffles take on a thicker coat of chocolate, so the contrast between the hard shell and the soft center is dramatic.

Classic ganache truffles dipped in tempered chocolate, on the other hand, are at their best at room temperature. They have a firmer interior consistency and usually a greater intensity of chocolate flavor, because they are made with one part cream to two parts chocolate or three parts cream to five parts chocolate. Rather than cold and creamy, their texture is satin-smooth, like slightly soft butter. Using the classic methods, it is possible, in fact highly desirable, to achieve a very thin coating of chocolate that, when set, offers the barest, audibly crisp resistance to your teeth before you encounter the smooth chocolate center. This is the type of truffle I make when I am using highest-quality chocolate with unique flavor characteristics that I don't want to hide with too much cream.

So I make both types of truffles, depending on the occasion, the chocolate I am using, etc. Regardless of method, however, I usually prefer small to large truffles, and I gravitate once again to the most traditional presentation of all: unadorned chocolate-dipped truffles rolled in a bed of cocoa or chocolate shavings.

CLASSIC GANACHE IS AN EMULSION

An emulsion is a combination of two substances that normally do not mix together. Oil and vinegar joined to make a salad dressing is an emulsion, as is the perfectly blended mixture of cream and chocolate that we call ganache. In both, tiny droplets of one ingredient are surrounded by and held in suspension within the other. When the emulsion in a salad dressing is formed, two otherwise transparent ingredients become a creamy homogeneous mixture. The emulsion is formed by shaking or whisking the two together so vigorously that the vinegar breaks into microscopic bubbles surrounded by oil; this is called a water-in-fat emulsion. The ganache emulsion is harder to see. In a ganache, vigorous whisking breaks the fat, from both the chocolate and the cream, into tiny droplets, which are then surrounded by the water in the cream; this is called a fat-in-water emulsion.

The ganache emulsion is far more stable than the oil and vinegar emulsion. However, any emulsion can break, or separate. This happens when the little droplets that were suspended in the other ingredient start bumping into each other and combining into bigger droplets, then pools, and then layers, and the heavier ingredient begins to shift and settle. In the oil and vinegar dressing, which is only a temporary emulsion, the two ingredients ultimately separate into distinct easy-to-see layers. A ganache is opaque to begin with and the fat and liquid don't separate quite so completely, but a broken ganache can definitely play havoc with the consistency of your truffles. Take heart, however. Unlike salad dressing, perfectly made ganache can be very stable. And if it is allowed to set without being disturbed, it will solidify into flawlessly smooth classic truffle centers.

This perfection requires chocolate and cream that are not too hot, mixed vigorously and thoroughly together (see Classic Ganache Truffles, page 151). It also requires a certain minimum ratio of cream to chocolate. In any emulsion, there must be enough of the surrounding substance to completely separate and suspend the droplets of the other. Because the dry cocoa particles in chocolate absorb some of the water in the cream, they remove some of what would otherwise be available to surround the fat drops. This means the minimum amount of cream required to form an emulsion with chocolate varies with both the fat content *and* the dry solid content of the chocolate. Luckily, we don't have to attempt to make what would probably be a complicated calculation for all the different chocolates. The percentage of chocolate liquor (cocoa butter plus nonfat dry solids) in chocolate is a fairly good indicator of the minimum amount of cream needed for an emulsion. This is true, thank goodness, even though two chocolates with the exact same percentage of chocolate liquor do not necessarily have the exact same ratio of dry particles to fat (see Chocolate Components, page 345).

TROUBLESHOOTING: WHAT TO DO WHEN GANACHE BREAKS

A perfectly emulsified ganache pulls itself together before your eyes as you whisk the chocolate and cream together. It thickens into a glossy homogeneous mass with a puddinglike consistency that shows distinct tracks in the wake of the whisk. If you pour the ganache into another container, it has enough body to hold a soft shape on the surface rather than flowing into a completely level mass. It sets at room temperature with a satiny gloss on the surface and is uniformly firm when pressed with a fingertip.

If the cream and chocolate are not mixed thoroughly, if you keep mixing after the emulsion is formed, if they are mixed at too cool a temperature (or even if the emulsion is disturbed much later when only partially set), it will break, and the fat will separate out. How can you tell if this is happening? You know that ganache is broken when, as you are whisking, it suddenly feels thinner and less viscous and the surface begins to look slightly curdled. Sometimes the change in texture is so slight that you have to lower your head and look closely at the way the light reflects off the surface. Sometimes an emulsion can seem only partially broken: It is mostly thick and emulsified but has fine streaks of oil or oiliness around the edges, and when you tilt it, the ganache slides as though the bowl were oiled. If you whisk harder and faster, hoping to correct or prevent further curdling, the ganache may start to appear stretchy and elastic. Broken genache gets worse after it sets. The surface may be mottled and dull or marred by streaks or puddles of yellow fat. When pressed it may be soft in some places and firm in others. The texture of a poorly made ganache is not smooth. Even the smallest invisible fat puddles will feel like fish scales in your mouth.

When the first signs of curdling appear in a bowl of ganache, instinct tells you to whisk harder and faster. That probably won't pay off, but is almost impossible to resist. After it (usually) doesn't work, there are three fixes to try. If the broken ganache has dropped to a temperature below 90°F, warm it several degrees without stirring, either in a water bath or in a microwave on Low (30%) power, using 5- to 10-second increments. Then whisk again and see if the emulsion forms as it should. If this doesn't work, you can whisk in either a tablespoon of corn syrup or a sprinkling of powdered sugar. Much better still (because I don't like the taste of corn syrup or powdered sugar), you can fix the ganache using the *mayonnaise method,* which I learned from Jim Graham, one of the very best chocolatiers that I know. (No mayonnaise is required, by the way.) Here is how it works: Regardless of the amount of ganache you are trying to fix, bring 3 to 4 tablespoons cream to a simmer. Pour it into a clean bowl and whisk in a few tablespoons of the broken ganache until the mixture looks smooth and thick. Continue to whisk, gradually adding the rest of the broken ganache, as though you were making mayonnaise. I have used this method to repair even fairly large batches of ganache.

TROUBLESHOOTING: WHAT TO DO WHEN GANACHE IS TOO SOFT TO SCOOP OR PIPE

After setting at room temperature for several hours, even perfectly mixed classic ganache may vary in firmness from batch to batch. Once again, this is a fact of life with chocolate. The reasons have to do with differences in the quantity of fat, dry cocoa solids, and sugar among even chocolates labeled with the same percentages. Observe the results and take notes each time you make ganache with a different brand of chocolate so you'll know whether to increase or decrease the amount of chocolate or cream the next time you make it.

To a certain extent, however, you can also adjust the texture and stiffness of a batch of ganache after it has set. A perfectly firm, smooth, shiny ganache can be formed into truffle centers as is, by scooping or piping it. Or you can lighten its color and flavor by whipping a little air into the ganache before you pipe or scoop. Because whipping also makes ganache stiffer, this technique is useful when your ganache turns out to be softer than you anticipated. Some chocolatiers whip as a matter of course; others do it only for certain flavors or varieties of truffle; others avoid whipping altogether.

If ganache for truffles is whipped, it must first be thoroughly set, so the fat has had a chance to crystallize and form a stable structure. This takes several hours, preferably overnight, at cool room temperature; don't rush this by chilling. (The very light whipped ganache cake filling on page 231 must be thoroughly chilled before whipping, but it is a different ganache altogether.) Disturbing the classic truffle ganache before it is set and stable will break the emulsion. Premature whipping will collapse and curdle the ganache completely; it will either never stiffen or it will stiffen with a grainy texture.

Once the ganache is set, you can whip it by stirring it vigorously with a rubber spatula or beating it with a hand-held mixer to lighten and stiffen it significantly. To avoid overwhipped (grainy) ganache, use a rubber spatula. How much you whip is a matter of preference, as long as you don't overwhip. Please note that whipping first softens the ganache—it doesn't stiffen until later, after you've stopped mixing, so you have to learn to anticipate. The color gives you clues; the lighter the color as you whip, the stiffer the ganache will be after it rests. Soft, freshly whipped ganache firms up in a matter of minutes, so if you are forming truffles with a pastry bag, pipe them while the ganache is soft. The piped centers will firm up nicely afterward. If you prefer to scoop the centers, let the whipped ganache firm up first. In either case, remember that the moist surface of truffle centers will dry and crust slightly after they set for an hour or so.

Yes, working with chocolate takes patience!

CLASSIC GANACHE TRUFFLES photograph on page 11

MAKES ABOUT 48 TRUFFLES

The key to absolute perfection in these classic truffles is to form a complete and perfect emulsion of the chocolate and cream by mixing thoroughly and taking the time to let the ganache cool, undisturbed, at room temperature, preferably overnight. I always begin at least one day ahead.

10 ounces (11 ounces if using brandy) bittersweet or semisweet chocolate, coarsely chopped

3/4 cup heavy cream

2 to 3 tablespoons brandy or liquor or liqueur of choice (optional)

1 1/4 pounds bittersweet, semisweet, milk, or white chocolate for dipping

SPECIAL EQUIPMENT

A shallow baking pan (such as a brownie pan) or plastic storage container

Miniature ice cream scoop (about 1 inch in diameter) or melon baller

Portable fan (optional)

Line the shallow baking pan with plastic wrap, overlapping two or more sheets as necessary and leaving a generous overhang on two sides (enough to cover the ganache once it is in the pan).

Place the 10 ounces chocolate in a medium heatproof bowl in a wide skillet of barely simmering water and stir frequently until most of the chocolate is melted. Remove from the heat and stir until completely melted and smooth. Set aside.

In a small saucepan, bring the cream to a boil. Remove from the heat and let it stand for 3 minutes to cool slightly. Pour the hot cream, and the brandy, if using, over the chocolate and whisk briskly, using a circular motion, keeping the whisk in contact with the bottom or the sides of the bowl to minimize splashing (which causes air bubbles), and alternately whisking in the center and around the sides of the bowl, until the cream is thoroughly mixed with the chocolate. Whisk only until the mixture appears completely homogeneous: smooth, glossy, and thickened slightly, like pudding. Stop instantly when the ganache looks completely emulsified. Immediately scrape the ganache into the plastic wrap–lined pan and let cool at room temperature, without stirring or disturbing it.

continued

Once the ganache is cool, fold the plastic wrap over it and let set at room temperature for at least several hours, preferably overnight, until firm enough to scoop or pipe. If you are in a hurry, you can refrigerate it to hasten the set, but the texture of the truffles will not be quite as silken. When the ganache has set, however, chilling won't hurt it; you can refrigerate it for a day or two (or freeze it for up to 2 months), until needed. Then let soften at room temperature until pliable enough to scoop or pipe. If piping, you may have to squeeze or knead the plastic-wrapped ganache gently until it is pliable enough.

To shape the truffles, use the miniature ice cream scoop or melon baller to form ¾- to 1-inch balls of ganache. If necessary, smooth the surface with your thumb, or the heel of your hand, before releasing the ganache from the scoop. (If it is difficult to release, between scoops, warm the back of the scoop gently with a hair dryer, or warm it by dipping it in hot water, wiping it dry each time.) Place the centers slightly apart on a tray lined with parchment or wax paper. Alternatively, scrape the ganache into a large pastry bag fitted with a ½-inch plain tip and pipe rounded mounds on the lined tray. Let stand at room temperature, uncovered, until the surface is dry and slightly crusted, at least 2 hours, preferably longer. Be sure that the centers are at a warmish room temperature before dipping them.

Melt and temper the dipping chocolate (see pages 357–361). Using the techniques on pages 161–162, dip the centers by hand or with a dipping fork, then finish as desired. Let set at room temperature, ideally in front of a portable fan. Store the truffles in a covered container at cool room temperature for up to 10 days, or refrigerate for up to a month. They can also be frozen for up to 3 months.

chocolate notes You can use standard bittersweet or semisweet chocolate (without a percentage on the label), or any marked 50% to 62%.

To use chocolate marked 64% to 66% instead of standard bittersweet: Increase the cream by 2 tablespoons.

To use chocolate marked 70% to 72% instead of standard bittersweet: Chocolate at this percentage level requires both more cream and a different mixing method. See Extra-Bittersweet Ganache Truffles (page 155) or Women of Taste Truffles (page 160) for the correct proportions and method.

CLASSIC GINGER TRUFFLES Increase the cream by 1 tablespoon. Combine the cream and 3 tablespoons finely chopped candied ginger in a saucepan and bring to a boil. Remove the pan from the heat, cover it, and let the mixture steep for 15 minutes. Line the shallow pan and melt the chocolate as directed. Reheat the cream to about 150°F, then pour it through a fine strainer onto the chocolate, pressing on the solids to extract all of the cream. Discard the ginger. Whisk the cream and chocolate together, proceeding as directed.

CLASSIC MINT TRUFFLES Two days before you plan to make the truffles, in a small bowl, stir ½ cup lightly packed coarsely chopped fresh mint leaves into ¾ cup cold heavy cream. Cover and refrigerate overnight. Strain the cream into a large glass measuring cup and press on the solids to release as much cream as possible; discard the mint. Add enough cream to make ¾ cup. Proceed as directed, substituting the mint-flavored cream for the plain cream.

CLASSIC JASMINE TRUFFLES These subtle, sexy truffles resulted from my collaboration with the artisan natural perfumer Mandy Aftel and artisan distiller Lance Winters. The three of us created an experimental sensory "experience" for a Berkeley Symphony fund-raising party at which guests were invited to taste a truffle, sip Lance's natural jasmine-infused vodka, and smell Mandy's jasmine, blood orange, and pink grapefruit perfume. We called it a "symphony of the senses."

Two days before you plan to make the truffles, in a small bowl or jar, combine 1 tablespoon best-quality loose jasmine tea (I use Peet's Downy Pearls) with 1 cup cold heavy cream. Cover tightly and refrigerate overnight to infuse the flavor. Strain the cream into a small saucepan, pressing on the tea to extract all the cream; discard the tea leaves. Substitute the infused cream for the plain cream.

continued

Proceed as directed, adding 1 teaspoon finely grated blood orange zest (organic or unsprayed) and 1½ teaspoons finely grated pink grapefruit zest (organic or unsprayed) to the chocolate with the infused cream.

Melt and temper the chocolate for dipping (see pages 357–361). Follow the instructions on pages 161–162 for double coating and rolling in cocoa. The truffles will keep at cool room temperature in a covered container for up to 10 days, or in the refrigerator for about a month. They can also be frozen for up to 3 months.

chocolate notes I used Scharffen Berger semisweet 62% chocolate for the ganache and coated the truffles with Scharffen Berger bittersweet 70%. Alternatively, you can use a standard bittersweet or semisweet chocolate (without a percentage on the label), or one labeled up to 64%.

To use chocolate 66% to 72% instead of standard bittersweet: Chocolate at this percentage level requires both more cream and a different mixing method. See Extra-Bittersweet Ganache Truffles (page 155) or Women of Taste Truffles (page 160) for the correct proportions and method.

EXTRA-BITTERSWEET GANACHE TRUFFLES
MAKES ABOUT 48 TRUFFLES

I don't flavor these truffles with liquor or anything that might detract from the taste of the chocolate—so the chocolate must be excellent to start with. In the interest of full disclosure, these truffles are not for beginners. Wait until you have mastered perfectly smooth Classic Ganache Truffles (page 151) before you venture here. Why? These high-percentage chocolate truffles contain less sugar (which normally helps chocolate emulsify with cream) and more nonfat dry cocoa solids (which normally hinder emulsification). If the chocolate and cream emulsion is not perfect, the ganache may curdle when you mix the ingredients. Or, even if the ganache appears smooth, it may later develop tiny hard bits of cocoa butter the size and shape of fish scales after it has cooled. These "fish scales" (my description for them) are hard to see, but you can feel them on your palate and they mar the perfection of the truffles.

Just to make the challenge more interesting, a small batch of these truffles is best mixed by hand and requires a little more cream than a larger batch—which works very nicely in the food processor. If you want to make a double recipe in the food processor, follow the method described for the intensely bittersweet Women of Taste Truffles (page 160). What follows here is the small batch, mixed by hand. All of the details matter: The temperature of both the chocolate and cream is important, and so is thorough but not excessive mixing. And, yes, the best, if not the most convenient, method is to pour the chocolate into the cream rather than vice versa. These small truffles are very bittersweet.

1 cup plus 2 tablespoons heavy cream
(1 1/4 cups if using 66% chocolate)

10 ounces bittersweet 66% to 72% chocolate, coarsely chopped

1 1/4 pounds bittersweet chocolate for dipping

About 1 cup premium unsweetened cocoa powder (natural or Dutch-process) (optional)

SPECIAL EQUIPMENT

Instant-read thermometer

A shallow baking pan
(such as a brownie pan)
or plastic storage container

Miniature ice cream scoop
(about 1 inch in diameter)
or melon baller

Portable fan (optional)

continued

In a small saucepan, bring the cream to a boil. Pour it into a medium bowl. Set aside to cool to 115°F.

Line the shallow baking pan with plastic wrap, overlapping two or more sheets as necessary and leaving a generous overhang on two sides (enough to cover the ganache once it is in the pan).

Meanwhile, place the 10 ounces chocolate in a medium heatproof bowl in a wide skillet of barely simmering water and stir frequently until most of the chocolate is melted. Remove from the heat and stir until completely melted and smooth. Let the chocolate cool until it is 115°F.

When the cream and chocolate temperatures are correct, begin pouring the chocolate slowly into the cream, whisking constantly in a circular pattern, in one direction only, keeping the whisk in contact with the bottom of the bowl to minimize splashing (which causes air bubbles). When about half of the chocolate is blended into the cream, stop whisking and scrape in the remaining chocolate. Resume whisking as before, alternately whisking at the center and around the sides of the bowl in order to blend the cream thoroughly and efficiently with the chocolate. Whisk only until the mixture appears completely homogeneous: smooth, glossy, and thickened slightly, like pudding. Stop immediately once the ganache looks completely emulsified. Immediately scrape the ganache into the plastic wrap–lined pan and let cool at room temperature, without stirring or disturbing it.

Once the ganache is cool, fold the plastic wrap over it and let set at room temperature for at least several hours, preferably overnight, until firm enough to scoop or pipe. If you are in a hurry, you can refrigerate it to hasten the set, but the texture of the truffles will not be quite as silken. Once the ganache has set, however, chilling won't hurt it; you can refrigerate it for a day or two (or freeze it for up to 2 months), until needed. Let soften at room temperature until pliable enough to scoop or pipe. If piping, you may have to squeeze or knead the plastic-wrapped ganache gently until pliable enough.

To shape the truffles, use the miniature ice cream scoop or melon baller to form ¾- to 1-inch balls of ganache. If necessary, smooth the surface with your thumb, or the heel or your hand, before releasing the ganache from the scoop. (If it is difficult to release, warm the back of the scoop gently with a hair dryer, or warm it between scoops by dipping it in hot water, wiping it dry each time.) Place the centers slightly apart on a tray lined with parchment or wax paper. Alternatively, scrape the ganache into a large pastry bag fitted with a ½-inch plain tip and pipe rounded mounds on the lined tray. Let stand at room temperature, uncovered, until the surface is dry and slightly crusted, at least 2 hours, preferably longer. Be sure that the centers are at a warmish room temperature before dipping them.

Melt and temper the dipping chocolate (see pages 357–361). Using the techniques on pages 161–162, dip the centers by hand or with a dipping fork, then roll in cocoa, or finish as desired. Let set at room temperature, ideally in front of a portable fan. Store the truffles in a covered container at cool room temperature for up to 10 days, or refrigerate for up to a month. They can also be frozen for up to 3 months.

WHITE OR MILK CHOCOLATE TRUFFLES

MAKES ABOUT 48 TRUFFLES

This recipe gives proportions and a simple method for making plain milk chocolate or white chocolate truffles, to which you can then add any flavorings you like. Another way to vary the truffles is to dip the truffle centers into a contrasting chocolate, milk or white or dark.

12 ounces white or milk chocolate (13 ounces if using liquor), chopped into small chunks

2 to 3 tablespoons rum or liquor or liqueur of choice (optional)

1/2 cup heavy cream

1 1/4 pounds white, milk, semisweet, or bittersweet chocolate for dipping

SPECIAL EQUIPMENT

A shallow baking pan (such as a brownie pan) or plastic storage container

Miniature ice cream scoop (about 1 inch in diameter) or melon baller

Portable fan (optional)

Line the shallow baking pan with plastic wrap, overlapping two or more sheets as necessary and leaving a generous overhang on two sides (enough to cover the ganache once it is in the pan).

Place the 12 ounces chocolate in a food processor and process to a crumb consistency. Add the liquor, if using.

Bring the cream to a boil in a small saucepan. With the food processor on, pour the cream through the feed tube, processing for a total of 20 to 30 seconds, until the chocolate is melted and the mixture is perfectly smooth.

Scrape the ganache into the plastic wrap–lined pan and let cool at room temperature, without stirring or disturbing it.

Once the ganache is cool, fold the plastic wrap over it and let set at room temperature for several hours, preferably overnight, until firm enough to scoop or pipe. If you are in a hurry, you can refrigerate it to hasten the set, but the texture of the truffles will not be quite as silken. Once the ganache has set, however, chilling won't hurt it; you can refrigerate it for a day or two (or freeze it for up to 2 months), until needed. Then let soften at room temperature until pliable enough to scoop or pipe. If piping, you may have to squeeze or knead the plastic-wrapped ganache gently until it is pliable enough.

To shape the truffles, use the miniature ice cream scoop or melon baller to form ¾- to 1-inch balls of ganache. If necessary, smooth the surface with your thumb, or the heel or your hand, before releasing the ganache from the scoop. (If it is difficult to release, warm the back of the scoop gently with a hair dryer, or warm it between scoops by dipping it in hot water, wiping it dry each time.) Place the centers slightly apart on a tray lined with parchment or wax paper. Alternatively, scrape the ganache into a large pastry bag fitted with a ½-inch plain tip and pipe rounded mounds on the lined tray. Let stand at room temperature, uncovered, until the surface is dry and slightly crusted, at least 2 hours, preferably longer. Be sure that the centers are at a warmish room temperature before dipping them.

Melt and temper the dipping chocolate (see pages 357–361). Using the techniques on pages 161–162, dip the centers by hand or with a dipping fork, then garnish as desired. Let set at room temperature, preferably in front of a fan. Store the truffles in a covered container at cool room temperature for up to 10 days, or refrigerate for up to a month. They can also be frozen for up to 3 months.

WHITE CHOCOLATE–LEMON TRUFFLES White chocolate is at its best when that sweet edge is offset with a crisp or tangy flavor with a little acidity. Lemon is perfect. Dip these in white chocolate or bittersweet. If you like, garnish each with a sliver of candied lemon peel.

Stir in 1 teaspoon finely grated lemon zest and 3 to 4 teaspoons fresh lemon juice immediately after straining the ganache.

GIANDUJA TRUFFLES Substitute 4 ounces gianduja (milk chocolate to which toasted hazelnut paste has been added; see Sources, page 366) and 8 ounces milk chocolate for the 12 ounces white or milk chocolate.

WOMEN OF TASTE TRUFFLES
MAKES ABOUT 144 TRUFFLES

The Women of Taste Quilt Show, sponsored by Girls Inc., opened in the spring of 1998 at the Oakland Museum. Fifty luminous quilts were exhibited, each a collaboration between a quilter and a chef. For me it was an opportunity to work with an extraordinary artist, Joan Schulze. For opening night, Alice Waters provided hors d'oeuvres from Chez Panisse, and I made one thousand of these bite-sized chocolate-coated, cocoa-dusted truffles with bittersweet 70 percent chocolate and natural cocoa powder from the then-two-year-old company Scharffen Berger Chocolate Maker. You do not have to make a thousand to enjoy them, but this recipe makes a little more than most because it works so well in a food processor; so freeze some if necessary. These are extra, extra bittersweet.

Begin at least one day in advance to allow the ganache to set overnight.

1 pound 6 ounces bittersweet 70% chocolate, chopped into small chunks

2 cups heavy cream

2 pounds bittersweet 70% chocolate for dipping

1 cup (or more) premium unsweetened cocoa powder (natural or Dutch-process) (optional)

SPECIAL EQUIPMENT

A shallow baking pan (such as a brownie pan) or plastic storage container

Miniature ice cream scoop (about 1 inch in diameter) or melon baller

Portable fan (optional)

Line the shallow baking pan with plastic wrap, overlapping two or more sheets as necessary and leaving a generous overhang on two sides (enough to cover the ganache once it is in the pan).

Place the 1 pound 6 ounces chocolate in a food processor and process to the consistency of crumbs. In a medium saucepan, bring the cream to a rolling boil. With the processor on, pour the cream through the feed tube, processing for a total of 15 to 20 seconds *including* the time it takes to pour in the cream. Immediately scrape the ganache into the plastic wrap–lined pan and let cool at room temperature, without stirring or disturbing it. Proceed as for Extra-Bittersweet Ganache Truffles (page 155).

DIPPING AND FINISHING TRUFFLES

Here are three methods for finishing truffles. The first turns out truffles with a paper-thin, crisp chocolate coating, cocoa-coated and irregular like the authentic fungus for which chocolate truffles were named. The centers are coated twice very thinly (between chocolate-covered palms) and then rolled in a bed of cocoa, finely chopped nuts, or chocolate shavings. (If you have taken a shortcut and chilled the mixture for the Classic Ganache, Extra-Bittersweet Ganache, Women of Taste, or any white or milk chocolate truffles, the double-coating method mitigates the problem of cracking that occurs when you dip a cold center into tempered chocolate: The first coat will crack, but the second probably will not. In any case, the cocoa hides a multitude of sins.)

The second method uses a dipping fork and gives smooth chocolate-dipped truffles sprinkled with cocoa or topped with other ingredients that go with the flavor of the truffle. The third method is similar to fork dipping, but it is done with your fingers.

HAND DIPPING METHOD: DOUBLE COATING, WITH OR WITHOUT COCOA Melt and temper the chocolate (see page 357-361) for the coating. If using cocoa (or nuts or shavings), spread it on a baking sheet in an even bed about ¼ inch deep. Line another baking sheet with wax or parchment paper. Use your fingertips to smear about a teaspoon of chocolate onto the centers of both palms. Pick up a truffle center and roll it gently between your palms to coat it very thinly with chocolate, and put it down on the lined baking sheet. Repeat with the remaining centers, dabbing more chocolate onto your palms as necessary. Work quickly so the chocolate on your hands doesn't harden. When all the truffles are lightly coated, start over again with the first one. Coat it lightly, as before, but once it is coated, place it in the bed of cocoa (or return it to the lined tray if you are skipping the cocoa). Repeat with 2 or 3 more truffles, then, as the coating is just beginning to set, use a spoon to push the first truffle across the bed of cocoa, rolling it over and over and leaving gentle wrinkles on its surface. Repeat with the remaining coated truffles. Continue to coat a few truffles at a time and roll them in the cocoa. As you get faster, you can increase the number you coat before rolling them. As the cocoa-covered truffle coatings set, or when the cocoa bed gets too crowded, transfer the truffles to a plate or another tray.

FORK DIPPING METHOD: WITH GARNISHES OR SPRINKLING Line a baking sheet with parchment or wax paper. Have ready any garnishes or toppings, such as slivers of candied ginger or candied citrus peel, chopped nuts, dried fruit, chopped chocolate or chocolate shavings, or cocoa. Melt and temper the coating chocolate (see pages 357–361). One at a time, place each truffle center in the tempered chocolate and submerge it by pushing it under the surface with the tines or the loop of the dipping fork. Slip the fork or loop under the center and lift it out of the chocolate. Quickly, with a little upward jerking motion, lift the fork up and down several times, touching the truffle lightly against the surface of the chocolate, to drain excess chocolate back into the bowl. If the fork has tines, wipe them against the edge of the bowl before sliding or rolling the truffle onto the lined sheet; if the fork has a loop, hold the loop close to the lined pan and flip it over to turn out the truffle. Before the chocolate sets on the truffles, top them with the chosen garnish. Place the truffles in front of a fan to set.

THREE-FINGER DIPPING METHOD This is just like fork dipping, but it is done with your fingers. Prepare a baking sheet, garnishes, and tempered chocolate as for fork dipping. Place a truffle center in the tempered chocolate and use your middle and forefinger to submerge and push the center around in the chocolate until it is thoroughly coated. Leaving the center in the chocolate, wipe the excess chocolate from your fingers on the side of the bowl. Using a little upward jerking motion, pick up the truffle with the two wiped fingers and your thumb, shake off the excess chocolate, and place the truffle on the lined baking sheet. Garnish as desired and place the truffles in front of a fan to set.

he bar of plain dark *chocolat à croquer* ("eating chocolate") from the *épicérie* tasted pretty good to me in the early seventies. It was nicely bittersweet, and I, like everyone else in France, bought it for both eating and cooking. A basic recipe for chocolate mousse was printed on the wrapper.

Chocolate mousse in its most elemental form in France was a classic dessert served in simple restaurants and cafés and frequently made at home as well. Americans thought it very elegant, but chocolate mousse was the chocolate pudding of France, savored by children and adults alike. *Mousse* simply means "foam." I recall my delight in discovering that shaving cream was called *mousse à raser,* that the curving ripple of froth at the edge of the surf was also *mousse,* and that sparkling wines were described as *mousseux* ("foamy" or "bubbly"). My linguistic discovery was one of the simple pleasures of learning French in France.

Chocolate foam, then. Creamy and smooth, but foamy. A mousse could be dense foam or light fluffy foam, but foam it was. Not pudding, not cream, not custard. Foam—it was supposed to have tiny air bubbles in it.

REDISCOVERING CHOCOLATE MOUSSE

The recipe on the chocolate wrapper had only four ingredients, with instructions to melt the chocolate with coffee or water (it was OK to add some brandy too), whisk in egg yolks, and then, to lighten it, fold in egg whites, beaten *en neige* ("into snow"). Divide among dessert glasses, chill, and serve. Top with whipped cream (*crème chantilly*) if desired. Grandma, if yours was French, used to make it. It didn't have butter in it, or cream (unless you count the topping), and I don't recollect adding sugar. All the flavor and sweetness of the mousse came from the perfectly satisfactory bar of dark chocolate.

What happened to that minimal but delicious old-fashioned chocolate mousse?

In France, chocolate mousse got more complex when it began keeping fancier company. It appeared as the signature of a new more modern school of pâtisserie, at the vanguard of which were Le Nôtre in Paris and Yves Thuries in Cordès, in the form of a filling for very elegant multilayered desserts. Mousse has a lighter texture but deeper chocolate flavor than classic buttercream, and chefs could pile it higher. At least one venerable establishment was accused (by jealous competitors?) of discovering how to sell "air" at a high price, as foamier fillings edged out denser creams and custards. Then came the many and sometimes splendid variations on the simple mousse. Additions of butter and/or cream multiplied the flavor and texture possibilities enormously.

What happened to chocolate mousse in America was less sublime. Sweeter chocolate, more and more sugar, and the frequent and frightful addition of gelatin destroyed the poetry of a simple but magnificent bittersweet chocolate dessert-in-a-dish.

Then, even as the American palate began to appreciate better and more intense chocolate, the specter of salmonella raised its toque. Culinary classics that contained uncooked eggs were abandoned (or went underground). Real chocolate mousse and real Caesar salad took a big hit. Magazines refused to publish recipes using uncooked eggs; book publishers and cookbook authors hedged by printing disclaimers. Some chefs and authors tried to salvage recipes by heating the eggs, but pouring a little hot sugar syrup over eggs does not necessarily heat them adequately, so such revisions didn't solve the problem. And, valid or not, such revisions made recipes more complicated and often sweeter. A few of my own early attempts to reinvent a chocolate mousse recipe required thirty-eight steps (or so it seemed), an eagle eye, and the hands of a surgeon. Even I didn't enjoy making mousse very much anymore. The simplest and best classic chocolate dessert had become a real pain in the neck.

Now some people have returned to eating uncooked eggs, although there is a lingering belief that they are not entirely safe for young children, the elderly, or people with immune deficiencies. Although I still taste raw batter and I will eat an authentic Caesar salad if the right person makes it, I hesitate to serve uncooked eggs to unknowing guests or the public.

But I have so missed simple old-fashioned chocolate mousse, especially in this era of ever-more-interesting and extraordinary chocolate. I was back in the kitchen trying once again to make a simple egg-safe chocolate mousse when my brother, Albert, arrived. And it was his birthday. Imagine a former ice cream lover who can no longer tolerate milk or cream without severe pain. I had a new mousse idea ready to test when I realized that the cream in it was going to be a problem for the birthday boy. Now, I appreciate a good spicy tofu dish as much as the next person, but I don't do chocolate tofu. So I tried something else. I made the mousse by replacing the cream with water. I ate mine with whipped cream on top; Albert didn't. Both of us loved the superb light texture and the clean deep chocolate flavor of mousse made with water! I should have known. After all, what had I done but accidentally rediscover (and reorganize) *mousse au chocolat à l'ancien:* old-fashioned French chocolate mousse. Again I was reminded that the simplest things are often the best, that the flavor of chocolate is truest when it is not mixed with dairy products. The cream on top? A perfect way to accentuate the bittersweet chocolate flavor.

With Albert's "water mousse," I returned to square one, back to the most basic chocolate mousse. From there, I tried new variations made with cream, and even crème frâiche, and with butter. Each affects the flavor and texture in various pleasing ways, offering the cook and chocolate lover room to play.

From the egg-safety point of view, by the way, the breakthrough that eliminated thirty-six (forgive the exaggeration) of thirty-eight "safe-egg" mousse-making steps was the realization that the eggs did not need to be separated and the whites and yolks heated separately. It is easy (especially compared to working with egg whites alone) to heat whole eggs, with water and sugar added, to 160°F. They are less likely to scramble, and they whip to a foam sturdy enough to fold into melted chocolate without deflating.

Once I'd developed the new mousses, Maya Klein asked, "Have you tried baking them yet?" Voilà, warm mousse, exquisitely pure and elegant. And the whole egg-heating step was eliminated! Then we also played with all sorts of ways to dress up the mousses: with caramelized molds, with spoonfuls of cream or raspberry puree in the bottom, and more.

I still love basic chocolate mousse spooned from a little dessert glass, with its coffee and liqueur variations, but I now have a new way to create it and its myriad variations, from the simplest to the most elegant. All are safe and simple to make (you will need a thermometer). If egg safety is not an issue, simply beat the eggs without the water and skip heating them.

ALBERT'S MOUSSE photograph on page 22

MAKES ABOUT 4 CUPS; SERVES 6 TO 8

This is a lovely light (and nondairy if you want it to be) chocolate mousse with intense chocolate flavor. It is the lightest mousse of all if you make it with water or coffee. Milk or cream adds a little body. Either way, you can top it with whipped cream, unless you are serving Albert himself.

6 ounces bittersweet or semisweet chocolate, finely chopped

1/4 cup water, coffee, or milk, or 1/2 cup heavy cream

1 1/2 tablespoons brandy, rum, or liquor of choice (optional)

3 large eggs, at room temperature

3 tablespoons water

3 tablespoons sugar

Whipped cream or Cocoa Bean Cream (page 304) (optional)

SPECIAL EQUIPMENT

Instant-read thermometer

Six to eight 4- to 6-ounce ramekins or dessert cups

Place the chocolate and the 1/4 cup water (or liquid of your choice) in a medium heatproof bowl in a wide skillet of barely simmering water. Stir frequently until the chocolate is nearly melted. Remove the bowl and stir until completely melted and smooth. Stir in the liquor, if using, and set aside.

In a medium heatproof bowl, whisk the eggs with the 3 tablespoons water and the sugar until well blended. Set the bowl in a skillet of not-even-simmering water and, stirring constantly to prevent the eggs from scrambling, cook until they register 160°F on an instant-read thermometer. (You will have to remove the bowl from the skillet to check the temperature unless you are agile enough to both stir and hold and read the thermometer at the same time!) Remove the bowl and beat with an electric mixer at high speed for 3 to 4 minutes, until the eggs have a texture like softly whipped cream. Fold about one-quarter of the eggs into the chocolate. Scrape the chocolate mixture onto the remaining beaten eggs and fold just until evenly incorporated. Divide the mousse among the ramekins.

Chill for at least 1 hour, or until set, before serving. If you are not serving the mousses within a few hours, cover them with plastic wrap.

Serve topped with the whipped cream, if desired.

chocolate notes You can use standard bittersweet or semisweet chocolate (without a percentage on the label), or any marked 50% to 62%.

To use chocolate marked 64% to 66% instead of standard bittersweet: Use 5¼ ounces chocolate. Increase the sugar to ¼ cup.

To use chocolate marked 70% to 72% instead of standard bittersweet: Use 4½ ounces chocolate, and increase the sugar to 4½ tablespoons. If you are using water or milk, add 1 tablespoon unsalted butter in the melting step.

WARM BITTERSWEET MOUSSE

MAKES ABOUT 4 CUPS; SERVES 6 TO 8

Baking transforms chocolate mousse in wonderful subtle ways, deepening its flavor and making it more melt-in-your-mouth. It also allows you the luxury of eating warm chocolate mousse straight from the cup it was baked in, garnished with whipped cream or Cocoa Bean Cream, fresh berries, or nothing at all. Baking eliminates the egg-heating step, and the extra three tablespoons of water necessary to accomplish it, but otherwise these two recipes are the same!

The mousses can be prepared ahead and refrigerated for as long as overnight before baking. And the baked mousses are also delicious served cold.

6 ounces bittersweet or semisweet chocolate, finely chopped	Whipped cream or Cocoa Bean Cream (page 304) (optional)
1/4 cup water, coffee, or milk, or 1/2 cup heavy cream	SPECIAL EQUIPMENT
1 1/2 tablespoons brandy, rum, or liquor of choice (optional)	Six to eight 4- to 6-ounce ramekins or dessert cups
3 large eggs, at room temperature	Instant-read thermometer
3 tablespoons sugar	

If you are planning to bake the mousses right away, position a rack in the lower third of the oven and preheat the oven to 325°F. Put a teakettle of water on to boil.

Place the chocolate and water (or liquid of your choice) in a medium heatproof bowl in a wide skillet of barely simmering water. Stir frequently until the chocolate is almost completely melted and smooth. Remove the bowl from the skillet and stir to finish melting the chocolate. Stir in the liquor, if using. Set aside.

In a medium bowl, whisk the eggs with the sugar until well blended. Beat with an electric mixer at high speed for 3 to 4 minutes, until the eggs have a texture like softly whipped cream. Fold one-quarter of the eggs into the chocolate. Fold in half of the remaining eggs until nearly blended. Add the rest of the eggs and fold just until evenly incorporated. Divide the mousse among the ramekins. (The mousse can be prepared to this point, covered with plastic wrap, and refrigerated for up to 24 hours before baking; bake right out of the fridge.)

To bake, place the ramekins in a large baking pan. Pull out the oven rack, put the pan on the rack, and carefully pour in enough boiling water to come about halfway up the sides of the ramekins. Slide the rack back in and bake until the center of the mousses registers 155°F on an instant-read thermometer (this will be about 3 minutes after it registers 140°F), 14 to 16 minutes. Remove the pan from the oven and remove the ramekins with tongs. Let the mousses cool for at least 10 minutes before serving hot, or let cool and refrigerate until chilled. If you are not serving the mousse within a few hours, cover with plastic wrap.

Serve topped with the whipped cream, if desired.

chocolate notes You can use standard bittersweet or semisweet chocolate (without a percentage on the label), or any marked 50% to 62%.

To use chocolate marked 64% to 66% instead of standard bittersweet: Use 5 1/4 ounces chocolate. Increase the sugar to 1/4 cup.

To use chocolate marked 70% to 72% instead of standard bittersweet: Use 4 1/2 ounces chocolate, and increase the sugar to 4 1/2 tablespoons. If you are using water or milk, add 1 tablespoon unsalted butter in the melting step.

✿ BITTERSWEET DECEPTION

SERVES 10 TO 12

Cake doesn't really begin to do justice to this dense, moist, melt-in-your-mouth bittersweet chocolate dessert. There's remarkably little fat here, but no one ever notices. Make it at least one day before serving.

5 ounces bittersweet or semisweet chocolate, finely chopped

1/2 cup unsweetened cocoa powder (natural or Dutch-process)

2 tablespoons all-purpose flour

1 cup sugar

Pinch of salt

3/4 cup plus 2 tablespoons water

1 tablespoon rum or cognac

1 teaspoon pure vanilla extract

2 cold large eggs

1 cold large egg white

Powdered sugar for dusting (optional)

Lightly sweetened whipped cream (optional)

Raspberry puree or fresh raspberries (optional)

SPECIAL EQUIPMENT

An 8-inch round cake pan (not a springform)

Position a rack in the lower third of the oven and preheat the oven to 350°F. Grease the sides of the cake pan and line the bottom with a round of parchment paper. Put a kettle of water on to boil.

Place the chocolate in a large bowl and set aside.

Combine the cocoa, flour, 1/2 cup of the sugar, and the salt in a small heavy saucepan. Whisk in enough of the water to form a smooth paste, then whisk in the remaining water. Cook over medium heat, stirring constantly (especially around the edges of the pan) to prevent scorching, until the mixture begins to simmer. Simmer very gently, stirring constantly, for 2 minutes. Immediately pour the hot mixture over the chopped chocolate. Stir until the chocolate is completely melted and smooth. Whisk in the rum and vanilla.

In a medium bowl, beat the eggs, egg white, and the remaining $1/2$ cup sugar with an electric mixer at high speed until nearly doubled in volume, 5 to 6 minutes. The eggs will be very foamy but still liquid rather than thick. One-third at a time, fold the eggs into the chocolate mixture. Scrape the batter into the cake pan and smooth the top.

Set the cake pan in a large baking pan at least 2 inches deep. Pour enough boiling water into the baking pan to come halfway up the sides of the cake pan. Bake until the cake rises and crusts slightly on top and the surface springs back when gently pressed, about 30 minutes. The cake will still jiggle in the center, like very firm Jell-O, and the interior will be still quite gooey. Remove the cake pan from the water and cool completely on a rack. Cover with plastic wrap and refrigerate overnight before serving. (The cake can be refrigerated for up to 2 days or frozen, wrapped airtight, for up to 2 months.)

To unmold, run a thin knife around the edges to release the cake from the pan. Cover the top with wax paper and an upside down plate, invert the cake onto the plate, and peel off the parchment liner. Invert onto a serving patter and remove the wax paper. Refrigerate.

At serving time, using a fine-mesh sieve, sift a light dusting of powdered sugar over the top, if desired. Serve unaccompanied or accompanied with a dollop of whipped cream and/or raspberry puree or fresh raspberries.

chocolate note I prefer a bittersweet in the 70% range here, as it delivers the most flavor, but you will have good results with standard bittersweet or semisweet chocolates (without a percentage on the label), or any marked from 50% to 72%. No adjustments are needed.

CHOCOLATE MARQUISE photograph on page 22

MAKES ABOUT 4½ CUPS; SERVES 8 TO 10

A richer chocolate mousse that includes butter, Chocolate Marquise is excellent on its own and positively glamorous with Caramel Shards (page 243) and Spun Sugar. Because it sets firm enough to slice, it is also perfect for filling a ladyfinger-lined mold or spreading between cake layers. Or top with two contrasting mousses to make Triple Mousses (page 177).

8 ounces bittersweet or semisweet chocolate, coarsely chopped	Whipped cream or Cocoa Bean Cream (page 304) (optional)
8 tablespoons (1 stick) unsalted butter, cut into chunks	Spun Sugar (page 244) (optional)
4 large eggs	SPECIAL EQUIPMENT
¼ cup sugar	Instant-read thermometer
¼ cup water	Eight to ten 4- to 6-ounce ramekins or dessert cups

Place the chocolate and butter in a medium heatproof bowl in a wide skillet of barely simmering water. Stir frequently until the chocolate is nearly melted. Remove the bowl from the heat and stir until completely melted and smooth. Set aside.

In a medium stainless steel bowl, whisk the eggs with the sugar until well blended. Whisk in the water. Set the bowl in the skillet of barely simmering water and, stirring constantly to prevent the eggs from scrambling, cook until they register 160°F on an instant-read thermometer. (You will have to remove the bowl from the skillet to take the temperature unless you are agile enough to both stir and hold and read the thermometer at the same time!) For safety, rinse the thermometer stem in the hot skillet water between readings. Remove the bowl from the skillet.

With an electric mixer, beat the eggs at high speed for 3 to 4 minutes, or until they have a texture like softly whipped cream. Fold one-quarter of the eggs into the chocolate. Fold in half of the remaining eggs until nearly blended. Add the rest of the eggs and fold just until evenly incorporated. Immediately, before the mousse can begin to stiffen and set, divide it among the ramekins, or use it to fill a cake or other dessert. Chill for at least 1 hour, or until set.

Serve with whipped cream or Spun Sugar, if desired.

chocolate notes You can use standard bittersweet or semisweet chocolate (without a percentage on the label), or any marked 50% to 62%.

To use chocolate marked 64% to 66% instead of standard bittersweet: Increase the sugar to 1/4 cup plus 2 teaspoons, and the water to 1/3 cup.

To use chocolate marked 70% to 72% instead of standard bittersweet: Increase the sugar to 1/3 cup, and the water to 1/3 cup.

WHITE OR MILK CHOCOLATE MOUSSE

MAKES 4 CUPS; SERVES 6 TO 8

This mousse has the consistency of extra-thick whipped cream rather than the more aerated structure of even the richest classic bittersweet or semisweet chocolate mousse. After waxing rhapsodic about taste and texture of classic chocolate mousse made with eggs, and the use of milk or water instead of cream, why am I backsliding with this eggless recipe loaded with cream? Because white and milk chocolates taste and behave quite differently from dark chocolate in recipes. Years ago I tried a dozen recipes for white and milk chocolate mousses. In recipes that called for eggs, I found the flavors less clean, and I didn't like the sticky, slightly elastic texture caused by the eggs. Cream interfered less with the flavors of the chocolate and improved the texture.

On the face of it, the recipe is no more than whipped cream folded into chocolate, but there are critical details that ensure that the mousse turns out perfectly creamy rather than grainy textured. Melting the chocolate first with water (or another liquid) to loosen it is essential, and then you must positively restrain yourself when whipping the cream: It must be so soft that you are certain it can't be right—but it is.

Made with white chocolate, this mousse is perfect with tart sweet berries or stone fruits. Both the white and milk chocolate versions invite simple flavor variations, including infusions, and experimentation.

Serve the mousse in dessert glasses, or use it as a filling for cakes and desserts. If you want to use the mousse to fill cake layers, or as an element in a composed dessert, have everything else ready, then prepare the mousse immediately before you need it to assemble the finished product. The mousse begins to set very quickly and the texture is damaged if you spread or stir or move it after it has begun to set.

9 ounces white or milk chocolate, finely chopped

6 tablespoons water (or half water and half eau-de-vie, brandy, or other liqueur)

1 1/2 cups heavy cream

Place the chocolate and water in a medium heatproof bowl. Bring 1 inch of water to a simmer in a wide skillet. Turn the burner off (if your stove is electric, remove the skillet from the burner) and wait for 30 seconds, then set the bowl of chocolate in the hot water. Stir constantly until the chocolate is melted and smooth. White chocolate is especially fragile and burns easily; do not turn the heat on again under the skillet unless absolutely necessary. Remove the bowl of chocolate from the hot water. Or, melt the chocolate with the water in a microwave on Low (30%) power for about 3 minutes. Stir until completely melted and smooth.

Let the chocolate cool to about 85°F (a small dab on your upper lip should feel slightly cool, not cold). If the chocolate mixture is too cold, the mousse may turn out grainy; if necessary, set the bowl in the pan of warm water for a few seconds before the next step.

Whip the cream in a medium bowl only until it is thickened and barely beginning to hold a shape—when you tilt the bowl, it should flow to one side, fluffy but still pourable and not at all stiff. Scrape the cream into the bowl of chocolate and fold carefully but quickly just until the two are incorporated. The mousse should seem too soft; it will firm up later. Immediately, while the mousse is still soft, divide it among dessert glasses or spoon into a serving bowl. Cover and chill until set, at least an hour; more if it is in a single large dish.

GIANDUJA MOUSSE Make the mousse with 9 ounces gianduja (milk chocolate with toasted hazelnut paste; see Sources, page 366) and reduce the water to ¼ cup. Top with lightly sweetened whipped cream and chopped toasted hazelnuts.

MOCHA MOUSSE Make the mousse with milk chocolate and substitute freshly brewed espresso for the water, or add 4 teaspoons instant espresso powder to the water. Top each serving with an espresso bean.

WHITE CHOCOLATE MOUSSE WITH FRESH MINT Start a day ahead.
Stir ¾ cup lightly packed coarsely chopped unsprayed mint leaves into the cream. Cover and refrigerate overnight. Strain and reserve the cream, pressing gently on the leaves in the strainer to release as much cream as you can; discard the leaves. Proceed with the recipe.

continued

WHITE CHOCOLATE–CITRUS MOUSSES Citrus zest adds welcome sparks of flavor to sweet white chocolate. Use organic, or at least unsprayed, fruit if possible. You can play around by combining flavors as marmalade makers do, using a mélange of several fruit peels. Pink grapefruit and blood orange is lovely, for example. Citrus peels are most aromatic in their season, which is winter and early spring. My first inclination was to use a little of the acidic fruit juice, as well as the zest, just as I do in white chocolate–lemon truffles. The truffles are successful, but citrus juice curdles the whipped cream in the mousse and ruins its texture. So I've resorted to liqueur instead!

Orange or Blood Orange: Use white or milk chocolate. Substitute ¼ cup Grand Marnier or Cointreau for ¼ cup of the water and add 1 teaspoon lightly packed finely grated orange zest.

Lemon, Lime, or Grapefruit: Use white chocolate. Substitute ¼ cup white rum, vodka (try one infused with citrus), tequila, or gin for ¼ cup of the water and add 1 teaspoon lightly packed finely grated orange zest.

TRIPLE MOUSSES photograph on page 133

MAKES 8 TO 10 SERVINGS

It's fun to play with three mousses in one dessert. The key to greatness, whether it is an individual serving or a large cake, is to use much more of the darkest, most intense flavor—bittersweet, of course—as an anchoring flavor on the bottom, and top it with lesser amounts of the two lighter, sweeter mousses. I like the bittersweet layer to have a different texture from the others. Here, bittersweet Chocolate Marquise is topped with layers of Gianduja Mousse and White Chocolate–Orange Mousse. But you could substitute Mocha Mousse or Milk Chocolate–Orange Mousse for the Gianduja and use plain White Chocolate Mousse for the top, and so forth. Prepare each mousse just before using it.

Instead of individual desserts, you can make one large dessert. A full recipe of each mousse will fill a chocolate-lined pan, as for Strawberry Celebration Cake (page 211), or simply an 8-inch springform pan lined with a plastic strip, also described in the Celebration Cake recipe.

2 ounces any bittersweet or semisweet chocolate, finely chopped if using dessert rings

1/2 recipe Chocolate Marquise (page 172)

1/3 recipe Gianduja Mousse (page 175)

1/3 recipe White Chocolate–Orange Mousse (page 176)

Ruffled chocolate fans (see page 238) or chocolate cigarettes (see page 241), or strips of candied orange peel (store-bought) or caramel-glazed hazelnuts (page 245) for decoration

SPECIAL EQUIPMENT

Eight to ten 2- by 2-inch dessert rings, (see Note), or 5- to 6-ounce martini glasses or parfait glasses

If using dessert rings, melt the chocolate in a medium heatproof bowl set in a wide skillet of barely simmering water, stirring frequently until the chocolate is almost completely melted and smooth. Remove from the heat.

continued

Meanwhile, cut ten 3-inch squares of foil and trace a 2-inch circle on each; lay the foil on a cookie sheet. Divide the melted chocolate among the foil squares, spreading it to cover each traced circle. Set a dessert ring over each chocolate circle. Refrigerate to harden the chocolate. If not using rings, set out martini or parfait glasses.

Prepare the Chocolate Marquise. Spoon it neatly into the rings or glasses, filling each one almost half full—there is no need to make an even layer. (Leftover marquise can be refrigerated and nibbled on later.) Refrigerate the rings or glasses.

Prepare the Gianduja Mousse. Spoon it neatly into the rings or glasses, leaving room for the final mousse. (Scrape any extra mousse into the bowl with the leftover marquise.)

Prepare the White Chocolate–Orange Mousse. Spoon it onto the gianduja; if using rings, fill them completely, heaping the mousse slightly above the top, then use a metal icing spatula to spread the mousse level in each ring. (Add any leftover mousse to the others.) Refrigerate for at least 1 hour, or until set, before serving.

To unmold the mousses: Pick up one dessert ring and peel off the foil. Set it on a serving plate. Warm the ring carefully with a hair dryer, or wrap a wrung-out hot wet washcloth around it, then pull the ring off the mousse. Repeat until all of the mousses are unmolded.

Serve each mousse topped with a chocolate fan or cigarette, or a strip of orange peel or a caramelized hazelnut, if desired.

NOTE: Rings this size hold $\frac{1}{2}$ cup mousse; if your rings are larger, count on fewer servings. You can figure out how much mousse you need for any size ring by lining one with foil and measuring how much water it holds filled to the top. Multiply by the number of rings you want to fill, and consult the yield of each mousse recipe.

I've always liked plain white, crisp, light meringue. I like to treat it in ways that offset its extraordinary sweetness, either by contrasting it with fillings or sauces or by adding something to the meringue to make it flavorful and interesting **LOOKING FOR THE PERFECT CHOCOLATE MERINGUE** even before it is filled.

For years I've been looking for the perfect chocolate meringue. Every now and then I'd try adding different amounts of cocoa or comparing natural versus Dutch-process cocoa. But I never was happy with the results, so I always returned to plain meringue, to which I'd sometimes add nuts or powdered espresso.

Finally I realized that the perfect chocolate meringue would be plain white meringue with loads of ground bittersweet or semisweet chocolate in it. Use your favorite dark chocolate. Try the nutty variation too.

Some bakers make meringues with powdered sugar or with half powdered and half granulated sugar. I use only granulated sugar, because I do not like the flavor or texture of the cornstarch in the powdered sugar. This is also why I do not add cornstarch to my nutty meringues, as some do. To ensure that meringues made with granulated sugar (and without starch) will be tender rather than hard or tough, it is essential that some of the sugar remain undissolved. Yes, undissolved. If the meringue is beaten long enough for all of the sugar to dissolve—as cookbooks sometimes instruct—the results can be as hard as china plates. Folding a portion of the sugar in by hand after the meringue is beaten stiff is a simple way to ensure that some of the sugar remains undissolved. In the recipes that follow, the tenderizing sugar is folded in with the chocolate. Easy.

Good meringues are a dessert maker's secret stash. Make layers in advance and store them airtight (they keep for at least two months). Then, for a fast easy dessert, fill them with whipped cream and berries, or buttercream, or ice cream, or use them to make an elaborate "pâtisserie"-style dessert by stacking them between layers of liqueur-moistened génoise and buttercream. You pick the flavors and build the layers as high as you like.

CHOCOLATE MERINGUE

MAKES TWO 9-INCH MERINGUES, THREE 7-INCH MERINGUES,
OR TWENTY-FOUR 2½- TO 3-INCH MERINGUES

5 ounces bittersweet or semisweet
chocolate, coarsely chopped

⅔ cup sugar (see Note)

3 large egg whites, at room temperature

⅛ teaspoon cream of tartar

⅛ teaspoon salt

1 to 2 tablespoons unsweetened
cocoa powder (optional)

SPECIAL EQUIPMENT

A large baking sheet

A large pastry bag fitted with
a ⁷/₁₆- to ³/₈-inch plain tip
(Ateco #5) (optional)

Position a rack in the center of the oven and preheat the oven to 200°F. Line the baking sheet with parchment paper and use a heavy pencil to trace two 9-inch circles or ovals on the paper. (Or, if you want to make a smaller but taller dessert, trace three 7-inch circles. For about a dozen individual desserts, trace 24 or more 2½- to 3-inch circles.) Turn the paper over so that the pencil marks cannot transfer to the meringue.

Pulse the chocolate with about one-third of the sugar in a food processor, until it looks like fine crumbs. Set aside.

In a clean, dry bowl, beat the egg whites, cream of tartar, and salt on high speed (medium speed if using a heavy-duty stand mixer) until soft peaks form when the beaters are lifted. Gradually beat in the remaining sugar, taking 1 to 1½ minutes. The meringue should stand in very stiff glossy peaks when the beaters are lifted. (Remove the bowl if using a stand mixer.)

Pour all of the ground chocolate mixture over the meringue and fold it in with a large rubber spatula just until incorporated. If you are using a pastry bag, scrape the meringue into the bag. Starting at the center of one of the traced circles, pipe an ever-widening spiral of meringue (counterclockwise if you are right-handed) to cover the entire circle. Or, scrape half of the meringue (or one-third if making 3 layers, or a dollop if making small meringues) into the center of each traced circle and spread it evenly with a spatula. Use a fine strainer to sprinkle the tops of the meringues lightly with cocoa, if desired.

Bake for 2 hours. Turn off the oven and let the meringues cool completely in the turned-off oven. Store in an airtight container for up to 2 months.

NOTE: The granulated cane sugar that I use (C&H) is visibly finer than ordinary table salt, and I have not found it necessary to use extra-fine or special bakers' sugar for making meringues. However, you can substitute either of those with confidence, or you can process regular granulated sugar in a food processor for a few seconds if it seems too coarse.

NUTTY CHOCOLATE MERINGUE Reduce the chocolate to 4 ounces. Pulse the chocolate (without any sugar) to the size of crumbs. Scrape into a bowl. Pulse 1/2 cup walnuts (or toasted skinned hazelnuts [see page 40] or almonds or pecans) with one-third of the sugar until fine. Add to the ground chocolate. Proceed with the recipe.

WHITE MERINGUE Sometimes plain is still best. Properly made plain white meringue is lighter and stiffer than chocolate meringue, so it holds tall, dramatic, or sharply defined shapes with ease. Use it for Carmen Meringay (page 226) or other inventive meringue shells, or whenever crisp classic meringue is needed.

Omit the chocolate and the food processor step. Set aside one-third of the sugar. Beat the remaining sugar into the egg whites as directed. Fold in the reserved sugar and proceed as directed in the recipe.

chocolate note No alternations are necessary for different percentage chocolates. The ground-up chocolate remains in the form of tiny flecks rather than mingling or melting into the other ingredients, so you can make your choice based on flavor alone. I like to use a bittersweet 70% since the meringue is so sweet.

CHOCOLATE MERINGUES WITH BERRIES AND CREAM
SERVES 12

These are always delightful and simple as can be. If you use the Nutty Chocolate Meringue, try walnuts with strawberries, toasted hazelnuts with blackberries.

Although you should assemble this dessert within an hour of serving, you can have all of the elements ready: Rinse and pat the berries dry, and whip the cream and sugar in advance. Keep berries and cream in the fridge until needed, and give the cream a few strokes of the whisk just before using to reincorporate any liquid that has separated.

2 cups heavy cream

2 tablespoons sugar, or more to taste

1 teaspoon pure vanilla extract

Chocolate Meringue (page 180) or Nutty Chocolate Meringue (page 181): twenty-four 2 1/2- to 3-inch meringues to make 12 individual desserts or two 9-inch meringues to make one large dessert

2 pints berries, rinsed and patted dry

Powdered sugar for dusting (optional)

SPECIAL EQUIPMENT

A large pastry bag fitted with a medium star tip (such as Ateco #856) (optional)

Whip the cream with the sugar and vanilla until almost stiff. Cover and refrigerate until ready to use.

Set aside the best-looking meringue(s) for the top. Spread or pipe about two-thirds of the cream over the other meringue(s) and distribute most of the berries over it. Spread or pipe the remaining cream over the berries and top with the remaining meringue layer(s). Scatter the extra berries on top and sieve a little powdered sugar over them, if you like.

STRAWBERRY CHOCOLATE MERINGUE WITH CINNAMON GANACHE Substitute Whipped Mexican Cinnamon Ganache Filling (page 233), chilled but not yet whipped, for the heavy cream, sugar, and vanilla. Use sliced or quartered strawberries. With an electric mixer, beat the chilled ganache until it stiffens to the consistency of very thick, stiff whipped cream. Proceed with the recipe.

MERINGUES GLACÉES WITH THE WORKS photograph on page 22
SERVES 12

If you are one who dismisses meringues as too sweet, too old-fashioned, or too boring, you have never eaten meringues glacées with whipped cream and chocolate sauce. Nothing quite compares. Imagine light and rich, warm and cold, smooth and crunchy, sweet and tart, all at the same time.

The first time I tried one, I had just eaten cassoulet in a small town renowned for that dish and was so full I had no business even looking at dessert. But there it was on the plate. Melting. It appeared unassuming—it wasn't even served with chocolate sauce—and I didn't expect much. More than twenty years ago, and I still remember it.

Here's a new twist, with ice cream and chocolate sauce, and berries too.

1 quart ice cream (vanilla, chocolate, coffee, or any favorite)

Chocolate Meringue (page 180) or Nutty Chocolate Meringue (page 181): twenty-four 2½- to 3-inch meringues to make 12 individual desserts or two 9-inch meringues to make one large dessert

Lightly sweetened whipped cream

Alice's Chocolate Sauce (page 292), warmed

1 to 2 pints berries, rinsed and patted dry

Soften the ice cream in the refrigerator for 15 to 20 minutes, or in the microwave with 10-second bursts. It should be just pliable but not melting.

For individual meringues, spoon 3 to 4 tablespoons of ice cream over the top of one meringue and level it with a spatula, then press a second meringue gently on top. Immediately place on a baking sheet in the freezer. Continue until you have used all of the meringues. For one large dessert, spread all of the ice cream onto one meringue and top with the second layer. To avoid breakage, rotate the top layer gently to seat it rather than pressing it.

Freeze the meringue(s) for several hours, until firm. Pipe whipped cream around the sides or on top and serve with warm chocolate sauce and berries.

GÂTEAU DIANE photograph on page 134
SERVES 10 TO 12

In the very earliest days at Cocolat, we made an old-fashioned classic dessert called Gâteau Diane. It was just two spiraled layers of tenderly crunchy white meringue sandwiched with buttercream. The sides were encrusted with toasted sliced almonds and the top stenciled with a design in cocoa and powdered sugar. It was simple, rich, and sweet, and it had a small but passionate following. One customer, Mr. R, placed an order for Gâteau Diane most weeks when we offered it and went away looking forlorn when we didn't.

Here it is with bolder flavors and lots more texture. It's still rich and sweet, but even better. I think Mr. R, wherever he is, would approve.

Because buttercream does not soak through meringue, you can prepare the dessert and refrigerate it (wrapped gently in plastic wrap or in an airtight container) for up to 2 days. You could sieve a little cocoa powder on top and then stencil with powdered sugar. I serve this with strong coffee to offset the sweetness.

Nutty Chocolate Meringue (page 181): two 9-inch meringues

1 cup chocolate ice cream or Whipped Chocolate Ganache Filling (page 231)

1/2 cup chopped or sliced nuts or chocolate shavings (optional)

Cocoa and powdered sugar for dusting (optional)

SPECIAL EQUIPMENT

Stencil (optional)

Set the better-looking meringue aside for the top. Spread all of the filling on the bottom layer with a spatula before setting the top layer in place. Or, spread two-thirds of the filling between the layers, then spread the sides of the cake with the remaining filling and press the nuts into it. Refrigerate to firm the filling.

For a crunchy dessert, serve within the hour. Otherwise, cover and refrigerate for up to 2 days, allowing the meringue to soften and merge with the filling. If you like, dust the dessert with cocoa or powdered sugar before bringing it to the table.

From making my first chocolate truffles, I learned that the simplest recipes demand the best chocolate. Because they are made with so few ingredients, truffles let the chocolate reveal itself, for better or worse! **ON FLAVORING** Thirty years later, with more chocolates to choose from, this is especially exciting. If you make a dozen batches of "plain" chocolate truffles today, each with a different brand of chocolate, you will end up with a dozen different truffle "flavors," simply because each chocolate maker selects, roasts, blends, and carries out the process of making chocolate a little differently. If I had a chocolate shop today, that is exactly how I would create at least a few of my truffle flavors.

In my cooking classes, we frequently taste and talk about the different flavors in different chocolates. The flavors are often described in terms of other familiar foods, such as almond, toasted nuts, cherry, coffee, vanilla, honey, spices, citrus, and so forth, or with adjectives like *grassy*, *tannic*, or *fruity*. I am always careful to clarify that I am talking about the natural tastes inherent in the chocolate, flavors that have been nurtured and developed by the farmer and chocolate maker, rather than those that come from added extracts, oils, or essences. If I am not specific about this, I am sure to be misunderstood, because so many people confuse flavors with flavorings.

Flavorings, in the form of liquids and powders and pastes, are pervasive in the food industry. They are used to "enhance" everything from coffee beans to snack foods, but they are also found in dairy products and natural and organic foods. Whether the flavorings are "natural" or artificial, the food often ends up tasting like a caricature of the real thing. Flavorings corrupt the palate. They distance us from the pure taste of real food made only from real ingredients. Cheese powder comes to mind. How many people mistake the flavor of cheese powder for Cheddar because they were raised on macaroni and cheese from a box?

My experiences taught me that people who are passionate about chocolate love chocolate first and chocolate with other flavors second, if at all. Of the twelve truffle flavors (rotated each month from a list of more than fifty) always offered at Cocolat, the most popular was plain Dark on Dark: bittersweet ganache dipped in bittersweet chocolate (see Cold Creamy Truffles, page 142). These were never rotated off the menu. But other flavors were also essential to keep our clientele excited and interested.

We flavored truffles in a very simple, rather expensive way. We added good sipping-quality liqueurs such as Grand Marnier, Myers's Rum, and the exquisite high-proof fruit brandies called eaux-de-vie, made by the California craft distiller St. George Spirits. I avoided the bottled extracts, flavorings, compounds, and pastes that were being used increasingly in Europe and may now be even more widely used here. I didn't think much about it at the time: They simply didn't taste good enough to me.

Almost a decade after I sold my business, I had an opportunity to see the direction that "fine" chocolates had taken, especially in the hands of large companies. I spent two years tasting and selecting chocolates for a monthly chocolate club. I opened hundreds of boxes and ballotins of fancy filled chocolates and chocolate truffles, looking for the best among them. I found that too many reeked of their flavorings. The aroma of chocolate, if it was there at all, was secondary. I didn't have to take the first bite (although I did) to know that the flavorings would also dominate the taste of the chocolates in an unpleasant way. Most of the filled chocolates and chocolate truffles you buy are made with flavorings. Even natural flavorings are unnaturally strong, and it is apparently hard to use them with finesse!

Only a small handful of the very best chocolatiers flavor their truffles with pure, real ingredients, yet there is no reason in the world why a home cook can't do the same. In addition to liquors or liqueurs, I like to use freshly grated citrus peel, fresh fruit purees, coffee beans, teas, herbs, even rose petals. One of the most exciting ways to flavor ganache, or any cream-based mixture, is with aromatic ingredients, real ones rather than extracts, steeped in the cream and then removed before the cream is mixed with the chocolate. Some flavors are best when infused overnight in cold cream, others are better steeped in hot liquid. The results are incomparable. Fresh mint from the garden, cold-infused, makes an unforgettable mint truffle. You would have to go far to find something as good in a shop. Freshly grated citrus zest (from organic fruit) added to ganache or steeped in the hot cream, depending on the desired effect, adds a flavor that cannot be matched by even the highly touted citrus oils. These same techniques are used throughout this book to flavor sauces, mousses, and ice creams with chiles, toasted coconut, vanilla beans, cocoa nibs, and more.

The difference between chocolates or desserts flavored with natural ingredients and those containing artificial flavorings, or even prepared natural flavorings, is the difference between edible poetry and barely palatable advertising jingles. Flavorings and extracts from a bottle are more convenient, but once you've tasted real flavors from real ingredients, convenience doesn't seem so important anymore. Your own truffles can be far better than 99 percent of what can be bought in the marketplace. This I know.

5

Less Is More

Soufflés and Other Confections

If you want great attendance at a healthy cooking class, ask a known chocolate dessert chef to teach it. Before I was invited to do that several years ago, I had never considered making chocolate desserts with less fat or less of anything. When they asked for something "lighter," I regularly told customers to eat a smaller piece. I said that a tiny piece of rich chocolate torte made with superb ingredients would be more satisfying than a big piece of something made of compromises.

At the time, commercial low-fat desserts were unbearably sweet and filled with weird fat "replacers" from industrial food laboratories, modified food starches, and artificial flavors to camouflage it all. Meanwhile, home cooks were learning to replace as well—prune puree for butter, egg whites for egg yolks, dietetic chocolate or nonfat cocoa for the good stuff, and heaven-knows-what for sugar. Results were dismally dry or rubbery.

MAXIMIZING THE MINIMUM

With the exception of foods inherently low in fat, like fresh fruit, sorbet, or meringues, low-fat dessert choices were more like punishment than pleasure. I wondered if I could make superb chocolate desserts with superb ingredients, but less fat and no compromises. I knew I could at least do better than the current offerings.

I knew I was on the right track after the second class when I saw students oohing and aahing as though they were tasting decadent desserts! And, they were excited about serving the new desserts without a disclaimer or even mentioning that they were lower in fat. Lighter desserts were fooling people, including my friends and customers accustomed to the richest faire.

I was hooked. I spent the next two years working on *Chocolate and the Art of Low-Fat Desserts,* for which I won the James Beard Cookbook of the Year Award. What really took my breath away was that the award was for not the best low-fat book of the year, but for the best cookbook! Almost better still, the work taught me about tasting and flavor, lessons that would change and improve all of my cooking—both lean and rich.

I'd always known, as everyone does, that fat enhances flavors and textures. What I had not known until I worked with a limited fat budget was how fat can also dull and blur flavors and how subtracting some fat can add flavor. What began as a set of strict "takeaways" (less fat) and limitations (fewer calories) turned into positive techniques for creating bigger and better flavors in desserts.

The most important lessons from the low-fat experience are summarized below. If you consider them without limiting your thinking to low-fat recipes, they will enhance your understanding and the quality of everything you cook or bake.

• Quality ingredients are essential in all fine cooking. They are especially important in low-fat recipes. You can't hide any flaws. Bad flavors, poor balance, artificial flavors—all these show up more in a dish with less fat. So if you cut down on fat, you need ingredients with the most and best flavor: good dairy products, fresh nuts, sipping-quality liqueurs (if you use them), and natural flavoring. If chocolate, which is inherently high in fat, is to be the starring ingredient, you must choose one with lots of flavor, intensity, and complexity, because you will be limited in how much you can use.

• When too much fat or all the fat is eliminated, a dessert no longer tastes or feels indulgent. (That's when your guests feel like leaving your table and immediately going out for hot fudge sundaes.) You can cut some fat without replacing it, but cut wisely. Most rich chocolate desserts are conveniently loaded with other high-fat ingredients, so you have lots of choices. Different recipes require different strategies, of course, but in general, the idea is to cut the rich ingredients that contribute the least flavor and texture to the dessert.

• Contrast is also a valuable tool. Where and how you use a particular fat in a dessert can make an enormous difference. For example, I like to serve a little dab of real whipped cream as a final touch on my Fallen Chocolate Soufflé Cake (page 112). It's great without the cream, but astonishing with it. This illustrates something valuable to know about chocolate desserts, regardless of how rich or lean they are. Through sheer contrast of color, flavor, and texture, even a little whipped cream intensifies the flavor of chocolate. The impact of this contrast can be more dramatic than using three times the amount of cream blended into the dessert itself. (I use this trick even when I am not intentionally creating reduced-fat desserts.)

• Flavor layering, the opposite of contrast, can add a perception of richness. To reinforce and deepen a flavor, use more than one ingredient to make the statement. Forced to cut down on chocolate, I may add cocoa. I also get different effects by combining different brands of chocolate with different cocoas (both natural and Dutch-process), because all have different flavors.

• Watch out for upstaging the chocolate when creating low-fat chocolate desserts with other assertive flavors. To keep chocolate in the starring role, make sure that other potentially strong notes such as liqueurs, citrus zest, or mint are kept sotto voce or eliminated.

• Finally, desserts made with less fat are less forgiving. Check your oven temperature and pay attention to timing, because these desserts will overbake and dry out faster. Measure carefully (especially dry ingredients) to prevent heavy desserts.

This book is lightly sprinkled with lower-fat desserts (indeed, there is only one in this chapter), but it is even more liberally laced with the lessons about flavor that I learned in creating them. By the time I turned my attention to better-quality chocolates with more distinctive flavors, those lessons were so fully integrated into my baking that I sometimes forgot how effective they can be.

✻ CHOCOLATE-FLECKED COCOA SOUFFLÉS
SERVES 8

I like chocolate soufflés to be more rich and chocolatey than light and ethereal. Those here push the limits with flavor and richness, even though each has less than 7 grams of fat and only 180 calories. Individual dishes work better than a single large soufflé here; that way each guest gets to enjoy the contrast of crunchy sugared edges and gooey interior without having to share. Unlike many soufflés, these come with a do-ahead feature: You can cover and refrigerate the unbaked soufflés for up to a day. Preheat the oven toward the end of the meal, then pop the soufflés in the oven for less than 15 minutes. Voilà!

About 2 tablespoons sugar
for coating the ramekins (optional)

$1/2$ cup unsweetened cocoa powder
(natural or Dutch-process)

2 tablespoons all-purpose flour

$3/4$ cup sugar

$1/2$ cup 1% milk

2 large eggs, separated

1 teaspoon pure vanilla extract

Pinch of salt

2 large egg whites

$1/8$ teaspoon cream of tartar

3 ounces bittersweet chocolate,
finely chopped

Powdered sugar for dusting

SPECIAL EQUIPMENT

Eight 4- to 5-ounce ramekins

If baking immediately, position a rack in the lower third of the oven and preheat the oven to 350°F. Lightly butter the sides and bottom of the ramekins. If you are sugaring them, pour the sugar into one ramekin. Hold it over a second ramekin to catch any spills, and tilt and rotate the sugar-filled ramekin until the bottom and sides are coated with sugar. Tap the excess sugar into the second ramekin. Repeat until all the ramekins are coated, adding more sugar if necessary. Set on a baking sheet.

In a small saucepan, combine the cocoa, flour, and $\frac{1}{2}$ cup of the sugar. Stir in enough of the milk to form a smooth paste, then stir in the remaining milk. Heat slowly, stirring constantly, until the mixture bubbles slightly around the edges. Continue to cook and stir, scraping the bottom and sides of the pan to prevent scorching, for about 2 more minutes, until the mixture is slightly thickened. Scrape into a large bowl. Whisk in the egg yolks, vanilla, and salt. Set aside.

In a large clean, dry bowl, beat the egg whites and the cream of tartar with an electric mixer at medium speed until soft peaks form when the beaters are lifted. Gradually add the remaining $\frac{1}{4}$ cup sugar, and continue to beat at high speed until the eggs whites are stiff but not dry.

Fold about one-quarter of the egg whites into the batter to lighten it. Scrape the remaining egg whites into the bowl and fold just until the egg whites are partially blended. Sprinkle in the chopped chocolate and fold until the egg whites and chocolate are blended. Divide the mixture among the ramekins, filling them nearly full. (The soufflés can be covered with plastic wrap and refrigerated overnight before baking.)

Bake, on the baking sheet, for 15 to 16 minutes (cold soufflés will take a minute or two longer to bake), until the soufflés puff up above the rim of the ramekins and crack on top and a toothpick inserted in the center of each emerges with thick, creamy batter still clinging to it. Do not overbake.

Using a fine-mesh sieve, sift powdered sugar over the tops, and serve immediately.

chocolate notes I have had good results with both natural and Dutch-process cocoa, except "black" cocoas.

For the chopped chocolate, you will get the most flavor from a bittersweet in the 70% range, but you will have good results with standard semisweet or bittersweet chocolates (without a percentage on the label), or any marked from 50% to 72%. Chocolate chips are acceptable as well, just not as wonderful. No adjustments are needed.

I lead a "chocolate tour" class at the Sur La Table store nearest my house. After a brief lecture on the history of chocolate and the cultivation of cacao, we take a private tour with one of the owners of the Scharffen Berger Chocolate Factory. When we return to the kitchen, I demonstrate several "minimalist" desserts made with each of the three Scharffen Berger chocolates.

At the outset, I always ask if anyone ever plunks down a small fortune to buy sensational extra virgin olive oil. Many hands shoot up and there are smiles and murmurs of pleasure. (I know this Berkeley audience well.) I ask if anyone ever whisks that precious green-gold elixir with mustard and honey and Worcestershire sauce and twenty-seven different herbs and spices to make salad dressing. That is the cue for knowing chuckles and head shaking, because in this rare corner of the world, people understand that such divine oil needs only a splash of good vinegar or squeeze of citrus, a judicious sprinkling of sea salt, and a grind or two of the peppermill. We save more complicated recipes for lesser oils. I make the similar point about chocolate: Good distinctive chocolate begs not to be crowded by too many ingredients or overwhelmed with an excess of sugar, butter, or cream.

If, as I originally learned by making chocolate truffles, the simplest recipe calls for the best chocolate, then the reverse is also true: The best chocolate requires the simplest recipe. A "minimalist" recipe, like the simplest vinaigrette, lets the inherent qualities of the ingredients shine. Sure of myself in this regard, I was unprepared for what happened one day and rudely awakened, when the concept was played out to its logical conclusion.

At the end of one class, amidst oohs and aahs produced by the Intensely Bittersweet Soufflés (page 198) made with Scharffen Berger chocolate and topped with Cocoa Bean Cream (page 304), one brave woman admitted that the soufflés tasted too tart and bitter. Her daughter, sitting next to her, agreed. My spirits sagged like their two half-eaten soufflés; I could no longer hear the sighs and moans of delight all around me. Someone hadn't loved my dessert? I asked the traitors (very politely) if they had enjoyed the chocolate by itself. They said it was too tart, too bitter. Then I realized that my dessert had not failed: I meant to create a recipe that revealed the chocolate, and I had done it well enough that someone who didn't like the chocolate had not liked the dessert either. (I wanted to shout, "Ah ha!" Actually I did shout, "Ah ha.") I suggested that the two women go home and try the recipe, using *their* favorite chocolate. I knew that the recipe would deliver the flavors they loved best in the chocolate that they loved best. I had made my point after all.

INTENSELY BITTERSWEET SOUFFLÉS

SERVES 8

This recipe is positively a showcase for the chocolate you make it with, so you must use a chocolate of distinction. Choose one that you adore eating, one with flavors that beg to be savored rather than masked with excess butter, sugar, or cream. Such a chocolate inspired the recipe in the first place, which, as it has evolved, reads more like mousse (no flour) than a classic soufflé. No matter, it produces a dessert that acts and tastes like a soufflé, and it is easier to make. I make these a day or so ahead and refrigerate them, unbaked, until shortly before I want to serve them. Preheat the oven toward the end of dinner, then bake the soufflés while you clear the table and make the coffee. Expect big chocolate flavor and extravagant praise.

About 2 tablespoons sugar for the ramekins

8 ounces bittersweet 70% chocolate, finely chopped

1 tablespoon unsalted butter

1/3 cup milk

3 large eggs, separated, at room temperature

1 large egg white, at room temperature

1/8 teaspoon cream of tartar

1/3 cup sugar

FOR THE TOPPING

1 cup heavy cream

1/2 teaspoon pure vanilla extract

1 tablespoon sugar

Powdered sugar for dusting (optional)

SPECIAL EQUIPMENT

Eight 6-ounce ramekins

If you are baking the soufflés right away, position a rack in the lower third of the oven and preheat to 375°F. Butter the ramekins and sprinkle with sugar.

Place the chocolate, butter, and milk in a large heatproof bowl in a large skillet of barely simmering water. Stir until the chocolate is melted and the mixture is smooth. Remove the bowl from the water bath and whisk in the egg yolks. (Don't worry if the mixture stiffens slightly or is less than perfectly smooth at this point.) Set aside.

In a medium, dry bowl, beat the egg whites and cream of tartar with an electric mixer on medium speed until soft peaks form when the beaters are lifted. Gradually sprinkle in the ⅓ cup sugar and beat at high speed until the whites are stiff but not dry. Fold one-quarter of the egg whites into the chocolate mixture to lighten it, then fold in the remaining egg whites.

Divide the mixture evenly among the prepared ramekins, filling each three-quarters full. (The soufflés can be prepared to this point, covered, and refrigerated for up to 2 days. Bake directly from the refrigerator.)

Place the soufflés on a cookie sheet. Bake until they rise and crack on top and a wooden skewer plunged into the center emerges very moist and gooey (but the centers should not be completely liquid), 14 to 16 minutes, perhaps a minute or so longer if the soufflés have been refrigerated.

Meanwhile, make the topping: Beat the cream with the vanilla and sugar until it holds a soft shape (or stiffer, if you like it that way). Transfer to a serving bowl and refrigerate until ready to serve.

When they are done, remove the soufflés from the oven, and serve immediately, with a little powdered sugar sifted over the top, if you'd like. Pass the whipped topping separately.

BITTERSWEET CHOCOLATE SOUFFLÉS WITH COCOA BEAN CREAM Sometimes I top the soufflés with lightly sweetened Cocoa Bean Cream (page 304) instead of plain whipped cream. The effect is sensual and subtle, as opposed to the sharp dramatic contrast with whipped cream. It's hard to choose which is better; you will have to try both.

chocolate note This is a remarkably versatile recipe. You can substitute a lower-percentage bittersweet or semisweet chocolate if you prefer a sweeter, less intense chocolate flavor; or reduce the sugar to ¼ cup to partially compensate for the sweeter chocolate, if desired. There is no need to make other changes in the recipe.

BITTERSWEET ROULADE photograph on pages 254–255
SERVES 12

Thin flourless chocolate soufflé layers have always been among my favorite and most useful "building blocks," whether I am making this simple roulade or the most intricate ten-layer extravaganza. My newest soufflé sheet was designed especially for bittersweet 70 percent chocolate. It yields an intensely flavorful layer (slightly cakey because of the higher percentage of cocoa solids—there is still no flour in the recipe!) that is not so sweet as what we used to make.

FOR THE BITTERSWEET CHOCOLATE
SOUFFLÉ SHEET

6 ounces bittersweet 70% chocolate,
coarsely chopped

1/3 cup water or freshly brewed espresso,
or 1 teaspoon instant espresso powder
(such as Medaglia d'Oro) dissolved in
1/3 cup hot water

1 teaspoon pure vanilla extract

6 large eggs, separated,
at room temperature

1/4 teaspoon cream of tartar

3/4 cup sugar

1 to 2 tablespoons unsweetened
cocoa powder

1 cup cream or Cocoa Bean Cream
(page 304), chilled but not whipped,
with 2 to 3 teaspoons sugar, or 1/2 recipe
Whipped Chocolate Ganache Filling
(page 231)

Cocoa powder and/or powdered sugar
for dusting

SPECIAL EQUIPMENT

An 11-by-17-inch or 12-by-17-inch
jelly-roll or half sheet pan

Position an oven rack in the lower third of the oven and preheat the oven to 375°F. Line the baking sheet with parchment paper.

Place the chocolate and water in a large bowl set in a wide skillet of barely simmering water and stir frequently until the chocolate is completely melted and the mixture is smooth. Or microwave on Medium (50%) power for about 1 minute and 15 seconds, then stir until smooth. Stir in the vanilla and set aside.

Place the egg whites and cream of tartar in a large dry bowl and beat with an electric mixer on medium speed until soft peaks are formed. Gradually sprinkle in the sugar and continue to beat at high speed until the whites are stiff but not dry.

Whisk the yolks into the melted chocolate mixture. Fold one-quarter of the egg whites completely into the chocolate mixture to lighten it. Add the remaining egg whites and fold in gently but completely. Spread the batter evenly in the prepared pan.

Bake until the cake springs back when pressed lightly with your fingertips and a toothpick inserted into the center comes out moist but not gooey, 8 to 10 minutes. Cool completely in the pan on a rack. (The soufflé sheet can be covered tightly and refrigerated for up to 2 days or frozen for up to 3 months.)

To unmold, first run a small knife around the inner edges of the pan to release the cake. Using a fine-mesh sieve, sift a very light dusting of cocoa over the surface. Cover with a sheet of foil. Holding the foil and pan edges together at both ends, invert the pan onto the counter. Remove the pan and peel off the parchment liner.

Whip the cream or cocoa cream with sugar to taste until nearly stiff. Or, whip the ganache until nearly stiff. Spread the filling evenly over the cake. Starting at one short edge and using the foil to help you, roll up the cake. At first the pastry will crack severely, but the cracking will get less severe as the roulade gets fatter; a little cracking on the finished roulade ends looks like tree bark and is quite appetizing. Wrap the roulade tightly in the foil and refrigerate it up to a day.

To serve, unwrap the roulade and transfer it to a platter, seam side down. Using a fine-mesh sieve, sift on a little more cocoa and/or a little powdered sugar.

BITTERSWEET PAVÉ For a dressier cake, cut the soufflé sheet into 6 equal layers and construct a rectangular layer cake with any of the fillings. Omit the cocoa. Glaze or frost with Bittersweet Chocolate Glaze (page 235) or Sarah Bernhardt Chocolate Glaze (page 236).

chocolate notes I let the chocolate determine how sweet or bittersweet the outcome will be, so I don't adjust the amount of chocolate or sugar for higher-percentage chocolates. Only water and baking details need adjustment. The lower the chocolate liquor percentage, the less cakey the texture will be.

To use chocolate marked 64% to 66% instead of bittersweet 70%: Use ¼ cup water.

To use standard bittersweet or semisweet chocolate (without a percentage on the label), or any marked 50% through 62% instead of bittersweet 70%: Reduce the water to 3 tablespoons. Bake the sheet for 10 minutes, then reduce the oven temperature to 350°F and bake for another 5 to 7 minutes, or until the surface of the sheet seems firm to the touch.

MELTING CHOCOLATE MERINGUES

MAKES ABOUT THIRTY 2-INCH COOKIES

Deceptively light and delicately crusted, these cookies are moist and meltingly bitter-sweet within. Without butter or egg yolks, they are the soul of simplicity, and a nice way to use a distinctive chocolate.

6 ounces bittersweet or semisweet chocolate, coarsely chopped

2 large egg whites ($1/4$ cup), at room temperature

$1/8$ teaspoon cream of tartar

$1/2$ teaspoon pure vanilla extract

$1/4$ cup sugar

$3/4$ cup chopped walnuts

Position the racks in the upper and lower thirds of the oven and preheat the oven to 350°F. Line two cookie sheets with parchment or wax paper.

Melt the chocolate in a medium heatproof bowl set in a wide skillet of barely simmering water, or in the microwave on Medium (50%) power for $3^{1}/_{2}$ to 4 minutes. Stir frequently until the chocolate is almost completely melted, then remove from the heat or microwave and stir to complete the melting. Set aside.

In a large bowl, beat the egg whites with the cream of tartar and vanilla until soft peaks form when you lift the beaters. Gradually add the sugar, continuing to beat until the eggs whites are stiff but not dry. Pour the nuts, then all of the warm chocolate, over the egg whites and fold in with a rubber spatula until the color of the batter is uniform. *Do not let the batter wait.*

Drop tablespoonfuls of the batter at least 1 inch apart onto the cookie sheets. Bake for 8 to 10 minutes, rotating the sheets from front to back and top to bottom about halfway through the baking period. The surface of the cookies should look dry and feel slightly firm but still gooey inside when you press them. Slide the paper pan liners onto racks to cool. Let cool completely before storing. (The cookies are best on the day they are baked, but still delectable for another 2 to 3 days; store in an airtight container.)

chocolate notes You can use standard bittersweet or semisweet chocolate (without a percentage on the label), or any marked 50% to 62%.

To use chocolate marked 64% to 66% instead of standard bittersweet: Use 5 ounces chocolate.

To use chocolate marked 70% to 72% instead of standard bittersweet: Use $4\frac{1}{2}$ ounces chocolate, and increase the sugar to $\frac{1}{3}$ cup.

RICH HOT CHOCOLATE photographs on pages 14 and 19
SERVES 6 TO 8

You may be surprised that a chocolate recipe labeled "rich" calls for water and milk rather than for all milk or even half milk and half cream. But here I am making a point about the flavor. My goal was to show off the chocolate. Less milk, less creaminess, and less fat allow us to taste more of the complex and subtle flavors that make one chocolate distinct from another. Try this with your favorite chocolate and you will see what I mean. If you want a creamier drink, or one so thick your spoon stands up in it, you can make the obvious changes. But I suggest that if you insist on cream, try serving it whipped on top, rather than stirred in; the contrast will be dramatic and satisfying, and it won't diminish the chocolate flavor.

I often make this in advance and reheat it using the steamer of my espresso machine. Delicious, and foamy too.

6 ounces bittersweet or semisweet chocolate, coarsely chopped	1½ cups boiling water
	1½ cups milk

Place the chocolate in a small saucepan. Pour about half of the boiling water over the chocolate and stir until the chocolate is melted and smooth. Stir in the rest of the boiling water and the milk. Heat over medium heat, whisking continuously, until hot but nowhere near boiling (the texture and flavor are both best if the hot chocolate never exceeds 180°F). Serve immediately, or set aside and reheat just before serving.

MOCHA HOT CHOCOLATE The recipe invites variations. Make it mocha using only ¾ cup water and adding the other ¾ cup espresso or strong coffee with the milk.

ANCHO CHILE HOT CHOCOLATE Dried ancho chiles are also called *pasillas*. They are deep chocolate red and heady with an earthy musk. After seeing the film *Chocolat* a friend and I came directly home for hot chocolate. From drawers and cupboards, little jars of dried ground chiles were unearthed from past bouts of Indian and Mexican cooking. Between sips of chocolate, we began to inhale from each jar. The anchos beckoned, and we stirred pinches into our cups—just enough to feel the heat. Try it.

SPICED HOT CHOCOLATE Following the sniffing ritual described above for Ancho Chile Hot Chocolate, experiment with other spices, such as anise, cinnamon, nutmeg, Chinese five-spice, ground vanilla beans, pieces of dried citrus peel, or grated fresh citrus zest. One spice blend will suggest another to you, as they do to me.

chocolate note Let the chocolate you choose determine how sweet or intense your results will be. No alterations are necessary. I like it with a bittersweet 70% chocolate.

Glitz and Glamour

Grand Cakes, Fillings, and Glazes

The heart and soul of Cocolat were the chocolate truffles and the sleek-looking bittersweet chocolate tortes, exemplified by the Queen of Sheba, beautifully glazed and encrusted with toasted shaved almonds. But there was glitz and glamour on the menu too: special-occasion desserts with complex multiple layers and contrasting textures of génoise and sponge cake, ganaches and glazes, mousses, and meringues. The most memorable were variously wrapped in chocolate, enveloped with halos of spun sugar, topped with ruffled chocolate fans, or gilded with gold leaf. Dream desserts.

DESSERTS WORTH CELEBRATING

Hardly a week goes by without someone in the grocery store, at a party, or on the street reminding me that I (we) made the cake for their wedding, anniversary, or birthday, or all of the above!

From the beginning, however, I never liked cake decorating in the traditional sense, and I still don't. But I love to design desserts, to choose and plan the construction of the layers, flavors, and textures so that when everything is put together, the result looks spectacular and tastes even better. The engineer and architect buried somewhere in me is still enthralled with the pastry chef's craft—the special effects and fancy feats—and the ingenuity involved in putting it all together.

So, while I normally serve simple desserts at home, I'm still a show-off. I think every cook needs a dramatic, spectacular dessert up his or her sleeve, to pull out on special occasions. One of my favorite pastry chef tricks—because it looks much harder than it is—involves assembling the elements of the dessert in a pan that has been lined with a band of chocolate spread on a plastic strip (see page 211). Once the chocolate liner is in the pan, the assembly is easy. You fill the lined pan with cake layers, fruit, and cream, or layers of cake and mousse, or three different mousses, or ice creams with meringues and sauce; it's entirely up to you. Top the whole affair with a bouquet of ruffled chocolate fans or an arrangement of thin abstract (meaning not so perfect) attempts at ruffled chocolate fans or simple chocolate curls, or just handfuls of fresh berries. When the dessert is unmolded and the plastic strip peeled away to reveal a shiny wall of chocolate, you may gasp involuntarily at the perfection of your own work (as I still sometimes do). The dessert can be prepared ahead, and the whole thing screams for invention. Having done it once, you will do it again and again, perhaps differently each time. Use the mousses and fillings and cake bases and meringues and ices creams from this book as you like, or use favorite components from your own repertoire. Now you are designing desserts and thinking like a pastry chef.

STRAWBERRY CELEBRATION CAKE photograph on page 127

SERVES 12 TO 16

My celebration cake is a chocolate shell filled with rum-splashed cake, ripe straw-berries, and whipped mascarpone and cream. But, for the latter, you could use Whipped Mexican Cinnamon Ganache Filling (page 233), or crème frâiche, or Albert's Mousse (page 166), or Chocolate Marquise (page 172). You could substitute black-berries for the strawberries or omit them altogether. Once you learn the method for lining the pan with chocolate and assembling the layers, you can go wild with flavors and textures. Master the technique for shaving chocolate off a cookie sheet, and you will be in great demand whenever a show-off dessert is needed.

3 ounces bittersweet or semisweet chocolate, chopped medium-fine

FOR THE SOAKING SYRUP

1/3 cup sugar

1/3 cup water

1/3 to 1/2 cup rum

2 cups mascarpone cheese

1 cup heavy cream

1/4 cup sugar

2 teaspoons pure vanilla extract

Chocolate Génoise (page 229)

About 2 pints ripe strawberries, rinsed, patted dry and hulled

Ruffled chocolate fans (see page 238) or chocolate ruffles (see page 240)

Powdered sugar for dusting (optional)

SPECIAL EQUIPMENT

A 26-by-3-inch strip of plastic shelf liner (see Note)

An 8-by-3-inch springform pan or cheesecake pan with a removable bottom

Instant-read thermometer

To line the pan with chocolate: Fit the plastic strip around the inside of the cake pan. Mark and then trim the ends so that it fits exactly, with the ends butted together: It should not overlap at all, nor should there be a gap. Tear off a sheet of wax paper longer than the plastic strip and place it on the counter. Place the plastic strip on the wax paper, with the smoother side facing up.

continued

Melt the chocolate in a small bowl set in a wide skillet of not quite simmering water, stirring frequently until melted and smooth. Or microwave on Medium (50%) power for about $2\frac{1}{2}$ minutes, stirring once or twice. The chocolate should be 115° to 120°F. If you used a water bath, wipe the bottom of the chocolate bowl dry.

Pour all of the chocolate in a thick band down the center of the plastic strip from one end to the other. Spread the chocolate evenly with an offset spatula, covering the plastic completely and allowing the excess to run over onto the wax paper. Use the point of a paring knife to locate and lift one end of the chocolate-coated strip. Slip your hand under the strip and hold it by the edges about a quarter of the way from one end. Slide your other hand under the strip and hold it by the edges about a quarter of the distance from the other end. Lift the strip and carefully fit it into the pan, chocolate facing the inside, ends butted together. Repair any gaps in the chocolate caused by your fingers with a little additional chocolate applied with your fingertips or a spatula. Refrigerate the chocolate-lined pan until needed.

To make the soaking syrup: Combine the $\frac{1}{3}$ cup sugar and water in a small saucepan. Stir just to moisten all the sugar, then bring to a simmer for about 2 minutes to dissolve the sugar. Let cool, then add rum to taste.

Combine the mascarpone, cream, $\frac{1}{4}$ cup sugar, and vanilla in a large bowl and whip until the mixture holds a good shape—almost stiff peaks.

Use a serrated knife to cut the chocolate génoise horizontally into 2 layers. Fit the bottom layer, cut side up, into the chocolate-lined pan. Brush the layer with about 3 tablespoons of rum syrup. Spread half of the cream evenly over the cake layer. Arrange and press the strawberries, lying on their sides, into the cream with a little space between them. Spread enough of the cream between and over the berries to just cover them. Spread a little extra cream about $\frac{1}{2}$ inch up the sides of the pan.

Moisten the second génoise layer lightly with about 2 tablespoons syrup and fit it, moist side down, in the pan. Press it into place. Moisten the top of the génoise with the remaining syrup and cover with any remaining cream. Cover the pan and refrigerate for several hours or overnight.

Remove the sides of the springform pan, or set the pan with the push-up bottom on a canister and pull the sides down and off the cake. (If, as is occasionally the case, there was little or no mascarpone filling left to spread on the top génoise layer, you can either beat a little extra whipping cream and spread it on; or melt 2 ounces bittersweet or semisweet chocolate with 3 tablespoons unsalted butter or cream and spread the cake with the resulting glaze, then add the chocolate sheets or fans.) Set the cake on a serving dish. Carefully peel the plastic strip off the cake. Arrange over-lapping chocolate sheets or ruffles on top of the cake to cover the cream, extending beyond the sides of the cake. Refrigerate until ready to serve.

If desired, using a fine-mesh sieve, sift a little powdered sugar over the top to highlight the chocolate just before serving. Cut with a sharp serrated knife dipped in hot water and wiped dry between slices.

NOTE: Plastic shelf liner is a flexible plastic sheet with a ribbed side and a smooth side. It is sold on a roll, like Contact paper, in the housewares section of most hard-ware stores. An 8-inch pan requires a length of at least 26 inches, but if you think that you will make larger chocolate-banded cakes, buy 36 inches instead. The liner is wide enough so you will have some left over in case you don't cut it quite right the first time, with plenty left to cut longer or shorter or wider strips to fit other pans. The strips are reusable.

chocolate note You can use any bittersweet or semisweet chocolate that you like, regardless of percentage, to line the pan and make the sheets or ruffles for decoration. You could even subsitute white or milk chocolate in this dessert.

TRIBUTE CAKE photograph on page 129
SERVES 14 TO 16

A few years ago I collaborated with my friend Flo Braker, a wonderful baker and cookbook author, on an eightieth-birthday cake for Chuck Williams, founder of Williams-Sonoma. The party was a hearty family-style luncheon in Boston, where three hundred members of the American Institute of Wine and Food were gathered for a conference. Flo and I describe the cake we made as "Flo's cake with Alice's goops": four thin layers of Flo's sensational devil's food cake, filled with my light whipped ganache and glazed with my Sarah Bernhardt Chocolate Glaze. Each serving had a handmade fan-shaped chocolate ruffle anchored by a little chocolate medallion with Chuck's name on it.

That cake for three hundred took us days to make and decorate in the bowels of an unfamiliar and not-too-luxuriously appointed hotel kitchen. We missed a number of the conference activities because we were up to our ears in, well, Flo's batter and my goops. We came up from the depths each day for a stiff drink and a giggle about the adventures below. But when it was finally served, Chuck looked touched, and Julia Child stood up spontaneously to pay her respects. We were thrilled.

Let me try to convey the true brilliance of this cake. The individual elements were excellent, but the idea of putting them together was pure Flo Braker genius. There were three (four, if you count the ruffled chocolate fans) different textures and intensities of chocolate, and they were perfection together. It was very chocolatey but not heavy; rich and yet light. It was a poem. I loved it and I continue to make it for all kinds of special occasions.

The cake inspired me. I love to take good ideas and use them as a springboard for new and different desserts. But there was one problem here. Flo's cake is the best devil's food I have ever eaten. It is sweet and tender and moist in the best American cake tradition without the equally traditional flavor of overalkalized cocoa (a taste I do not like) that results from too much baking soda. And, it happens to go perfectly with the less-sweet European-style fillings and chocolate glazes I like. I admit I tried to improve on the cake, but I just wasn't able to. So I asked Flo if I could publish our cake.

Here it is, with her blessing, the way I made it at home, with three layers to serve 14 to 16 rather than 300. You can prepare the ganache up to four days in advance, and you can assemble the cake up to two days before glazing and serving it.

FOR THE CAKE

2 cups (7 ounces) sifted
(before measuring) cake flour

1 teaspoon baking soda

1/4 teaspoon salt

1/2 cup sifted cocoa powder
(natural or Dutch-process)

1/2 cup lukewarm water

1/2 cup buttermilk, at room temperature

1/2 cup water

2 teaspoons pure vanilla extract

2 large eggs, at room temperature

8 tablespoons (1 stick) unsalted butter,
at room temperature

1 cup sugar

1 cup packed light brown sugar

Whipped Chocolate Ganache Filling
(page 231), chilled but not whipped

Sarah Bernhardt Chocolate Glaze
(page 236), cooled to frosting consistency

1 ounce chocolate, melted,
for piping the greeting

Ruffled chocolate fans (see page 238)
(optional)

3 (unsprayed) roses (optional)

SPECIAL EQUIPMENT

Three 9-inch round cake pans

A 9-inch cardboard cake circle

Instant-read thermometer

Decorating turntable or lazy Susan
(optional)

Position a rack in the lower third of the oven and preheat the oven to 350°F. Line the bottom of the cake pans with rounds of parchment paper.

In a medium bowl, mix together the flour, baking soda, and salt, then sift onto a sheet of wax paper. In a small bowl, whisk together the cocoa and lukewarm water; set aside to cool. In a glass measure, combine the buttermilk, the remaining 1/2 cup water, and the vanilla. In a small bowl, whisk the eggs briefly to combine the whites and yolks.

In a large bowl, beat the butter with an electric mixer for a few seconds, until creamy. Gradually add the sugars and beat until light and fluffy, 6 to 7 minutes. With the mixer on medium, slowly add the eggs, taking about 2 minutes in all. Continue to beat, scraping the bowl as necessary, until the mixture is fluffy and velvety.

continued

Stop the mixer and scrape in the cocoa mixture, then beat on medium speed just until combined. Stop the mixer, add one-third of the flour mixture, and beat on low speed only until no flour is visible. Stop the mixer and add half of the buttermilk mixture, and beat only until the liquid is absorbed. Repeat with half of the remaining flour, then all of the remaining buttermilk, and finally the remaining flour. Scrape the bowl as necessary, and beat only enough to incorporate the ingredients after each addition.

Pour the batter into the pans and spread it level. Bake until the layers spring back slightly when lightly pressed with your fingers and a toothpick inserted into the centers comes out clean, about 20 minutes. Cool the layers on a rack for about 5 minutes before unmolding to cool completely, right side up, on the rack.

To assemble the cake: Beat the chilled ganache with an electric mixer on medium speed just until it stiffens and holds its shape like very thick whipped cream but can still be easily spread. Do not overbeat.

Place one cake layer, upside down, on the cardboard cake circle. Spread with half of the ganache. Place the second cake layer upside down on the ganache and press into place. Spread with the remaining ganache and top with the third layer of cake (upside down). Chill the cake at least 1 hour, or up to 2 days, before glazing it.

Spread a very thin layer of the cooled glaze over the top and sides of the cake. This layer is called the crumb coat; it is just to smooth the surface, glue on any crumbs and fill any cracks. Chill the cake for a few minutes to set the crumb coat.

Set the bowl of the remaining glaze in a pan of barely simmering water and reheat very gently, stirring with a rubber spatula, until it is fluid and shiny; it should be no warmer than 90°F. Center the cake on the turntable or lazy Susan. Have a clean, dry, metal icing spatula ready. Pour all of the glaze over the center of the cake. Working quickly, using just 3 or 4 strokes and rotating the turntable, spread the glaze over the top of the cake so that it runs down to coat the sides. If there are any bare spots left uncoated, use the spatula to scoop up excess glaze and touch it to those spots, but don't spread it: spreading the glaze as it begins to set will make it look dull. Refrigerate the cake immediately, and save the excess glaze.

After the glaze is set, write a birthday greeting on top of the cake with the melted chocolate and attach the optional chocolate fans to the sides of the cake with the reserved glaze or more melted chocolate. Decorate the cake with the roses, if desired. Refrigerate the cake until about 1 hour before serving.

TRIBUTE CAKE VARIATIONS AND IDEAS It's hard *not* to play with even a great cake. Whipped ganache is a perfect vehicle for infused flavors: Ideas and recipes follow.

Gianduja: Fill the cake with Whipped Gianduja Ganache Filling (page 231) or Gianduja Mousse (page 175). Decorate with toasted hazelnuts (see page 40), shards of toasted hazelnut praline (see page 245), or caramel-glazed hazelnuts (see page 245) instead of chocolate fans.

Espresso: Fill the cake with Whipped Mocha Ganache (page 232) and glaze it with Glace à l'Eau (page 237) made with espresso. Top the cake with Mendiants (page 341) decorated with cocoa nibs.

Canela: Fill the cake with Whipped Mexican Cinnamon Ganache (page 233). Garnish with chocolate cigarettes (see page 241) dusted with cocoa and ground cinnamon to look like cinnamon sticks, or use real cinnamon sticks, dipped halfway in chocolate. Accompany the cake with sliced strawberries or a sauce of pureed strawberries.

Raspberry: Embed ½ pint fresh raspberries in the filling between each layer.

JULIA'S CAKE

SERVES 12 TO 14

This is another stunning adult birthday cake. Crème frâiche and eau-de-vie de framboise add an extra dimension and plenty of sophistication to everyone's favorite raspberry-and-chocolate combination. The cake is a kissing cousin to the one that I made on the PBS series *Baking with Julia*. But in this version, instead of a chocolate wrapper and a crown of ruffles, the cake is cloaked with a chocolate glaze. It remains an elegant and dramatic presentation and quite tailored enough to serve as a man's birthday cake, especially with deep red roses and your best chocolate script.

FOR THE SOAKING SYRUP

1/3 cup sugar

1/3 cup water

1/3 cup eau-de-vie de framboise (not sweet raspberry liqueur), or 2/3 cup Chambord (or other sweet raspberry liqueur)

2 cups crème frâiche, chilled

1 1/2 teaspoons pure vanilla extract

One 8-inch Chocolate Génoise (page 229)

3 tablespoons boiling water

5 ounces bittersweet or semisweet chocolate, very finely chopped

12 to 16 ounces fresh raspberries, rinsed and patted dry

Sugar to taste

Sarah Bernhardt Chocolate Glaze (page 236) or Glace à l'Eau (page 237), cooled to the consistency of soft frosting

Ruffled chocolate fans (see page 238) (optional)

2 or 3 (unsprayed) roses (optional)

1 ounce white chocolate, melted, for piping the greeting

SPECIAL EQUIPMENT

An 8-by-3-inch springform pan or cheesecake pan with a removable bottom

Instant-read thermometer

Decorating turntable or lazy Susan (optional)

If using eau-de-vie, make the soaking syrup. Combine the sugar and water in a small saucepan. Stir just to moisten all the sugar, then bring to a simmer, and simmer without stirring, about 2 minutes. Let cool, then add the eau-de-vie.

To assemble the cake: In a medium bowl, beat the chilled crème frâiche with the vanilla until very thick but not stiff. Refrigerate until needed.

Use a serrated knife to cut the génoise horizontally into 3 layers. Fit the top layer, cut side up, into the bottom of the cake pan. Brush it with up to 3 tablespoons of the framboise syrup or the Chambord. Set aside.

In a small bowl, pour the boiling water over the chopped chocolate. Whisk until the chocolate is completely melted and smooth. Immediately fold ¼ cup of the crème frâiche into the chocolate mixture, then fold in another ½ cup. Right away, before the mixture stiffens, spread all of the chocolate crème frâiche evenly over the moistened génoise.

Moisten a second génoise layer very lightly with up to 2 tablespoons syrup and fit it moist side down into the pan. Press it in place. Moisten the top very lightly. Arrange a layer of berries over the génoise, leaving just a little space around each.

Fold sugar to taste into the remaining crème frâiche and beat it a little to stiffen it slightly. Scoop the cream onto the berries. Spread and press it over and between them.

Moisten the third chocolate génoise layer very lightly with up to 2 tablespoons syrup and fit it moist side down into the pan. Press it in place. Moisten the top of the génoise with the remaining syrup. Cover and refrigerate for several hours, or overnight.

Release and remove the sides of the springform, or set the cheesecake pan on a canister or can of food and pull the sides of the pan down and off the cake. Set the cake on a tray or flat dish. Spread the top and sides with a very thin crumb coating of the glaze. Chill the cake for a few minutes to set the crumb coat.

Reheat the remaining glaze to just 90°F. Place the chilled cake on a decorating turntable, lazy Susan, or on a rack set over a large tray. Pour all of the glaze over the top of the cake, allowing it to run down the sides. Use a metal icing spatula and as few strokes as necessary to make sure that the cake is completely covered. If there are bare spots left uncoated, use the spatula to scoop up excess glaze and touch it to those spots, but don't spread it: Spreading glaze as it cools will cause it to look dull. If desired, press chocolate fans into the sides of the cake before the glaze is completely set; you can also glue the fans on later with warmed leftover glaze. Refrigerate the cake to set the glaze.

continued

When the glaze is set, decorate the top of the cake with 2 or 3 fresh roses and write "Happy Birthday" with melted white chocolate. Refrigerate until ready to serve.

chocolate notes You can use standard bittersweet or semisweet chocolate (without a percentage on the label), or any marked 50% to 60%. Or, for even more bittersweet results, use higher-percentage chocolates as follows:

To use chocolate marked 61% to 62% instead of standard bittersweet: Use 4 ounces chocolate.

To use for chocolate marked 70% to 72% instead of standard bittersweet: Increase the water to 3$\frac{1}{2}$ tablespoons, and dissolve 1 tablespoon sugar in it before adding the chocolate. Use 3$\frac{1}{2}$ ounces chocolate.

MOLTEN CHOCOLATE–RASPBERRY CAKES

SERVES 6

Have you ever ordered one of these sexy little desserts in a restaurant only to find that the anticipated molten center has morphed into cake instead of flowing sauce? Because small desserts are more easily overbaked than large ones, and because baking times vary with different kinds of chocolate, I've concluded that the best and simplest insurance against disappointment (congealed sauce) is the buried-truffle method. During the short time in the oven, the truffle in each small cake melts to form a luscious sauce, while the cake gets fully baked. Although it sounds like a completely separate step, the truffles are actually created with a portion of the cake batter, so the whole process is quite efficient.

Sugar for the custard cups

8 ounces bittersweet or semisweet chocolate, coarsely chopped

6 tablespoons unsalted butter

1/4 cup strained raspberry puree (from fresh or frozen unsweetened raspberries)

3 tablespoons plus 2 teaspoons sugar

2 tablespoons unsweetened cocoa powder (natural or Dutch-process)

2 large eggs, separated

1 large egg white

1/8 teaspoon cream of tartar

Fresh raspberries for garnish (optional)

Powdered sugar for dusting

SPECIAL EQUIPMENT

Six 6-ounce custard cups or ramekins

Put a pie plate or cake pan in the freezer to chill. Liberally butter the insides of the custard cups, sprinkle with sugar, and tap out the excess.

Melt the chocolate and butter in a medium heatproof bowl in a wide skillet of barely simmering water, stirring frequently until smooth. Remove the bowl from the skillet. Transfer 5 tablespoons of the chocolate mixture to a small bowl, and set aside the remaining chocolate. Add the raspberry puree and 2 teaspoons of the sugar to the 5 tablespoons chocolate and stir to blend. Scrape the raspberry mixture into a puddle in the chilled pie plate or pan and place in the freezer for 10 minutes or so to firm.

continued

When the raspberry-chocolate mixture is firm enough to hold a shape, use a teaspoon (or a tiny ice cream scoop) to form it into 6 truffles (they need not be perfectly round). Return the truffles to the freezer.

Rewarm the remaining chocolate mixture in the skillet of water over low heat until warm to the touch. Remove from the heat and whisk in the cocoa and egg yolks.

In a dry medium bowl, beat the egg whites and cream of tartar with an electric mixer until soft peaks form when the beaters are lifted. Gradually beat in the remaining 3 tablespoons sugar and continue beating until the whites are stiff and glossy but not dry. Fold about one-quarter of the egg whites into the batter. Scrape the remaining whites into the bowl and fold until blended. Using half of the batter, fill each cup about half-full. Press a truffle about halfway into the batter in the center of each cup. Top with the remaining batter and level the tops; make sure the truffles are completely covered by batter. Cover the cups with plastic wrap. Refrigerate for at least 3 hours or up to 3 days.

Position a rack in the lower third of the oven and preheat the oven to 400°F.

Twenty minutes before you want to serve the cakes, remove the plastic wrap and place the cups on a cookie sheet. Bake 12 to 14 minutes, until the cakes are puffed and the truffles are melted (a toothpick inserted in the center of each should meet no resistance and the chocolate on the toothpick should feel warm rather than cool when you touch it to your lip). Let the cakes cool for about 3 minutes.

Run a knife around the sides of each cup. Holding each cup with a potholder, invert the cakes onto serving plates. Garnish with a few raspberries, if desired, and, using a fine-mesh sieve, sift a light dusting of powdered sugar over all. Serve immediately.

chocolate notes I developed this dessert using standard bittersweet chocolate, with 55% chocolate liquor, and loved the outcome. When I tested it with a 62% chocolate, it was even better because, in addition to being more bittersweet, the difference in texture between the slightly cakey outside and the gooey inside is more pronounced and exciting.

You can use standard bittersweet or semisweet chocolate (without a percentage on the label), or any marked 50% through 62%.

To use chocolate marked 64% to 66% instead of standard bittersweet: Use 7$\frac{1}{2}$ ounces chocolate. Add 2 teaspoons water to the raspbery puree. Increase the sugar added to the raspberry-chocolate mixture to 1 tablespoon. Reduce the cocoa to 1 tablespoon.

To use chocolate marked 70% to 72% instead of standard bittersweet: Uses 7 ounces chocolate. Add 1 tablespoon water to the raspberry puree. Increase the sugar added to the raspberry-chocolate mixture to 1 tablespoon. Omit the cocoa. Increase the sugar added to the egg whites to 4$\frac{1}{2}$ tablespoons.

COCONUT SARAS photograph on page 128

MAKES 20 TO 24 PASTRIES

A Danish pastry chef created Sarah Bernhardt cookies to honor that divine late-nineteenth-century French actress. My version was a tall kiss of light whipped ganache atop a soft almond macaroon enveloped in bittersweet glaze, more an individual dessert than a cookie. Now I've returned them to a dainty size and reinvented them as chewy toasted coconut macaroons filled with soft light ganache and capped with a crisp coat of pure chocolate instead of the softer glaze. And they are more divine than ever.

FOR THE MACAROONS

4 large egg whites

3 cups (9 ounces) sweetened shredded coconut

3/4 cup sugar

2 teaspoons pure vanilla extract

Scant 1/4 teaspoon salt

1/2 recipe Whipped Chocolate Ganache Filling (page 231)

5 ounces bittersweet or semisweet chocolate, coarsely chopped

SPECIAL EQUIPMENT

Cookie sheets

A pastry bag fitted with a plain tip with a 7/16- to 1/2-inch opening

Instant-read thermometer

To make the macaroons: Position the racks in the upper and lower thirds of the oven, and preheat the oven to 350°F. Line two cookie sheets with parchment paper.

Combine all of the ingredients in a large heatproof bowl, preferably stainless steel (which conducts heat much better than glass). Set the bowl in a wide skillet of barely simmering water and stir, scraping the bottom to prevent burning, until the mixture is very hot to the touch and the egg whites have thickened slightly and turned from translucent to opaque, 6 to 7 minutes. A scoop of batter dropped onto a cookie sheet should hold a soft shape without a puddle of syrup forming around it. Remove the bowl from the skillet.

Scoop tablespoonfuls of the mixture about 2 inches apart onto the cookie sheets. Use your finger to make a hollow depression in the center of each cookie so it looks like a little nest. Bake for 13 to 15 minutes, or until the edges of the cookies—and any protruding coconut shreds—are deep golden brown. Rotate the sheets from front to back and top to bottom halfway through the baking time.

Slide the cookies on the parchment onto cooling racks. Cool completely before removing them from the paper. (They can be stored in an airtight container at room temperature for 4 to 5 days, or frozen for up to 3 months.)

To fill and dip the macaroons: Beat the chilled ganache just until the color lightens and the mixture becomes stiff enough to hold its shape—if you overbeat the ganache, it will have a granular texture. Scrape the ganache into the pastry bag. Pipe a 1-inch-high kiss-shaped mound (about 1 tablespoon of ganache) into each macaroon "nest." Refrigerate until well chilled, at least 1 hour.

Place the chocolate in a medium heatproof bowl set in a wide skillet of almost simmering water. Stir until the chocolate is nearly melted, then remove from the heat and continue to stir until the chocolate is completely smooth. Wipe the moisture from the bottom of the bowl and transfer the chocolate to a very small bowl or cup. If necessary, let the chocolate cool to about 105°F. Hold a macaroon upside down and dip only the ganache kiss into the chocolate. Then turn the macaroon right side up, hold it over the bowl, and use a fork to drizzle a little chocolate around the edges. Set the macaroon on a tray. Repeat until all of the macaroons are dipped. Refrigerate to set the chocolate.

chocolate notes For the ganache, you can use standard bittersweet or semisweet chocolate (without a percentage on the label) or any marked 50% to 58%. For an increasingly bittersweet filling, use higher-percentage chocolates as follows:

To use chocolate marked 60% to 62% instead of standard bittersweet: Use 3½ ounces chocolate.

To use chocolate marked 66% to 72% instead of standard bittersweet: Use 3 ounces chocolate, and stir 4 teaspoons sugar into the cream before heating it. Pour only half of the hot cream and sugar over the chocolate, and stir well to melt the chocolate before adding the remaining cream.

For dipping, you can use the same chocolate you use in the ganache, or any other chocolate. No alterations are necessary.

CARMEN MERINGAY photograph on pages 130–131
SERVES 12 TO 14

Meringue is irresistible to me as a sculptural medium as well as a dessert component. Although I've gotten some big laughs (howls, actually) for attempting to make trompe l'oeil meringue asparagus, I always get raves for meringue shells. Named for the fun of it, Carmen Meringay is for show-offs: Meringue is piped straight up the sheer walls of a vertical form, baked until dry and crisp, then removed from the form. You can fill it with chocolate mousse, whipped cream, and chocolate curls, or with layers of softened chocolate ice cream drizzled with chocolate sauce and interspersed with crushed praline (see page 245). Or you can fill the shell with ripe berries or sliced stone fruit, toasted nuts, and whipped cream, custard, or vanilla ice cream. Cubes of liquor-drenched sponge cake can be layered in, if you like.

For this stunt you want plain (not chocolate) meringue because it is stiff enough to hold a defined shape and light enough to cling to the sides of the form without sagging in the oven. The following instructions are for creating the form and piping the meringue. The filling is up to you. Use recipes from this book or other favorites.

White Meringue (page 181)

SPECIAL EQUIPMENT

A large baking sheet

A piece of flexible corrugated cardboard 25 to 30 inches long and 5 to 6 inches wide

Cellophane tape

A large pastry bag fitted with a medium small star tip (Ateco #843 or #9824)

Position a rack in the lower third of the oven and preheat the oven to 200°F. Cut a piece of parchment paper to cover the baking sheet, then cut the paper crosswise in half. Set one piece aside.

To make the form: Bend the corrugated cardboard into a cylinder 7 to 8 inches in diameter and secure the overlapping edges with tape. Stand the cardboard cylinder in the center of the parchment on the baking sheet. Push the cylinder into an oval shape (or keep it round), taping the bottom edges securely to the parchment in several places to preserve the shape. Cut a piece of parchment big enough to wrap around and cover the cardboard cylinder completely. Secure the overlapping end of the parchment with tape but do not tape the parchment to the cardboard or you will not be able to slip it off later.

Make the meringue and scrape it into the pastry bag. Starting at the bottom of the form, pipe a line of meringue up the outside of the form. Near the top, jerk the tip of the pastry bag upward to form a point. Starting at the bottom again, pipe a second line of meringue parallel to and touching the first. Repeat until the form is covered with meringue. (If there are gaps in coverage or places where the piping barely touches, pipe some extra lines of meringue as necessary. Don't worry, this will look beautiful and reinforces the structure!)

Slide the parchment with the form placed on it to one end of the baking sheet. Place the reserved parchment next to it. Pipe or spread the remaining meringue on the parchment to make a thin oval layer slightly smaller than the form.

Bake for 2 hours. Turn off the oven and leave the meringue inside for at least another hour or overnight.

Carefully detach the baked (and very fragile) meringue shell from the form as follows: Lift the meringue and attached parchment upward, sliding them off of the cardboard. Set the meringue on a flat tray. Carefully, without bumping the meringue, reach in and grasp the end of the parchment. Gently pull the parchment off the meringue, pulling toward the center of the shell.

Slide a metal spatula under the meringue layer to separate it from the parchment underneath. If necessary, trim the layer with a serrated knife so the meringue shell (lifted and set down carefully with two hands) fits completely over it. Store the shell and the bottom layer in an airtight container for up to several weeks, until needed.

Basic Wardrobe for Designing Desserts

Anyone who loves to create desserts with multiple elements must have a short list of reliable basic cake layers and cake sheets that can be split and sandwiched, layered, or rolled up around an endless menu of fillings, frostings, mousses, and creams. The recipes that follow are a few of my favorite chocolate basics, revised or reinvented to reflect my current preferences or to enable you to make them successfully with higher-percentage chocolates. Voilà, the best chocolate génoise I know (page 229), my favorite light whipped chocolate ganache filling (page 231), and more. You will also need some of these for other recipes in this book. All are equally valuable for countless other desserts, suggestions for which are given after each recipe. And additional basics, desserts unto themselves, can be found throughout the book:

Ice Creams (pages 77–89)

Albert's Mousse (page 166)

Chocolate Marquise (page 172)

White or Milk Chocolate Mousse (page 174)

Chocolate Meringue (page 180)

White Meringue (page 181)

Nutty Chocolate Meringue (page 181)

Cocoa Bean Cream (page 304)

Bittersweet Chocolate Soufflé Sheet (page 200)

CHOCOLATE GÉNOISE

MAKES ONE 8-INCH ROUND LAYER

The bakery workhorse and primary building block of dozens of classic European layer cakes, chocolate génoise can be flavorless and dry as dust until it gets its designated drenching with liqueurs and syrups and/or slathering with buttercream. But it doesn't have to be. After years of making chocolate génoises, I like this one best. It is light but very flavorful, moist enough to snack on when it is naked, but still more splendid splashed and slathered, filled, and/or frosted. Before you begin, remember that when you make a génoise, all of the details matter. Yes, please sift the flour and cocoa before measuring, and again and again and again afterward as instructed. Take no shortcuts. Use a stand mixer fitted with the whisk attachment if you have one.

4 tablespoons unsalted butter

1 teaspoon pure vanilla extract

1/3 cup sifted (before measuring) all-purpose flour

1/3 cup sifted (before measuring) unsweetened cocoa powder (I like Dutch-process in this)

4 large eggs

2/3 cup sugar

SPECIAL EQUIPMENT

An 8-inch round cake pan

Position a rack in the lower third of the oven and preheat the oven to 350°F. Line the bottom of the cake pan with parchment paper.

To clarify the butter: In a very small saucepan, or in a narrow glass jar in the microwave, heat the butter, without stirring, until it is melted and very hot. The butter will separate into foam on top, clear yellow oil beneath, and water plus some milk solids on the bottom. Simply spoon off and discard the foam on the surface (tilt the pan if necessary). Transfer 3 tablespoons of the clear yellow butter (avoid the watery liquid on the bottom) to a medium heatproof bowl. Add the vanilla to the bowl and set aside.

Sift the flour and cocoa together three times; return to the sifter and set aside.

continued

In a large heatproof bowl, preferably the bowl of your electric mixer, use a whisk to combine the eggs and sugar thoroughly. Place the bowl in a wide skillet of barely simmering water. Whisking constantly, heat the eggs to lukewarm (about 105°F). Remove the bowl from the pan; leave the skillet on the stove but turn off the heat. With an electric mixer, beat the egg mixture at high speed until it has cooled, is tripled in volume, and resembles softly whipped cream. This may take as little as 3 to 5 minutes in a heavy-duty mixer or much longer with a less powerful mixer.

Meanwhile, set the bowl of butter and vanilla in the skillet of hot water, with the burner off, to keep it warm.

Sift about one-third of the flour and cocoa over the whipped eggs. Use your largest rubber spatula to fold in the mixture—quickly but gently—until combined. Fold in half the remaining flour and cocoa, then fold in the rest. Remove the warm butter mixture from the skillet. Scoop about 1 cup of the batter into the bowl and fold together with a small rubber spatula until completely combined. Use the large spatula to fold the butter mixture completely into the remaining batter. Turn the batter into the prepared pan and tilt to level.

Bake until the cake begins to shrink slightly around the edges and the top springs back when pressed with your finger, 35 to 40 minutes. Cool the cake completely in the pan on a rack.

To unmold, run a small knife or spatula around the inner edges of the pan to release the cake. Invert it onto a rack and remove the parchment liner. Turn the cake right side up, so that the "skin" on top of the cake does not stick to the rack. (The génoise can be wrapped and refrigerated for up to 2 days, or frozen for up to 3 months.)

chocolate note Some chocolate génoise cakes turn out a little drier with natural rather than Dutch-process cocoa, but this one is so light and relatively moist (as génoise goes) that the difference is negligible. You can use either with good results. For inexplicable reasons—since I normally prefer natural cocoa—I like génoise best with Dutch-process.

WHIPPED CHOCOLATE GANACHE FILLING

MAKES ABOUT 3½ CUPS

This is one of my all-time favorite fillings for cakes and roulades. It is light, creamy, and rich, but not at all intense, so it makes a brilliant contrast to stronger, more bittersweet flavors and a nice offset to the texture of cake or something crisp or chewy. I use this in the Tribute Cake (page 214) and in Coconut Saras (page 224). You can spread it over a Bittersweet Chocolate Soufflé Sheet (page 200) and make a rich and simple roulade. Don't be alarmed if the chilled ganache looks too soft to spread (I've had late-night phone calls about this): It will not stiffen until you whip it just before you use it. It is essential that you consult the Chocolate Notes (page 232) if you plan to make this filling with high-percentage chocolates, or you will lose the poetry of its light creamy texture.

You can make this ganache, or any of the variations, up to four days in advance.

8 ounces bittersweet or semisweet chocolate, chopped medium-fine

2 cups heavy cream

To make the ganache: Place the chopped chocolate in a medium bowl. Heat the cream in a large heavy saucepan over medium-high heat until it comes to a gentle boil. Immediately pour the hot cream over the chocolate and stir until the chocolate is mostly melted. Let stand for 15 to 20 minutes to be sure all of the chocolate particles are completely melted.

Stir the ganache until perfectly smooth. Let cool. Cover the bowl and refrigerate the ganache for at least 6 hours (I usually leave it overnight); it must be very cold or it will curdle when it is whipped. (The ganache can be prepared up to 4 days ahead.)

When you are ready to use the ganache (and not before), whip it until it is stiff enough to hold a nice shape and seems spreadable, but don't overdo. Overwhipped ganache looks granular, so watch it carefully: I usually stop the mixer early and finish the whipping by hand. After whipping, the ganache will firm as it sits (and even more after it is chilled), so spread it immediately. If you accidentally overwhip, or if the ganache becomes too stiff to spread, warm your spatula by rinsing it under hot tap water and wiping it dry as necessary. (The warm spatula rescued me when I overwhipped ganache for three hundred during the Tribute Cake adventure—so don't worry.)

chocolate notes Unlike dense or intense ganaches, this one is meant to be whipped to a light, almost fluffy texture. High-percentage chocolates are superb in this recipe, but the quantity of chocolate must be decreased, or the texture of the ganache will be too dense to whip and the whole ensemble of cake, filling, and glaze will not be so exciting. I've fine-tuned this, one of my favorite fillings, so that at each level the flavor is less sweet but the texture is still divinely light.

You can use standard bittersweet or semisweet chocolate (without a percentage on the label), or any marked 50% to 60%.

To use chocolate marked 60% to 64% instead of standard bittersweet: Use 7 ounces chocolate.

To use chocolate marked 66% to 72% instead of standard bittersweet: Use 6 ounces chocolate, and add at least 4 teaspoons (or up to 3 tablespoons if you like) sugar to the cream before heating it. Without added sugar, the flavor of the ganache is a little flat. The minimal 4 teaspoons sugar lifts and opens up the flavor a little (almost the way salt lifts the flavor of savory food) without adding perceptible sweetness. You must also alter the technique slightly: Pour half of the hot cream and sugar over the chocolate first and stir until smooth before adding the rest.

WHIPPED GIANDUJA GANACHE FILLING Substitute 12 ounces gianduja (milk chocolate to which toasted hazelnut paste has been added [see Sources, page 366]). for the 8 ounces bittersweet or semisweet chocolate.

WHIPPED MOCHA GANACHE FILLING Substitute 12 ounces milk chocolate for the 8 ounces bittersweet or semisweet chocolate. Add 2 tablespoons regular roast (not espresso roast) coffee beans, coarsely crushed, to the cream and bring the cream to a simmer. Remove the pan from the stove, cover it, and allow to steep for 4 minutes. Pour the hot cream through a fine strainer onto the chocolate. Discard the coffee beans, and proceed with the recipe.

WHIPPED MEXICAN CINNAMON GANACHE FILLING Substitute 12 ounces milk chocolate for the 8 ounces bittersweet or semisweet chocolate. Add a crushed 6-inch piece of Mexican cinnamon (*canela*) stick (see page 41) to the cream and bring to a simmer. Remove the pan from the stove, cover, and allow to steep for 5 minutes. Pour the hot cream through a fine strainer onto the chocolate. Discard the cinnamon, and proceed with the recipe.

WHIPPED MINT-INFUSED GANACHE FILLING Begin this ganache a day ahead. For the best flavor, strain and discard the mint after 12 hours, even if you are not ready to proceed with the recipe. If necessary, the mint-infused cream can wait in the refrigerator for up to a day before you make the ganache.

Combine the cream and 1 cup lightly packed coarsely chopped mint in a bowl, cover, and refrigerate overnight (10 to 12 hours). Strain the cream into a small saucepan, pressing gently on the leaves to extract all the cream. Discard the mint and proceed with the recipe.

WHIPPED MINT-INFUSED WHITE CHOCOLATE GANACHE FILLING This is excellent in desserts with ripe strawberries. Begin this ganache a day ahead.

Prepare the Mint-Infused Ganache as directed, using ½ cup coarsely chopped mint instead of 1 cup and substituting 12 ounces white chocolate for the 8 ounces bittersweet or semisweet chocolate.

GANACHE GLAZE OR FROSTING

MAKES 1½ TO 1¾ CUPS

Pour it warm for a beautiful glaze, or cool it and slather it like a frosting.

8 ounces bittersweet or semisweet chocolate, chopped into small pieces

¾ cup heavy cream, plus ¼ cup extra (optional)

Make the ganache with the extra cream for frosting rather than glaze, because spreading cool ganche makes it much harder after it sets.

Place the chopped chocolate in a medium bowl. Bring the cream to a simmer and immediately pour it over the chocolate. Stir briskly until the chocolate is melted and smooth. For a pouring glaze, let the ganache cool (between 90° and 100°F). For frosting, let the ganache cool, without stirring, until it looks thick enough to spread.

To reheat, set the bowl in a pan of barely simmering water until the ganache is partly melted, then stir gently to the desired consistency. The consistency of the glaze or frosting can be adjusted with more hot cream as necessary.

chocolate notes You can use standard bittersweet or semisweet chocolate (without a percentage on the label), or any marked 50% to 60%. Because it has plenty of cream, you can adjust the sweetness of the ganache after you make and taste it.

To use chocolate marked 61% to 66% instead of standard bittersweet: Increase the cream to 1¼ cups. Pour only half of the cream over the chocolate and stir well before adding the rest.

To use chocolate marked 70% to 72% instead of standard bittersweet: Increase the cream to 1 cup, and reduce the chocolate to 7 ounces. Pour only half of the cream over the chocolate and stir well before adding the rest. Add about 1 tablespoon sugar to the cream before heating it. You can always taste and add more later.

As the chocolate liquor percentage increases, ganache becomes less stable. It may separate or curdle, especially when reheated. If this happens, try whisking in a few drops of cream or water. Or, try the mayonnaise trick as follows: Pour a tablespoon of hot cream into a medium bowl. Dribble a little of the lukewarm curdled ganache into the cream and whisk it briskly until perfectly smooth. Gradually whisk in the remainder of the curdled ganache.

BITTERSWEET CHOCOLATE GLAZE

MAKES ABOUT 1 CUP

For many years this was my "classic" rich butter glaze for chocolate tortes, which I now alternate with the Ganache Glaze (page 234) or Glace à l'Eau (page 237). This glaze sets firm but soft, with an even satiny appearance. Use it on any cake or torte that is kept and served at room temperature. For cakes that are chilled, use Sarah Bernhardt Chocolate Glaze (page 236) instead.

6 ounces bittersweet or semisweet chocolate, coarsely chopped

8 tablespoons (1 stick) unsalted butter, cut into several pieces

1 tablespoon light corn syrup

Place the chocolate, butter, and corn syrup in a small heatproof bowl set in a wide skillet of barely simmering water. Stir frequently and gently (to prevent air bubbles) with a spatula or wooden spoon until the chocolate is almost completely melted. Remove the glaze from the water and set aside to finish melting, stirring once or twice until the glaze is perfectly smooth. Or, melt in a microwave on Medium (50%) power for about 2 minutes. Stir gently until completely smooth; do not whisk or beat. Let the glaze cool, without stirring, until nearly set and the consistency of easily spreadable frosting.

chocolate note This glaze can be made with any bittersweet or semisweet chocolate, regardless of percentage, without modifying the recipe. Of course, the higher-percentage chocolates will produce a stronger and more bitter chocolate flavor. I often make this glaze with a bittersweet 70% chocolate.

SARAH BERNHARDT CHOCOLATE GLAZE

MAKES 1²/₃ CUPS

I designed this thin bittersweet-chocolate-and-butter pouring glaze for my version of Sarah Bernhardt pastries, which was one of my favorites at Cocolat. I use it on all kinds of cakes and desserts that require refrigeration because it does not harden to the point of cracking when chilled, and, if it is applied at the correct temperature, it stays beautiful even when cold. I use it on the Tribute Cake (page 214) and Julia's Cake (page 218), in place of the usual sweet fondant glaze on chocolate éclairs, and as a substitute for the pure chocolate coating on Coconut Saras (page 224).

8 ounces bittersweet or semisweet chocolate, cut into bits

12 tablespoons (1¹/2 sticks) unsalted butter

1 tablespoon light corn syrup

5 teaspoons water

SPECIAL EQUIPMENT

Instant-read thermometer

Place all the ingredients in a small heatproof bowl set in a wide skillet of barely simmering water and stir frequently until the chocolate is almost completely melted; do not overheat. Remove the glaze from the water bath and set aside to finish melting, stirring once or twice until perfectly smooth. Or, melt in a microwave on Medium (50%) power for about 2 minutes. Stir gently with a spatula or a wooden spoon until completely smooth; do not whisk or beat. If necessary, before using, cool the glaze to 88° to 90°F (or rewarm it gently in a water bath). It will be optimally shiny if you pour it at that temperature. (Any excess glaze may be refrigerated for up to a week or frozen. Reheat or defrost in the microwave or in a pan of barely simmering water.)

chocolate note You can make this glaze with any bittersweet or semisweet chocolate. Make it as intense as you like simply by choosing higher-percentage chocolates; there is no need to make alterations.

GLACE À L'EAU

MAKES ABOUT 1¾ CUPS

This intensely bittersweet glaze or frosting can be used as a substitute for Bittersweet Chocolate Glaze (page 235) or Sarah Bernhardt Chocolate Glaze (page 236). Glace à l'Eau, literally "water glaze," is simple to make and versatile. You can pour it like a glaze or cool it and spread it like frosting.

8 ounces bittersweet or semisweet chocolate, coarsely chopped

8 tablespoons (1 stick) unsalted butter, cut into several pieces

½ cup water or strong coffee

Pinch of salt

SPECIAL EQUIPMENT

Instant-read thermometer

Combine all the ingredients in a small heatproof bowl set in a wide skillet of barely simmering water; stir frequently until the chocolate and butter are almost completely melted. Remove from the heat and stir gently (to avoid creating air bubbles) until completely melted and smooth. Let cool to 90°F before using as a glaze. Or, to use as a frosting, let cool until spreadable. (The glaze can be kept, covered, at room temperature for several days or refrigerated for up to 2 weeks; freeze it in a sealed container for up to 6 months. Soften or defrost in a pan of barely simmering water or the microwave before using.)

chocolate note You can make this glaze with any bittersweet or semisweet chocolate. However, be forewarned! It naturally produces a very intense bittersweet flavor, even without using a high-percentage chocolate. If you decide to use high-percentage chocolate, feel free to adjust (thin) the consistency of the glaze by adding water as necessary. You can also sweeten the glaze with sugar if you find the flavor too intense and/or flat.

High-percentage chocolates may cause the glaze to separate or curdle. When this happens, the glaze will appear both grainy and watery. You can fix it with the mayonnaise method as follows: Put a tablespoon of water in a clean bowl. Whisk a tablespoon or two of the curdled glaze into the water. When blended, whisk in a little more of the curdled glaze. It the mixture looks smooth, whisk in the remaining glaze a little at a time. If not, start again with fresh water in the bottom of a fresh bowl.

Finishing Touches

CHOCOLATE FANS AND RUFFLES photographs on pages 129 and 127

Chocolate fans and ruffles take lots of practice. If you can't make them obey at first (and it's inevitable you won't), save the abstract shapes that you do get. They will look great arranged on the top or sides of your cake, either embedded in frosting or glued on with a little melted chocolate or leftover glaze. No one needs to know you were trying for fans and ruffles.

RUFFLED CHOCOLATE FANS These ruffled fans with ragged or deckled edges are my favorite, perhaps even my signature, show-off trick with chocolate. Because they are made of pure chocolate with nothing added, they are as delicious as they are sensational to look at. Decorate an individual dessert or even a dish of ice cream or pudding with a single fan, or arrange lots of fans to resemble a giant flower with ruffled petals on a larger dessert.

The amount of chocolate is approximate, and you may not need every bit of it. The idea is to spread a relatively thin even coat of chocolate on the cookie sheets. As you get more skilled, you will spread the chocolate thinner and scrape the excess back into the bowl.

9 to 10 ounces bittersweet, semisweet, milk, or white chocolate (no chocolate chips!), melted

1 to 2 ounces chocolate of a contrasting color, melted (optional)

SPECIAL EQUIPMENT

Three unwarped, undented heavy-duty cookie sheets with smooth surfaces (do not use pans with special coatings or nonstick surfaces)

An 8-inch offset metal icing spatula

Warm the back of one of the cookie sheets by holding it about 6 inches above a burner and moving it back and forth in a slow circle until the bottom of the pan feels very warm all over (when you touch the underside rather than the inside) but not hot enough to burn your fingers. Turn the pan upside down on the counter and pour about one-third of the chocolate onto it. Spread it very thin evenly with the offset spatula. Immediately, if desired, drizzle or streak the sheet randomly with a little of the contrasting chocolate. Refrigerate to harden the chocolate, for at least 20 minutes, or up to several hours. Repeat to coat the remaining cookie sheets.

Remove one chilled pan at a time from the refrigerator and let the chocolate soften until it is flexible when you try to scrape it from the pan. Line two baking sheets with parchment or wax paper, for the finished shapes.

For fans: Place one short edge of the pan of chocolate up along the edge of the counter in front of you. Lean forward (wearing an apron!) against the counter to brace the pan and keep it from sliding toward you as you work. If you are right-handed (if you are left-handed, reverse the directions as appropriate), start at the upper left-hand corner of the pan. Holding the handle of the offset spatula in your right hand with the blade parallel to the back edge of the pan, grab the end of the blade with your left hand—your third and fourth fingers should be against the back edge of the blade, thumb and index fingers in front of the blade to gather the fan (yes, it is an awkward position!). With the back edge raised only slightly off the pan, pull the front edge of the spatula firmly toward you, sliding it under the layer of chocolate. If all goes well (it probably won't at first), the chocolate will gather up against the thumb and index fingers of your left hand and open into a fan near the handle of the spatula. With practice, you may be able to make 10 to 15 good-sized fans from each cookie sheet of chocolate. Remember, whatever shapes you do get will look dramatic arranged on a cake.

For easier shapes: Brace the pan against the wall or the backsplash of your kitchen counter. Push the edge of a metal dough scraper or a putty knife away from you, at an angle against the chocolate, to make sheaves or curls or whatever ruffley shapes turn out.

Either way, place the finished fans or shapes on one of the lined pans and refrigerate as soon as possible. If the finished shapes start to melt as you work, work with two pans at a time, rotating one in and one out of the refrigerator as needed to hold your finished work.

continued

TIPS: If the chocolate is too cold, it will crack and splinter when you try to slide the spatula—wait a few minutes to let soften at room temperature. If the chocolate is too warm, it will gum up or melt against the spatula—return it to the refrigerator for only a minute or so to firm up before trying again. The right temperature makes a big difference: Don't fight it. Sheets can be rechilled over and over again or allowed to soften longer at room temperature as necessary. If the temperature of the chocolate is perfect but you still can't get the shape you want, try altering the angle at which you are holding the spatula blade as you scrape; beginners usually tilt the blade up too much, when it should be almost but not quite flat against the chocolate.

Once you have a feel for the perfect chocolate temperature, you can remove more than one pan at a time from the refrigerator, or remove the pans at short intervals, depending on the warmth of the room and the speed at which you work.

CHOCOLATE RUFFLES I normally just arrange ruffled chocolate fans together and call that a ruffle, but you can make an actual long ruffle using the fan technique by scraping the chocolate in longer pulls. Then, while the ruffle is still soft and flexible, arrange directly on the dessert, perhaps in a spiral from the center.

chocolate note Almost any chocolate will work here, regardless of percentage. Don't use chocolate chips.

CHOCOLATE CURLS OR CIGARETTES

This is a simple way to make perfect chocolate curls or cigarettes! Use clarified butter for the best-tasting curls, shortening for the easiest-to-handle. Clarified butter softens the chocolate more than shortening does—hence less is needed. Clarified butter is used because the water in regular butter makes the chocolate less flexible and harder to curl. (See Chocolate Génoise, page 229, for instructions on clarifying butter.)

6 ounces bittersweet or semisweet chocolate (no chocolate chips!), finely chopped

1½ teaspoons clarified butter (see headnote) or 1 tablespoon vegetable shortening

SPECIAL EQUIPMENT

Miniloaf pan (6 by 3½ inches)

Vegetable peeler

Line the loaf pan with plastic wrap, leaving an overhang along the long sides. Place the chocolate and clarified butter in a small heatproof bowl in a pan of barely simmering water and stir constantly until melted and smooth.

Scrape the chocolate into the plastic wrap–lined loaf pan. Chill for at least 2 hours or until firm.

Lift up the edges of the plastic wrap to remove the chocolate from the pan. Let stand for 10 to 15 minutes to soften slightly.

Cut the chocolate lengthwise in half to form two long bars no wider than the cutting blade of your vegetable peeler. Scrape the chocolate firmly with the peeler for curls and cigarette shapes. If the curls splinter or crack, the chocolate is too cold; wait a few more minutes and try again. If the chocolate becomes too soft, return it briefly to the refrigerator to harden. Handle the chocolate curls with a toothpick to avoid fingerprints. Store in a tightly covered container in the refrigerator or freeze.

chocolate note You can use standard bittersweet or semisweet chocolate (without a percentage on the label), or any marked 50% to 62%. It doesn't seem necessary to use more expensive higher-percentage chocolates for this decorative touch.

PIPING WITH MELTED CHOCOLATE

This is the easiest and most fun and elegant way to decorate birthday cakes or even cookies: with free-form curlicues, filigree, fancy borders, or birthday greetings.

Simply melt 1 ounce semisweet, bittersweet, or milk chocolate, or even white chocolate (but not chocolate chips). Make a small parchment or wax paper cone (see below). Prop the cone up in a small jar or bud vase and scrape the chocolate into the cone, filling it no more than halfway. Fold over and roll the top of the cone to seal, then snip off the tip. Press from the rolled-over paper at the top to pipe the chocolate.

Alternatively, you can scrape the chocolate into a small zipper-lock bag, bunch the excess plastic in your fist to push the chocolate into one corner, snip off the corner, and squeeze out the chocolate to pipe. A little practice yields wondrous results.

MAKING A PARCHMENT PIPING CONE Cut a 12-by-12-inch piece of parchment paper or wax paper. Fold across opposite corners to form a right triangle. Hold the triangle on the counter with one hand. With the other hand, slide a sharp knife between the layers and cut along the fold into 2 right triangles.

Hold a triangle in your left hand (if you are right-handed; the right angle should be the upper right corner opposite the hypotenuse). Place your thumb at the center of the hypotenuse. Grasp the acute angle on top with your other hand and roll it toward the bottom angle to form a cone. Be certain that the tip of the cone remains completely closed. Continue to roll the cone toward the bottom angle and fold the tip of the bottom angle over and into the open end of the cone to secure it.

The idea is to be able to fold the paper so that the cone does not come apart when you put it down. At first you may find this a bit awkward. Use some tape, if necessary, and master the finer points of cone making later.

chocolate note Use any bittersweet, semisweet, milk, or white chocolate—but not chocolate chips, which are not fluid enough when melted to flow beautifully from a piping cone.

CAREFREE CARAMEL

Inspired by a technique in *Cook's Illustrated* magazine, this is my version of the easiest way to caramelize sugar. Because the sugar is kept below the surface of the water, there is no need for the usual precaution of washing down sugar crystals on the sides of the pan with a wet pastry brush to prevent crystallization.

¹/₂ cup water	¹/₈ teaspoon cream of tartar
1 cup sugar	

Have a white saucer and a skewer at the side of the stove to test the color of the syrup.

Pour the water into a 1-quart saucepan and set it over medium heat. Mix the sugar and cream of tartar and pour the mixture carefully in a thin stream into the center of the pan to form a low mound. Without stirring, use your fingers to pat the sugar mound down until it is entirely moistened; any sugar at the edges of the pan will be safely below the water line. Cover the pan and cook for a few minutes (still without stirring), until when you lift the lid, the sugar has completely dissolved and the syrup looks clear. Uncover the pan and continue to cook, without stirring, until the syrup begins to color slightly. If the syrup seems to be coloring unevenly, swirl the pan gently, rather than stirring. To test the caramel, use the skewer to drop a bead of syrup onto the white saucer. When a drop of syrup looks pale amber on the saucer, turn the heat to low and pay close attention. Continue to cook and test drops of syrup until it has darkened to a slightly reddish amber color. Immediately remove the pan from the heat.

CARAMEL SHARDS Have ready a foil- or parchment-lined baking sheet and a metal icing spatula. Make the caramel and immediately scrape it onto the baking sheet and tilt the pan to spread the caramel, or spread it even thinner with the spatula. Allow to cool and harden.

Break the caramel into shards, or coarsely chop. Store in an airtight container (with silica gel if possible; see page 31) until needed.

continued

SPUN SUGAR (photograph on page 132) Spinning sugar is so easy that there is no reason to save it for the occasional showpiece dessert. Spun sugar turns a simple dish of ice cream or chocolate mousse into a celebration. You can make a reusable sugar-spinning tool from a wire whisk by snipping off the curved section of each wire (using a wire cutter) until the whisk resembles a bouquet of wire stems, or you can use a handful of skewers.

Have ready a pan of ice water, the altered whisk or a few wooden or metal skewers, and a sheet of foil- or parchment. If you plan to make caramel shards *and* spun sugar, have a foil- or parchment-lined cookie sheet ready for the shards.

Make the caramel. If you are making shards, immediately pour up to half of the caramel onto the foil-lined sheet and tilt or spread it into a thin layer for shards (as described on page 243). Set the sheet in the ice water for a few seconds to stop further cooking.

Remove the pan from the stove, and let the caramel cool and thicken for a minute or two. Dip the tips of the whisk or fanned skewers into the caramel and lift them 12 inches above the pan, watching how the caramel flows from the tips back into the pan. At first the caramel will form very fine threads as it flows off the whisk. As it cools, it will flow more slowly and form thicker golden threads: perfect spun sugar. Continue to dip and lift the whisk until this happens.

The drips and little globs of caramel that fall from the wires are extremely hot, but the threads are cool enough to touch. Grasp and pull the threads aside with your hand, coiling them into a pretty tangle directly on top of a dessert or onto the foil sheet. Continue to dip the whisk to make more spun sugar. After each dip, raise the whisk and wait until the heaviest flow of carmel subsides into threads before touching them. Pull the threads aside, out from under the whisk, so that any drops of caramel that fall cannot burn you. With your hands, shape the tangle of threads to form a nest, halo, or cloud. When the caramel becomes too thick, remelt it over the lowest heat, trying not to let it boil and scorch. Depending on the weather, spun sugar is short-lived. Serve desserts with spun sugar as soon as possible.

DO-AHEAD NOTE: Although simple to make, spun sugar demands last-minute attention. I consider it performance art—guests love to watch—but the show is much easier to put on if the caramel is made ahead (in the form of shards) so it needs only remelting and spinning at the crucial moment. You can make an entire batch of caramel shards several days ahead and store them as described on page 243. At serving time, reserve a few shards for garnish, if desired, and crush the rest into a small saucepan or microwave-safe bowl. Over very low heat, or with 10-second bursts in the microwave, reheat the caramel until most of it is melted; it is not necessary for all of it to melt. Then spin the sugar and serve dessert!

PRALINE Have ready a foil- or parchment-lined baking sheet, a metal icing spatula, and 1 cup small to medium whole or chopped nuts, such as walnuts, pecans, or macadamias or toasted almonds or toasted skinned hazelnuts (see page 40). Make the caramel up to the point where the syrup looks light amber on the white plate. Add the nuts to the pan and turn them gently, using a clean dry wooden spoon or silicone spatula, just until they are completely coated with syrup. (Brisk stirring will cause the caramel to crystallize). Continue to cook, pushing the nuts around gently if the syrup is coloring unevenly, until a drop of syrup looks deep reddish amber on the white plate. Immediately scrape the mixture onto the lined sheet and spread it as thin as possible with the spatula. Allow to cool and harden.

Break the praline into shards, or coarsely chop. Store in an airtight container (with silica gel if possible; see page 31) until needed.

CARAMEL-GLAZED NUTS WITH STEMS Have ready a pan of ice water, cellophane tape, and a large bowl with flared sides. Impale 30 to 40 walnut or pecan halves, whole hazelnuts, or almonds (blanched or with skins) on toothpicks. Make the caramel, and immediately set the saucepan in the ice water for a few seconds to stop the cooking and prevent the caramel from continuing to darken. Let the caramel cool to the consistency of honey. Remove the pan from the ice bath and hold it so that it is tilted at a 45-degree angle, making the caramel flow into a deep pool at one side. Dip the skewered nuts, one by one, into the hot caramel and hold each nut upside down, letting the caramel form a stem as it drips. Tape each toothpick to the rim of the bowl so that the nut dangles freely upside down while the caramel cools. When the caramel glaze is cool and hardened, trim the caramel stems with a pair of scissors. To store, tape each toothpick to a sheet of foil, keeping the nuts slightly apart. Store in an airtight container (with silica gel, if possible; see page 31) until needed.

Rediscovering

Rethinking, reinventing, and reimagining with an open mind, in a new way, with new chocolate… tasting again for the first time.

PAGE 247: Wild Mushroom Ragout (PAGE 327) over polenta. OPPOSITE: Nibby Asparagus with Prosciutto (PAGE 326). ABOVE, LEFT TO RIGHT: Roasted Squash Soup with Cocoa Bean Cream (PAGE 325); Crunchy Baby Greens (PAGE 322); A Little Sauce for Pasta (PAGE 331) with fettuccine.

Still life with cacao pod, beakers of cocoa and chocolate sauce, blocks of chocolate, chocolate chips, chocolate chunks on a spoon, cocoa nibs and beans. OPPOSITE: Warm buttered tortillas filled with cinnamon sugar and cocoa nibs.

Warm Mocha Tart (PAGE 278). **OPPOSITE:** Tiger Cake (PAGE 269).

LEFT TO RIGHT: Bittersweet Roulade (PAGE 200); Fallen Chocolate Soufflé Cake (PAGE 112); Bittersweet Tartlets with Ancho Chile and Cherry, with Cocoa Nibs, and with Hazelnuts, Orange, and Anise (PAGES 280–281).

Infusing cream with cocoa nibs.

OPPOSITE: Cocoa Nib Panna Cotta (PAGE 305).

FOLLOWING PAGE: Marble Cheesecake (PAGE 266).

7

Home Baking

Cakes, Pies, and Cookies

About two years after I had stopped working for the new owners of Cocolat, my second book, *Chocolate and the Art of Low-Fat Desserts,* was already a year old. I was teaching a lot, but I had not written a new book proposal, or anything but an occasional article. Professionally, I was dragging my feet. Mostly, I was being a mom.

(Regenerating and healing, I can say from this distance.)

Lucy was entering the first grade, already a reader and passionate writer of her own little books, and an artist. I daydreamed briefly about collaborating with her on an illustrated cookbook. But she was saved when I concluded that her young psyche might not survive being art-directed by her mother. Then my agent told me that *Joy of Cooking,* originally published in 1931, was being revised for the first time in twenty-five years, and its editor wanted me to help with two important chapters.

By the mid-1990s, the state of cooking and food in this country had become so diverse and so driven by specialized expertise and passion that there was no single supercook who could possibly revise all the recipes and text in every chapter of America's culinary bible. So the editor enlisted a team to rewrite the book on a chapter-by-chapter basis.

Work on the cake chapter alone was the equivalent of writing an entire book. I turned in over three hundred manuscript pages, including perhaps twice as many recipes as there was room to include in the new book. I didn't mind. Working on the new *Joy* turned out to be an unexpected midlife and career transition. I brought everything I had to the project and emerged from it with even more.

I came to the revision's American kitchen table with a wealth of knowledge and experience in the use of chocolate, mostly in European-style cakes, desserts, and chocolate truffles. What I didn't feel that I knew as much about, except for cheesecakes, was American cake making. I dove into the subject with a passion, learning as fast as I could by testing recipes and by studying the cookbook authors I trusted the most. My nearly obsessive tendency to experiment stood me in good stead. I felt it was essential to test and taste every single recipe before deciding to recommend that it be dropped, kept as is, or revised. In doing so, I saw, more clearly than ever before, how details make a difference, how even the smallest changes in techniques and measurements affect results.

The old *Joy* did not necessarily need all new dessert and cake recipes, but even some of the keepers required tuning up to get bigger, brighter flavors. When I finally ventured into the actual revisions, I instinctively began to use what I had learned about fat and flavor while working on low-fat recipes. I saw at once that the dessert recipes weren't flavorful enough for contemporary palates either, so I began judiciously decreasing sugar and fat, not for dietary purposes, but simply to create heightened flavors.

Quite apart from the enormous education I aquired during this period, the greatest gift from the experience was inadvertent. Because I physically could not make and taste every recipe, I recruited people to help: home bakers and professionals. Some were already friends or acquaintances, others were not. All were women. They turned up separately every other day or so bringing cake. Visits were brief and businesslike, yet wonderfully comfortable. Sipping coffee and taking notes, I discovered a new way of working, centered (in every respect) in my home kitchen.

As if by magic, we re-created a slice of life straight from the old *Joy of Cooking:* the casual dropping-in of women friends to share coffee for a moment, an interruption of the daily routine of keeping house and raising children. It was a thoroughly pleasant throwback to a time when women did not work outside the home as much as they do today, but still constantly shared information and experience with one another. It is now the way I order my professional life.

The recipes were a revelation as well. For years, I had been knee deep in chocolate and European desserts. I was now tasting and testing the American baker's repertoire, including classic butter cakes, pound cakes, American sponge cakes (with leavening!), chiffon cakes, and angel cakes. Muffins, scones, and corn breads came under scrutiny when I turned to the quick bread chapter, infusing it with some low-fat alternatives as well. To help with quick breads, I hired Maya Klein, who was planning to become a professor of economics but was starting a family instead, and whose real passion (aside from husband and babies) was cooking.

Working on biscuits was her introduction to my obsession with testing and comparing. We tested plain biscuits with four different amounts of baking powder, each baked at three different temperatures. We tried different amounts of fat and sugar too. We have continued to taste and test and say "what if" to each other through each successive book.

In addition to improving my baking techniques and finding a new way to work, the project also shifted my focus in an unexpected but quite natural direction: I began paying more attention to simpler recipes for home cooks while, at the same time, digging even deeper into the technical aspects of chocolate and cocoa. I seemed to be going in two opposite directions. But that duality was reconciled when I remembered a particularly valuable hallmark of the old and new *Joy of Cooking:* Options and variations were offered to the cook in the recipes themselves, and even more variations were suggested in separate sections titled "Ideas for. . . ." I loved that way of empowering the cook with choices and knowledge from experiments, testing, and experience. Now, years later, the Chocolate Notes for nearly every recipe in this book have become a way to accommodate the differences among chocolates and offer the cook a wealth of informed choices.

Testing and experimenting, the combined legacy of my upbringing, self-taught bakery experience, and stint with the *Joy,* have all helped me temper technical knowledge with hands-on experience. Research and reading alone could not have yielded the richness of detail and nuance that infuse the Chocolate Notes and the Dessert Maker's Guide to High-Percentage Chocolates (see page 344)—brand-new resources for the curious and chocolate-loving cook.

CHOCOLATE CHEESECAKE

SERVES 12 TO 16

The tart taste of cream cheese, sour cream, and dark chocolate really appeals to me, so you'll find this cheesecake less sweet and far more chocolatey than most commercial and restaurant offerings. I developed the original version for Cocolat years ago, when I had fewer chocolate choices to work with. I used to intensify the flavor by adding a little cocoa powder, still a good technique if you use a standard bittersweet or semisweet. The recipe got "lost" and then turned up again when I was working on the cheesecake section of the new *Joy*. A good recipe doesn't die, it just gets better. Now I make the cake with a fruity bittersweet 70 percent chocolate, skip the cocoa powder, and make my own wafers for the crust (but see the Chocolate Notes for other chocolate options). I've still never tasted a chocolate cheesecake that I like better.

FOR THE CRUST

1 1/2 cups chocolate wafer crumbs, homemade (page 284) or store-bought

5 tablespoons unsalted butter, melted

1/4 cup sugar

1 1/2 teaspoons instant espresso powder

FOR THE CHEESECAKE

1/3 cup boiling water

6 1/2 ounces bittersweet 70% chocolate, finely chopped

1 pound cream cheese, at room temperature

3/4 cup sugar

1 teaspoon pure vanilla extract

3 large eggs, at room temperature

One 16-ounce container sour cream

SPECIAL EQUIPMENT

A 9-inch springform pan or cheesecake pan with a removable bottom

To make the crust: Position a rack in the lower third of the oven and preheat the oven to 350°F. Grease the cake pan.

Use a fork to blend together all the crust ingredients in a medium bowl. Press evenly over the bottom and about halfway up the sides of the pan. Prick the bottom of the crust with the fork. Bake for 10 minutes. Let cool on a rack before filling (leave the oven on).

To prepare the cheesecake: In a small bowl, pour the boiling water over the chocolate and stir until the chocolate is completely melted and smooth. Set aside.

In a large bowl, beat the softened cream cheese with an electric mixer just until smooth, about 30 seconds at high speed (or use a heavy-duty stand mixer and beat on medium speed with the flat beater attachment). Scrape the bowl and beaters well. Turn the mixer back on medium-to-low speed and gradually add the sugar. Continue to beat until smooth and creamy, then add the vanilla. Add the eggs one at a time, beating just until each is incorporated and scraping the bowl and beaters before adding the next one. Add the sour cream and beat just until incorporated. Pour in the warm chocolate mixture and beat on low speed just until well blended. Pour the batter into the crust and place the pan on a cookie sheet.

Bake for 35 to 40 minutes, or until the cake has puffed and looks set about 1½ inches in from the sides of the pan but still jiggles in the center when the pan is tapped. Remove the cake from the oven. Slide the tip of a thin paring knife carefully around the top edge of the cake to detach it from the pan, but do not remove the pan sides. Place the pan on a rack and cover the pan and rack with a large inverted bowl or pot so that the cake cools slowly to room temperature.

Cover the cooled cake and chill for at least 5 hours, preferably 24, before serving. The flavors are even more intense after 48 hours.

chocolate notes To use standard bittersweet or semisweet chocolate (without a percentage on the label) or any marked 50% to 62% instead of bittersweet 70%: Use 8 ounces chocolate. Increase the sugar to ⅔ cup and add 1 tablespoon natural or Dutch-process cocoa powder with the sour cream.

To use chocolate marked 64% to 66% instead of bittersweet 70%: Use 7 ounces chocolate.

❋ MARBLE CHEESECAKE photograph on page 258

SERVES 10 TO 12

Updated and improved, this is one of the best cheesecakes I make, even though a slice has only about two hundred calories and less than eight grams of fat. What it does have is plenty of cheese flavor and a satisfying swirl of rich dark chocolate without the excessive sweetness of commercial cheesecake. I often teach this recipe alongside luxuriously rich and decadent desserts. It is only from the ingredients list, never from the taste or texture, that students realize that this cake has a fraction of the fat of a traditional cheesecake.

Avoid nonfat cream cheeses and spreads because they taste artificial. I like the flavor of Neufchâtel cream cheese and low-fat cottage cheese or quark, which is an excellent creamy type of yogurt cheese available at cheese shops and also at the best supermarkets. I have also added simple steps to make the texture richer and *less wet* (the bane of some low-fat homemade cheesecakes). Thus the cottage cheese or quark is drained and the cake pan is lined with absorbent coffee filters. And I use real ground vanilla beans (see Sources, page 366), if possible, rather than vanilla extract. It's still a simple recipe, but, as always, the details make a difference!

Instead of one 8-inch cake, you can make two 6-inch cheesecakes from this recipe. Bake 5 to 10 minutes less.

For best flavor and texture, make this one day before serving.

One 16-ounce container low-fat (2%) quark or small-curd cottage cheese

3 tablespoons premium cocoa powder (natural or Dutch-process)

1/4 teaspoon instant espresso or powder (such as Medaglia d'Oro) coffee powder

1 cup plus 1 tablespoon sugar

3 tablespoons water

1 1/2 teaspoons strained fresh lemon juice (if using cottage cheese)

One 8-ounce package Neufchâtel cream cheese (Kraft in the box is good—don't buy the kind in the tub)

3 cold large eggs

3/4 teaspoon ground vanilla beans, or 1 tablespoon pure vanilla extract

1/4 teaspoon salt

1/4 cup graham cracker crumbs or chocolate wafer crumbs, homemade (page 284) or store-bought

SPECIAL EQUIPMENT

An 8-inch round cake pan (not a springform), at least 2 inches deep

Four round coffee filters at least 8 inches in diameter (iron or weight them if necessary to flatten them), or several cone-shaped filters

An 8-inch cardboard cake circle (optional)

Line a sieve with several layers of folded paper towels topped with 1 of the coffee filters. Scrape the quark or cottage cheese on top and set the sieve over a bowl. Cover and refrigerate for at least 30 minutes to drain. (Don't worry if the cheese does not exude much liquid; some brands do, some don't.)

Position a rack in the lower third of the oven and preheat the oven to 350°F. Line the bottom of the cake pan with coffee filters: Lay the round ones on top of one another, or arrange cone-shaped filters in an overlapping pattern to cover the bottom of the pan. Lightly grease the sides of the pan. Put a kettle of water on to boil.

In a small bowl, whisk the cocoa, coffee powder, 1 tablespoon of the sugar, and the 3 tablespoons water until smooth. Set aside.

Place the drained cheese (if using cottage cheese, add the lemon juice now) in a food processor for 2 1/2 to 3 minutes, until silky-smooth, scraping the sides and bottom of the bowl once or twice as necessary. Leave the cheese in the processor.

Soften the Neufchâtel cheese in the microwave on High (100%) power for about 30 seconds. Or warm it gently in the top of a double boiler. Stir until smooth and soft, like thick mayonnaise. Scrape into the processor. Add the eggs, the remaining 1 cup sugar, the vanilla, and salt. Pulse only until all the ingredients are incorporated and the mixture is perfectly smooth. Do not overprocess or the batter will become too thin.

continued

Stir 1 cup of the batter into the cocoa mixture. Pour all of the plain batter into the prepared pan (on top of the coffee filters). To prevent the chocolate batter from sinking into the vanilla batter, pour or spoon it gently—in several puddles—over the top, making sure it doesn't cover all of the vanilla batter. Draw a knife or teaspoon through the puddles to marble the batters without really mixing them together. (The cake tastes best and most chocolatey with separate pockets of vanilla and chocolate rather than a blend.)

Place the cheesecake pan in a baking pan at least 1 inch larger all around than the cake pan, pull out the oven rack, and set the pans on the rack. Carefully pour boiling water around the cheesecake pan to a depth of about 1 inch. Slide the oven rack in gently and bake until the cheesecake has puffed and risen slightly around the edges and is just beginning to shrink from the edges of the pan, 40 to 45 minutes. Remove the cheesecake from the water bath and cool on a rack. When completely cool, cover and chill for at least 12 hours, or for up to 2 days, before serving.

To serve, run a thin knife blade around the side of the pan to release the cake. Cover the pan with tightly stretched plastic wrap. Place a flat dish upside down over the plastic. Invert the pan and dish and rap the pan gently until the cheesecake is released from the pan. Remove the pan and peel the coffee filters from the bottom of the cake. Place a cake circle or serving plate on the cake and carefully invert again so that the cake is right side up. Remove the plastic wrap. Press the crumbs around the sides of the cake. Cut with a sharp thin knife dipped in hot water and wiped dry between cuts.

chocolate note I get good results with either natural or Dutch-process cocoa. However, I don't like the Dutch-process cocoas called "black" cocoa.

TIGER CAKE photograph on page 253
SERVES 12

A chocolate marble cake made with extra virgin olive oil and a pinch of white pepper? Stay with me. The flavors are subtle and delicious, the cake is moist with a close-to-pound-cake texture, it's not too sweet, and the stripes are beautiful. The pepper does its work sotto voce, accentuating the olive oil flavor and somehow adding an elusive almond flavor with just a little heat. Too esoteric? The five-year-old boy who named the cake (for the stripes, of course) says it's his favorite, but grown-ups like it too. It's a little sneaky in that it seems plain at first, then you notice you've eaten the whole piece and have started slicing seconds.

This cake is even better on the second day. Toasting brings out more flavor too; try a slice for breakfast. Finally, the cake is easy to make and seems to be self-marbling: The liquid layers of batter sink and mingle in the oven of their own accord, with gorgeous results.

1/2 cup natural cocoa powder (not Dutch-process)

1/2 cup sugar

1/3 cup water

3 cups all-purpose flour

2 teaspoons baking powder

1/4 teaspoon salt

2 cups sugar

1 cup flavorful extra virgin olive oil

1 teaspoon pure vanilla extract

1/2 teaspoon finely ground white pepper

5 cold large eggs

1 cup cold milk

SPECIAL EQUIPMENT

A 10- to 12-cup tube or Bundt pan or two 6-cup loaf pans

Position a rack in the lower third of the oven and preheat the oven to 350°F. Grease and flour the cake pan or line the loaf pans with parchment.

In a small bowl, whisk the cocoa, sugar, and water together until well blended. Set aside.

Mix the flour, baking powder, and salt thoroughly and sift together onto a piece of wax paper. Set aside.

continued

In a large mixer bowl (with the whisk attachment if you have it), beat the sugar, oil, vanilla, and pepper until well blended. Add the eggs one at a time, beating well after each addition. Continue to beat until the mixture is thick and pale, 3 to 5 minutes. Stop the mixer and add one-third of the flour mixture. Beat on low speed just until blended. Stop the mixer and add half of the milk. Beat just until it is blended. Repeat with another third of the flour, the remaining milk, and then the remaining flour.

Pour 3 cups of the batter into another bowl and stir in the cocoa mixture. Pour one-third of the plain batter into the prepared tube pan (or divide it between the loaves) and top with one-third of the chocolate batter. Repeat with the remaining batters. Don't worry about marbling the batters—that happens beautifully during the baking.

Bake until a cake tester comes out clean, about 1 hour and 10 minutes for either the tube pan or loaf pans. Cool the cake in the pan(s) on a rack for about 15 minutes. Slide a skewer around the tube pan or slide a thin knife around the sides of the loaf pans to release the cake(s). Invert the pan(s) and invert again, setting the cake right side up on a rack to cool completely.

chocolate note Natural cocoa powder is a *must* here. Dutch-process adds an unpleasant taste because it reacts with the leavening and the olive oil in the cake.

✿ A LIGHT CHOCOLATE POUND

SERVES 12

Although this simple and delicious chocolate pound cake has very little fat, it still has the velvet texture and flavor of a real butter cake—because it is one! Beating the butter with the flour tenderizes the cake. Coating the flour particles with fat water-proofs them, which prevents the cake-toughening gluten that normally forms when the liquid is beaten into the batter. Using cold eggs and milk further tenderizes the cake.

1 cup plus 2 tablespoons sugar

1 cup all-purpose flour

1/2 cup unsweetened natural (not Dutch-process) cocoa powder

3/8 teaspoon baking soda

1/4 teaspoon salt

4 tablespoons unsalted butter, softened

1 cold large egg

2 cold large egg whites

1 teaspoon instant espresso powder (such as Medaglia d'Oro), or 1 1/4 teaspoons instant coffee powder or crystals

1 teaspoon pure vanilla extract

1/2 cup cold low-fat (1%) milk

Powdered sugar for dusting (optional)

SPECIAL EQUIPMENT

A 6-cup fluted tube pan

Position a rack in the lower third of the oven and preheat the oven to 350°F. Spray the tube pan with vegetable oil spray.

In a large bowl, whisk together the sugar, flour, cocoa, baking soda, and salt. Add the butter, egg, and egg whites. Set a timer for 2 minutes, and begin beating with an electric mixer on medium speed. When the dry ingredients are moistened but not wet, increase the speed to high and beat until the 2 minutes are up.

Combine the espresso powder, vanilla, and cold milk and add to the batter. Beat at high speed for exactly 2 more minutes. Scrape the batter into the pan and spread it evenly. Bake just until a wooden toothpick inserted in the center of the cake comes out clean, 35 to 40 minutes. Do not overbake. Cool in the pan on a wire rack for 10 minutes before unmolding onto the rack to cool completely. Serve dusted with powdered sugar, if desired.

chocolate note You must use a natural cocoa here: Dutch-process cocoa will interact badly with the baking soda.

RASPBERRY-LACED CHOCOLATE CAKE

SERVES 10

Substituting fresh raspberry puree for the buttermilk in my favorite chocolate loaf cake—on a whim, really—led to this soft-textured, moist little gem. Be sure that the raspberry puree, butter, and eggs are all at room temperature before beginning.

1 cup all-purpose flour

1/2 cup Dutch-process cocoa powder

1/4 teaspoon baking powder

1/4 teaspoon baking soda

1/2 teaspoon salt

1/2 cup seedless raspberry puree
(from frozen unsweetened raspberries
or from 3/4 pint fresh raspberries)

3 tablespoons brandy or rum

1 teaspoon pure vanilla extract

10 tablespoons (11/4 sticks)
unsalted butter, softened

11/3 cups sugar

3 large eggs

Powdered sugar for dusting
(optional)

SPECIAL EQUIPMENT

A 6-cup decorative tube pan, such as
a Turk's Head or Kugelhopf pan

A skewer, toothpick, or artist's brush
if making cupcakes

Position a rack in the lower third of the oven and preheat the oven to 350°F. Spray the tube pan with vegetable oil spray.

Whisk together the flour, cocoa, baking powder, baking soda, and salt in a bowl, then sift onto a sheet of wax paper. Set aside.

Combine the raspberry puree, brandy, and vanilla in a small bowl; set aside.

In a medium to large bowl, with an electric mixer, beat the butter on medium speed for a few seconds, until creamy. Add the sugar in a steady stream and continue to beat (on high speed with a hand-held mixer or medium speed with a heavy-duty mixer) until light and fluffy, about 4 to 5 minutes.

Break the eggs into a cup or small bowl and whisk to combine the whites and yolks. Take a full 2½ to 3 minutes to dribble the eggs gradually into the butter mixture, beating constantly.

Stop the mixer and add one-third of the flour mixture. Beat on low speed only until no flour is visible. Stop the mixer and add half of the raspberry mixture. Beat only until absorbed. Repeat with half of the remaining flour, all of the remaining raspberry mixture, and finally the remaining flour. Scrape the bowl as necessary and beat on low speed only enough to incorporate the ingredients after each addition.

Scrape the batter into the pan and spread it evenly. Bake until the cake starts to shrink away from the sides of the pan and a toothpick inserted in the center comes out dry, 40 to 45 minutes. Let the cake cool in the pan on a rack for 10 minutes, then invert onto a rack and let cool completely. (The cake can be wrapped well and kept at room temperature for 4 to 5 days, or it can be frozen for up to 3 months.)

Using a fine-mesh sieve, sift powdered sugar over the cake just before serving, if desired.

MOLTEN RASPBERRY–CHOCOLATE CUPCAKES WITH MARBLED GLAZE
(photograph on page 134) In a muffin tin with fluted paper liners, or greased, bake the batter, about 20 minutes. When the cupcakes are completely cool, make Bittersweet Chocolate Glaze (page 235) or Bittersweet Ganache Glaze (page 234). Melt 1 ounce milk chocolate and 1 ounce white chocolate in two small bowls. Dip one cupcake top (or bottom) into the glaze. Turn the cupcake glaze side up. Dip the tip of your finger or a rubber spatula into the melted chocolates and drizzle a little of each on the glaze. Swirl a skewer, toothpick, or tiny artist's brush through the wet glaze to marble the chocolates. Repeat with the remaining cupcakes. Let the glaze set at room temperature.

chocolate note Dutch-process cocoa is a must here; natural cocoa will not work with this leavening.

Although chocolate is my family's favorite flavor, it is not prominent on our Thanksgiving table. My mother's apple pie is the undisputed centerpiece of the holiday. Pumpkin and mince pies used to flank it, usually brought by family members or guests; they were essentially shills.

My father would make elaborate noises over those other pies, offering them first and with great enthusiasm, encouraging generous portions, all the while winking at us kids. The unspoken message was that there would be more apple pie left over for us if the guests filled up on the mince and pumpkin.

My family shares a deep sense of connection to that apple pie. We tell stories about it, joke about it, and argue passionately about every change in its fifty-year evolution. It has grown up and old with some of us and is now enjoyed by a generation that never tasted it with two crusts instead of one, or without a few cranberries, or whatever else my mother, never content with the status quo, has decided to do to it "this time." Although I've fought or at least rolled my eyes at some of her changes (puh-lease, not whole wheat flour!), the pie is always delicious. The recipe details are obviously not sacrosanct, but my mother does hold to one ritual. She produces enough extra pies to allow pie eating for breakfast, lunch, and dinner several days running during the holiday marathon. Even in my childhood, we were allowed to eat pie instead of breakfast on those few magical days.

I never want to see the apple pie take second place, but I thought it might be nice to put a chocolate dessert on the Thanksgiving table alongside it, if only to fulfill the role of the long-forgotten mince. What would be appropriate?

The real Thanksgiving chocolate challenge has to do with the mood and the flavors associated with the season, its crisp crackling air and brilliant sunlight, and the ritual nuts and apples and pumpkins of the greatest American food holiday of them all. (If you are waiting to hear about the turkey, I'll have to admit that my family of food lovers and epicureans includes vegetarians and other fish-loving folk, such that turkey went the way of the second pie crust long ago, and has been replaced with a magnificent whole wild salmon, barbecued to breathtaking perfection by my father.) Thanksgiving has never seemed like a day for my chocolate tortes or anything fancy, foreign, or Frenchified. No one, not even my family, watches football while eating leftover chocolate mousse.

I needed a thoroughly American dessert with some chocolate in it. It had to be rich and voluptuous without being too dressy for the Thanksgiving table. Chocolate pecan pie had possibilities, but the task was delicate. I could not let the chocolate ruin the pie, or vice versa: balance was key. The worst possible outcome would be a dessert that insulted the pecan pie lovers *and* disappointed chocolate lovers at the same time.

In fits and starts over a period of a dozen years, I worked on a recipe for chocolate pecan pie. This one, originally published in my book *A Year in Chocolate,* is the best to date. It is the essence of pecan pie with a rich undertone of chocolate and spirits. And the information in the Chocolate Notes allows you to use different types of chocolate without destroying the delicate balance of flavors in this pie. I thank Steven Schmidt again for teaching me that filling a hot prebaked crust with a warm filling results in a piecrust that is never soggy. Happy Thanksgiving!

CHOCOLATE PECAN PIE photograph on pages 20–21

SERVES 8 TO 10

FOR THE CRUST

1 1/2 cups all-purpose flour

3/4 teaspoon salt

10 tablespoons (1 1/4 sticks)
unsalted butter

4 to 5 tablespoons cold water

FOR THE FILLING

2 cups (7 ounces) pecan halves

2 ounces bittersweet or semisweet
chocolate, coarsely chopped

1/4 cup light corn syrup

1 tablespoon unsalted butter, melted

1 cup lightly packed dark brown sugar

1/4 teaspoon salt

1 tablespoon rum, bourbon, or brandy

1 teaspoon pure vanilla extract

3 large eggs

SPECIAL EQUIPMENT

A 9-inch glass pie pan

To make the crust: Thoroughly mix the flour and salt in a large bowl. Cut the butter into chunks and add it to the bowl. Using two knives or a pastry blender, cut the butter into successively smaller pieces, scraping the bottom of the bowl and tossing the pieces to coat and separate them with flour as you work, until the largest pieces of butter are the size of peas and the rest bread-crumb size. (Do not let the butter melt or form a paste.) Drizzle 1/4 cup cold water over the flour mixture, mixing with a rubber spatula or a fork, folding and pressing the dough to distribute the moisture. If necessary, drizzle in some or all of the remaining 1 tablespoon water, until the dough is just moist enough to hold together when pressed. Use your hands to compress the dough into a flat disk, pressing in any loose pieces. Wrap in plastic wrap and refrigerate for at least 30 minutes, or for up to 3 days.

Remove the dough from the refrigerator and let it stand until it is pliable enough to roll without cracking. On a lightly floured surface, roll the dough into a 14- to 15-inch circle about 1/8 inch thick, rotating and dusting the surface with flour to keep it from sticking. Brush the excess flour from the rolled-out circle, fold the circle into quarters, and transfer it to the pie pan. Unfold, easing the pastry into the pan without stretching it. Trim the overhang to about 1 inch. Turn the excess dough under and flute or crimp the edge. Refrigerate for least 30 minutes before baking. (Reserve a few dough scraps for later patching if necessary.)

Toast the nuts while the dough is chilling: Position a rack in the lower third of the oven and preheat the oven to 350°F. Spread the nuts on a baking sheet and bake for 6 to 9 minutes, until fragrant and lightly colored. Set aside.

Increase the oven temperature to 400°F and let preheat.

Press a 12-inch square of foil, shiny side down, against the bottom and up the sides of the crust. Tent the edges of the foil over (not touching) the edges of the crust, like an awning, to prevent overbrowning. Prick the bottom of the crust all over with a fork, piercing right through the foil. Fill the foil-lined crust with dried beans or pie weights.

Bake the crust for 20 minutes. Remove the foil liner and weights. Bake for 10 to 12 minutes more, until the bottom of the crust is golden brown.

While the crust is baking, make the filling: Combine the chocolate, corn syrup, and butter in the top of a double boiler over barely simmering water. Stir until the chocolate is completely melted and the mixture is smooth. Stir in the brown sugar, salt, rum, and vanilla. Add the eggs and stir until the mixture is well blended and hot to the touch. Set the double boiler aside, stirring the filling from time to time.

When the crust is baked, remove it from the oven. (Leave the oven on.) If necessary, press bits of reserved dough into any holes or cracks in the crust. Pour the pecans into the crust and the hot filling over the nuts.

Bake until the filling is puffed and cracked at the edges and brown in patches but still jiggles in the center when nudged, 10 to 12 minutes. A knife inserted in the pie will emerge very gooey. If the edges of the crust are browning too fast before the pie is done, cover with a 12-inch square of foil with a 7-inch circle cut out from its center. Cool the pie on a rack. Serve warm or at room temperature.

chocolate notes It takes very little chocolate to make the balance of flavors work. You can use standard bittersweet or semisweet chocolate (without a percentage on the label), or any marked 50% to 64%.

To use chocolate marked 66% to 72% instead of standard bittersweet: Use 1 1/2 ounces chocolate.

To use unsweetened (or 99%) chocolate instead of standard bittersweet: Use 1 ounce chocolate.

Tarts and Tartlets

Two weeks of nonstop shortbread testing produced an unorthodox surprise: perfect shortbread made with melted butter. That shortbread became an exquisitely crunchy and flavorful base for lemon bars, a crust for cheesecake, and, ultimately, my favorite sweet tart crust. I even bake brownie batter on top of it. It is simply mixed in a bowl and pressed into a tart pan or tartlet pans. Or you can roll it out in the usual way. I now make variations with ground nuts and even sesame seeds; it is nothing if not versatile. This remarkable crust barely shrinks in the pan, so there is no need to weight or even prick it before baking. To ensure that the bottom remains crunchy, bake the crust fully, to a deep golden brown, before pouring in the filling.

WARM MOCHA TART photograph on page 252
SERVES 8 TO 10

At the same time I was playing with my new tart crust, I was experimenting with different cocoas, tasting and comparing natural and Dutch-process in all kinds of recipes. Voilà, rich warm cocoa custard in the simplest crust.

FOR THE CRUST

8 tablespoons (1 stick) unsalted butter, melted

1/4 cup sugar

1/8 teaspoon salt

3/4 teaspoon pure vanilla extract

1 cup all-purpose flour

FOR THE FILLING

3 tablespoons unsalted butter, cut into chunks

1/2 cup sugar

1/4 cup unsweetened cocoa powder (natural or Dutch-process)

1 cup heavy cream

1 1/4 teaspoons instant espresso powder (such as Medaglia d'Oro), or 1 1/2 teaspoons instant coffee crystals

1/2 teaspoon pure vanilla extract

1 large egg, lightly beaten

SPECIAL EQUIPMENT

A 9 1/2-inch fluted tart pan with a removable bottom

Position a rack in the lower third of the oven and preheat the oven to 350°F.

To make the tart crust: Mix the butter, sugar, salt, and vanilla in a medium bowl. Add the flour and mix just until well blended. Don't worry if the dough seems too soft. Press all of the dough very thinly and evenly into the bottom and up the sides of the tart pan.

Bake for 20 to 25 minutes, or until the crust is a deep golden brown.

Meanwhile, make the filling: Place the butter, sugar, cocoa powder, and cream in a medium saucepan and cook over medium heat, stirring, until the mixture is blended and smooth and begins to simmer around the edges. Remove from the heat and stir in the espresso powder and vanilla.

Just before the crust is ready, whisk the egg thoroughly into the hot chocolate mixture.

Pour the filling into the hot crust and turn off the oven. Leave the tart in the oven until it quivers like tender Jell-O in the center when the pan is nudged, about 10 to 12 minutes. Cool on a rack.

Serve the tart warm or at room temperature.

ESPRESSO WALNUT TART The same tart in a walnut cookie crust produces a subtler but still delicious effect. You could also make it with toasted skinned hazelnuts—then I would omit the espresso powder.

Reduce the butter to 6 tablespoons and add 2 teaspoons brandy and 1 teaspoon instant espresso powder (or a heaping teaspoon instant coffee crystals) with the sugar, salt, and vanilla. In a food processor, pulverize ⅓ cup walnut pieces with ¾ cup flour until fine. Substitute this mixture for the flour. Proceed as directed.

chocolate note Either natural or Dutch-process cocoa works well here. The former has a livelier, more complex, fruity flavor, while the latter has a cozy old-fashioned flavor reminiscent of chocolate pudding. You choose.

BITTERSWEET TARTLETS WITH HAZELNUTS, ORANGE, AND ANISE photograph on pages 254–255

MAKES 8 TARTLETS

Here the filling is made with chocolate rather than cocoa, so you can try any of your favorite brands. These tartlets, garnished with aromatic ingredients, were inspired by a bout of mendiant making (see page 341). Restraint is the key to making the spice and chocolate a sublime experience. Mysterious understatement is better than a blow upside the head. Sensitivity to spices is highly variable from one person to the next; what is splendidly subtle to one may not be enough for others. If your gathering is informal and friendly, pass some crushed anise separately at the table. Let those who love it, or who find your treatment too elusive, add a pinch to their own portion. It creates a nice conversation topic, and fragrant fingertips, in any case.

For the less adventuresome but totally committed chocolate lovers, these tartlets are fabulous served on their own, without their exotic toppings, sprinkled instead with handfuls of cocoa nibs.

FOR THE CRUST

8 tablespoons (1 stick) unsalted butter, melted

1/4 cup sugar

3/4 teaspoon pure vanilla extract

1/8 teaspoon salt

1 cup all-purpose flour

FOR THE FILLING

1 cup half-and-half

2 tablespoons sugar

8 ounces bittersweet or semisweet chocolate, finely chopped

1 large egg, lightly whisked

3 tablespoons chopped, toasted, and skinned hazelnuts (see page 40)

1 ounce candied orange peel, slivered or chopped

1/2 teaspoon anise seeds, slightly crushed in a mortar

SPECIAL EQUIPMENT

Eight 4-inch (measured across the top) fluted tartlet pans (about 3/4 inch deep) with removable bottoms

Position a rack in the lower third of the oven and preheat the oven to 350°F.

To make the crust: Combine the melted butter, sugar, vanilla, and salt in a medium bowl. Mix in the flour just until blended. Don't worry if the dough seems too soft. Divide the dough into 8 or 10 equal pieces. Press one piece very thinly and evenly across the bottom and up the sides of each pan. This takes patience—the amount of dough is just right.

Place the pans on a cookie sheet. Bake for 15 to 20 minutes, until the crusts are a deep golden brown.

Meanwhile, make the filling: In a small saucepan, bring the half-and-half and sugar to a simmer. Remove the pan from the heat. Add the chopped chocolate and stir until completely melted and smooth.

Just before the crust is done, whisk the egg into the chocolate mixture.

When the crusts are ready, remove from the oven. Turn off the oven. Pour the hot chocolate filling mixture into the crusts. Return the tartlets to the turned-off oven for 5 to 10 minutes, or just until the filling begins to set around the edges but most of the center is still liquid when the pans are nudged. Set the sheet on a rack to let the filling continue to cool and set.

Remove the pan sides and serve the tartlets warm or let them cool completely. Just before serving, scatter the chopped hazelnuts and slivers of candied orange peel over the tarts, then sprinkle with the crushed anise. (The tarts are best on the day they are made.)

ANCHO CHILE AND CHERRY TARTLETS Substitute walnuts or pecans for the hazelnuts, a few dried sweet cherries for the orange peel, and ground dried ancho (if you have a choice) powder or a commercial chili powder for the anise seeds.

chocolate notes You can use standard bittersweet or semisweet chocolate (without a percentage on the label), or any marked 50% to 60%.

To use chocolate marked 62% to 64% instead of standard bittersweet: Use 7 ounces chocolate.

To use chocolate marked 66% to 72% instead of standard bittersweet: Use 5½ ounces chocolate, and increase the sugar to 5 tablespoons.

MELTING CHOCOLATE COOKIE TARTLETS

MAKES 8 TO 10 TARTLETS

These rustic-looking craggy-topped tartlets with a crunchy crust and chewy-yet-soft-centered chocolate filling were the inspiration of one of my students. Alicia Hitchcock makes thousands of tartlets by filling my melted butter shortbread crust with my melting chocolate meringue cookie batter. Here's "our" recipe.

FOR THE CRUST

8 tablespoons (1 stick) unsalted butter, melted

3 tablespoons sugar

3/4 teaspoon pure vanilla extract

1/8 teaspoon salt

1 cup all-purpose flour

FOR THE FILLING

6 ounces bittersweet or semisweet chocolate, coarsely chopped

2 large egg whites, at room temperature

1/8 teaspoon cream of tartar

1/2 teaspoon pure vanilla extract

1/4 cup sugar

3/4 cup chopped pecans or walnuts

SPECIAL EQUIPMENT

Eight 4-inch (measured across the top) or ten 3 1/2-inch fluted tartlet pans (about 3/4 inch deep)

Position a rack in the lower third of the oven and preheat the oven to 350°F.

To make the crust: Mix the butter, sugar, vanilla, and salt in a medium bowl. Add the flour and mix just until well blended. Don't worry if the dough seems too soft. Divide the dough into 8 or 10 equal pieces. Press one piece of dough very thinly and evenly across the bottom and up the sides of each tartlet pan. This takes some patience—there is just enough dough.

Place the pans on a cookie sheet. Bake for 15 to 20 minutes, until a deep golden brown.

While the crusts are baking, make the filling: Melt the chocolate in a medium heatproof bowl set in a wide skillet of barely simmering water, or in the microwave on Medium (50%) power for $3\frac{1}{2}$ to 4 minutes, stirring frequently until the chocolate is almost completely melted. Remove from the heat and stir until completely melted. Set aside.

In a large bowl, beat the egg whites with the cream of tartar and vanilla until soft peaks form when you lift the beaters. Gradually add the sugar and continue to beat until the egg whites are stiff but not dry. Pour the nuts and all of the warm chocolate over the egg whites and fold with a rubber spatula until the color of the batter is uniform.

As soon as the tartlet crusts are ready, divide the filling equally among them. Make sure that batter touches the crust all around the edges. Return to the oven and bake until the filling is dry or slightly cracked on top, about 10 minutes. Cool on a rack.

To unmold, use the point of a paring knife to loosen one edge of the crust from the pan, then tip the tarts into your hand. Serve warm or at room temperature.

IDEAS Fold into the filling 2 ounces crystallized ginger, finely chopped; 4 ounces moist prunes, chopped into $\frac{1}{4}$-inch pieces; or 4 ounces candied chestnuts, chopped.

Substitute toasted pine nuts for the pecans.

chocolate notes You can use standard bittersweet or semisweet chocolate (without a percentage on the label), or any marked 50% to 62%.

To use chocolate marked 64% to 66% instead of standard bittersweet: Use 5 ounces chocolate.

To use chocolate marked 70% to 72% instead of standard bittersweet: Use $4\frac{1}{2}$ ounces chocolate, and increase the sugar to $\frac{1}{3}$ tablespoon.

❋ REAL CHOCOLATE WAFERS

MAKES 40 TO 45 COOKIES

Plain and crisp, these are good served with the creamy crustless Marble Cheesecake (page 266). They also make the best cookie crumbs for the sides of the cake.

1 cup all-purpose flour	1/2 cup packed brown sugar
1/2 cup plus 1 tablespoon unsweetened cocoa powder (natural or Dutch-process)	1/2 cup plus 2 tablespoons granulated sugar
1/4 teaspoon baking soda	1 teaspoon pure vanilla extract
1/4 teaspoon salt	3 tablespoons low-fat (1%) milk or water
6 tablespoons unsalted butter, slightly softened	

In a medium bowl, whisk together the flour, cocoa, baking soda, and salt. Set aside.

In a medium bowl, beat the butter with an electric mixer until creamy. Add the sugars and vanilla. Beat on high speed for about 1 minute. Beat in the milk. On low speed, beat in the flour mixture just until incorporated. Gather the dough together with your hands and form it into a neat 9- to 10-inch log. Wrap it in wax paper, folding or twisting the ends of the paper without pinching or flattening the log. Chill for at least 45 minutes, or until needed. (The dough can be refrigerated for up to 3 days, or double-wrapped and frozen for up to 3 months.)

Place the oven racks in the upper and lower thirds of the oven and preheat the oven to 350°F. Lightly grease two baking sheets.

Use a sharp knife to slice rounds of chilled dough a scant 1/4 inch thick. Place them 1 inch apart on baking sheets. Bake for 10 to 12 minutes, rotating the baking sheets from top to bottom and front to back about halfway through. The cookies will puff and crackle on top, then settle down slightly when done. Use a metal spatula to transfer the cookies to wire racks to cool completely.

Store in an airtight container for up to 2 weeks, or freeze for up to 2 months.

chocolate note Use natural or Dutch-process cocoa, not "black" cocoa.

❖ SAUCEPAN FUDGE DROPS

MAKES ABOUT 32 COOKIES

These easy cookies have crunchy edges and chewy, fudgy centers.

1 cup all-purpose flour (bleached flour makes more tender cookies)

1/4 teaspoon baking soda

1/8 teaspoon salt

5 tablespoons unsalted butter

1/2 cup plus 1 tablespoon unsweetened cocoa powder (natural or Dutch-process)

2/3 cup granulated sugar

1/3 cup packed light brown sugar

1/3 cup low-fat or nonfat yogurt

1 teaspoon pure vanilla extract

2 to 3 teaspoons powdered sugar for dusting

Arrange the racks in the upper and lower thirds of the oven and preheat the oven to 350°F. Line two cookie sheets with parchment or wax paper.

Whisk the flour, baking soda, and salt together thoroughly. Set aside.

In a medium saucepan, heat the butter until it is melted and sizzling. Off the heat, stir in the cocoa until blended and smooth. Stir in the sugars until blended; the mixture will be stiff and sandy. Mix in the yogurt and vanilla. Add the flour mixture all at once and fold and stir just until it is entirely moistened and incorporated into the cocoa mixture—do not stir more than necessary.

Scoop level tablespoons of the dough 1 1/2 inches apart onto the lined cookie sheets. Use a fine strainer to sift powdered sugar over the tops.

Bake until the cookies look dry and cracked on top but still feel a little soft when pressed, 9 to 11 minutes. Rotate the sheets from top to bottom and front to back about halfway through the baking. Slide the cookies, on the paper, off the sheets and onto racks to cool; or set the pans on the racks and let cool.

The cookies will keep for 2 to 3 days in an airtight container, although they soften and lose their crunchy exterior.

chocolate note My preference here is for natural cocoa, which has the liveliest and most complex flavor, but use Dutch-process if you prefer it. I avoid "black" cocoas.

BITTERSWEET DECADENCE COOKIES photograph on page 15

MAKES 36 COOKIES

Ultrachocolatey and richer than sin, slightly crunchy on the outside with a divinely soft center, these are not delicate or subtle, but the jolt of bittersweet is irresistible. I reorganized and revised the original recipe from one in a newspaper—to make the cookies more chocolatey and intense—by reducing the sugar and butter. Now I've revised it again so that I can make it with higher-percentage chocolates without compromising that perfect contrast of textures. For the best cookies of all, chop your own chocolate for the chunks, or use a premium brand of chocolate chunks rather than ordinary chocolate chips. You can choose a chocolate for the chunks that contrasts in sweetness with the chocolate in the cookie batter.

1/4 cup all-purpose flour	1/2 cup sugar
1/4 teaspoon baking powder	1 teaspoon pure vanilla extract
1/8 teaspoon salt	2 cups walnuts or pecans, broken or chopped into large pieces
8 ounces bittersweet or semisweet chocolate, coarsely chopped	6 ounces bittersweet or semisweet chocolate, chopped into chunks, or store-bought chocolate chunks
2 tablespoons unsalted butter	
2 large eggs	

Position the racks in the upper and lower thirds of the oven and preheat the oven to 350°F. Line two cookie sheets (see Note) with parchment or wax paper.

In a small bowl, mix the flour, baking powder, and salt together thoroughly; set aside.

Place the 8 ounces of chocolate and the butter in a large heatproof bowl in a wide skillet of barely simmering water and stir frequently just until melted and smooth. Remove the chocolate from the skillet and set it aside. Leave the heat on under the skillet.

In a large heatproof bowl, whisk the eggs, sugar, and vanilla together thoroughly. Set the bowl in the skillet and stir until the mixture is lukewarm to the touch. Stir the eggs into the warm (not hot) chocolate. Stir in the flour mixture, then the nuts and chocolate chunks.

Scoop slightly rounded tablespoons of batter 1$\frac{1}{2}$ inches apart onto the cookie sheets. Bake until the surface of the cookies looks dry and set but the center is still gooey, 12 to 14 minutes. If you used parchment (or wax paper), carefully slide the cookies, still on the parchment, onto racks, or set the pans on the racks. Otherwise, let the cookies firm up on the pans for a minute, then transfer them to the racks with a metal pancake turner. Let cool completely. Store in a tightly sealed container.

NOTE: I am fussy about cookie sheets. These cookies will have the best flavor and texture if they are baked on sheets lined with parchment paper, or even wax paper, which insulates them just enough but still allows the cookies to be a little crusty on the outside and soft within. Cushioned pans and silicone liners make the texture of the cookies too uniform for my taste. Pans with dark surfaces (even if they are non-stick) tend to scorch rich chocolate cookie bottoms before the centers are cooked.

chocolate notes For the batter, you can use standard bittersweet or semisweet chocolate (without a percentage on the label), or any marked 50% to 60%. Adjusting the recipe for higher-percentage chocolates, I tried to increase the intensity of the flavor without sacrificing the texture or the pretty gloss on the surface of the cookies.

To use chocolate marked 61% to 64% instead of standard bittersweet: Use 7 ounces chocolate. Increase the sugar to $\frac{1}{2}$ cup plus 1 tablespoon.

To use chocolate marked 66% instead of standard bittersweet: Use 6$\frac{1}{2}$ ounces chocolate. Increase the butter to 3 tablespoons and the sugar to $\frac{1}{2}$ cup plus 2 tablespoons.

To use chocolate marked 70% to 72% instead of standard bittersweet: Use 5$\frac{1}{2}$ ounces chocolate. Increase the butter to 3 tablespoons and the sugar to $\frac{3}{4}$ cup.

For the chunks, use any chocolate you like, the same as or different from the batter, higher percentage or not. No alterations are necessary.

CREAM SCONES WITH
CHOCOLATE CHUNKS photograph on page 13
MAKES 8 TO 12 SCONES

Like plain bread and chocolate, there is something at once elemental and sumptuous about these flaky scones made entirely with cream, instead of butter, and laced with chunks of the best (your favorite) dark chocolate.

2 cups all-purpose flour

1/4 cup sugar, plus sugar for sprinkling

2 1/2 teaspoons baking powder

1/2 teaspoon salt

3 to 4 ounces bittersweet or semisweet chocolate, coarsely chopped

1 1/4 cups heavy cream

1 tablespoon milk or cream for brushing the tops

Position a rack in the center of the oven and preheat the oven to 425°F. Line the baking sheet with a double layer of parchment paper.

In a large bowl, whisk the flour, sugar, baking powder, and salt together thoroughly. Stir in the chopped chocolate. Make a well in the center and pour the cream into it. Use a rubber spatula to push the dry ingredients from the sides of the bowl into the well, cutting and turning the mixture just until the dry ingredients are almost entirely moistened and the dough looks rough and shaggy. Gather the dough into a lump and knead it gently against the sides of the bowl five or more times, pressing in the loose pieces, until the dough just holds together (it should not be smooth) and the sides of the bowl are fairly clean.

On a lightly floured board, pat the dough into an 8 1/2-inch round about 3/4 inches thick. Cut into 12 wedges. Place them at least 1 inch apart on the lined baking sheet. Brush the tops with milk or cream and sprinkle lightly with sugar.

Bake until the tops are golden brown, 12 to 15 minutes. Let cool on a rack, and serve warm or at room temperature.

chocolate note Because the chocolate does not melt and mingle with the other ingredients, you can use any bittersweet or semisweet chocolate you like.

TRULY CREAMY EGG CREAM

An egg cream is an exquisitely refreshing drink made with a little milk or cream, chocolate syrup, and topped with a generous spritz of seltzer. It is not very sweet and not very rich, nor does it contain eggs. A California girl raised in non-Jewish suburbs, I didn't taste my first egg cream until I was in college at Berkeley. The effect was Proustian just the same. The egg cream tasted exactly like the cold fizzy liquid sipped from countless childhood chocolate ice cream sodas, when just enough of the ice cream had melted and mingled with the chocolate syrup and soda water. In my soda days, there was never enough of that thirst-quenching counterpoint to the sweet rich ice cream in the tall glass. Years later, the humble egg cream was, and still is, a fitting riposte. There's plenty of bubbly liquid, it's remarkably low in calories and fat, and it's wonderfully satisfying, especially when made with your own syrup.

Bottled seltzer water is fine, but if you love egg creams, you'll want to buy a siphon to turn ordinary (or filtered) water into seltzer. (Soda siphons are available from cookware stores or mail-order catalogs; see Sources, page 366.) Egg creams are made to order, one glass at a time. This "recipe" is flexible, and you will quickly fine-tune the variables (fizzy, creamy, chocolatey) to your own taste.

Milk, half-and-half, or cream

Cold seltzer water
(bottled or from a siphon)

Cocoa Syrup (page 295)

Fill a 12-ounce glass one-quarter to one-half full of milk or whichever cream you are using. (I use the lesser amount of half-and-half to get maximum fizz with enough creaminess for my taste.) Now, there are two ways to go: Either stir 2 to 3 tablespoons of cocoa syrup into the milk before filling the glass with seltzer, or add the seltzer to the milk first and then add the cocoa syrup. Stir briskly. If syrup is added before seltzer, the foam on the egg cream will be cocoa-colored. If syrup is added after seltzer, the foam will stay white! Delicious either way.

At my house, it is important to have a really good chocolate sauce recipe available in case of emergency. Even if your house doesn't have emergencies of this nature, you can still use this recipe. Good chocolate sauce and a little good vanilla ice cream make a dessert more delicious and satisfying than 90 percent of those you could order in even a top-flight restaurant. Good chocolate sauce and an assortment of ripe fruits and chunks of cake will get you chocolate fondue. And when things look bleak, good chocolate sauce and a spoon will make you smile.

LESSONS FROM A
CHOCOLATE SAUCE

The recipe that follows immediately is one I have used for at least a dozen years. It is flexible and contains some interesting lessons about flavor, perhaps about life.

There is a simple secret to good chocolate sauce: You need good chocolate. Don't buy the individually wrapped squares of chocolate at the supermarket. Buy chocolate you love to eat because the sauce is mostly chocolate and you are going to eat it. A recipe like this shows off all of the qualities, good or bad, of the chocolate you use. The many options and imprecise measurements in this recipe may suggest either that I can't make up my mind or that I don't think the details really matter. Neither is true. I know what I like, and every detail is important.

But what do you like? Depending on the choices you make, you can have a sauce that is rich and creamy or intensely bittersweet, or anything in between. You can have a thin sauce that mingles pleasantly with the melted ice cream in the bottom of the bowl, or one that thickens like fudge and makes you groan a little with pleasure. You can make the sauce with a standard semisweet chocolate or a powerful 70 percent bittersweet—it all depends on your tastes.

Once you've selected your chocolate, you are ready to consider the milk versus cream question. Milk is the more convenient choice if you don't usually keep cream in the refrigerator (and that's what I used when I first made this sauce). So you might make the sauce with milk, all the while thinking that cream would be better if only you felt like going to the store. But you might be wrong. Richer is not always better. Milk allows the tastes of the chocolate to come through more—but that also means it does less to hide flavor flaws. Chocolate sauce made with milk has the most intense bittersweet chocolate flavor. So, if you are using a harsh or mediocre-tasting chocolate, don't make your sauce with milk! If your milk-based sauce is delicious but a tad too tart or austere, stir in bits of the optional butter to round out the flavor. Way over at the other end of the taste spectrum, chocolate sauce made with heavy cream—although still bittersweet— is positively voluptuous and creamy. It is also decidedly milder, less chocolatey, and less bittersweet. Half-and-half or a combination of milk and cream lands you somewhere between. If you've read my story about the nectarine (see page 68), you will rightly guess that I have also made this sauce with water! A versatile sauce indeed.

ALICE'S CHOCOLATE SAUCE

MAKES 1¾ CUPS

10 ounces bittersweet or semisweet chocolate, finely chopped

½ to 1 cup milk, half-and-half, heavy cream, or any combination

2 tablespoons unsalted butter (if using milk instead of cream, but optional)

½ teaspoon pure vanilla extract

Pinch of salt

Put the chocolate and ½ cup of the milk or cream in a large heatproof bowl set in a wide skillet of barely simmering water and stir frequently until the chocolate is melted and smooth. If the sauce is too thick or looks curdled, add more milk. Or add more liquid if the sauce hardens more than you want it to when you spoon a little "test" over ice. If you have used milk (or even water), taste the sauce and, if you like, tone down the flavor intensity by adding some or all of the butter, bit by bit. Remove the sauce from the water and stir in the vanilla and salt.

Use the warm sauce immediately, or set it aside and rewarm it briefly in a pan of hot water when you need it. (The sauce keeps in a closed container for several days in the refrigerator, and it can be frozen for up to 3 months.)

chocolate notes This extremely accommodating recipe can be made with any bittersweet or semisweet chocolate. The range given for the milk or cream and the recipe instructions will guide you to adjust the liquid upward as needed for higher-percentage chocolates.

BITTERSWEET HOT FUDGE SAUCE

MAKES ABOUT 2 CUPS

Here's a more traditional hot fudge sauce, but updated (with less butter and sugar) so you can really taste the flavors in the chocolate. This is a pretty adult sauce, breathtaking over vanilla ice cream, but the children of my acquaintance don't seem to turn it down!

9 to 10 ounces bittersweet 70% chocolate, finely chopped

3/4 cup heavy cream

1/4 cup plus 2 tablespoons sugar

3 tablespoons corn syrup

2 tablespoons water

SPECIAL EQUIPMENT

Instant-read thermometer

This sauce is foolproof so long as you heat it slowly: Combine all of the ingredients in the top of a double boiler over (and touching) barely simmering water. Stir frequently until all the chocolate has melted. Then stir occasionally until the sauce is thick and glossy and is between 160° and 165°F (the exact temperature is not critical so long as you are close), 15 to 20 minutes (going slowly is the key here). Remove from the heat.

Serve the sauce immediately or set it aside until needed. It can be kept, in a covered container, refrigerated for at least a week, or frozen for 3 months. Reheat in a double boiler or microwave on Medium (50%) power, using short bursts and stirring frequently. Do not simmer or boil.

chocolate notes You can use any chocolate marked 66% to 72%. Or adjust the recipe for other chocolates as follows:

To use chocolate marked 61% to 64%: Use 12 ounces chocolate. Reduce the sugar to 1/4 cup and the corn syrup to 1 tablespoon.

To use standard bittersweet or semisweet chocolate (without a percentage on the label), or any marked 50% to 60%: Use 14 1/2 ounces chocolate. Reduce the sugar to 2 tablespoons and the corn syrup to 1 tablespoon.

SCHARFFEN BERGER COCOA FUDGE SAUCE

MAKES 1½ CUPS

I created this recipe for Scharffen Berger natural cocoa powder, which is especially fruity and aromatic, but any good-quality cocoa powder can be used. Cooled to spreading consistency, this sauce makes a great cake frosting or filling for butter cookies or graham crackers.

½ cup premium unsweetened cocoa powder (natural or Dutch-process)

½ cup sugar

½ cup heavy cream

3 tablespoons unsalted butter, cut into bits

½ teaspoon pure vanilla extract (optional)

Place the cocoa and sugar in a small heavy saucepan. Stir in just enough of the cream to make a smooth, thick paste, then stir in the rest of the cream and add the butter pieces. Stir over low heat until the butter is melted and the sauce is smooth and hot but not simmering. Taste and add the vanilla, if desired.

Spoon the warm sauce over ice cream. Or, for frosting, cool until spreadable. (The sauce keeps in a covered container in the refrigerator for a week, or it can be frozen for up to 3 months.) To reheat (and thaw), put the sauce in a heatproof bowl set in a wide skillet of barely simmering water, and stir occasionally until the sauce is the desired consistency. Or microwave on Medium (50%) power, using short bursts and stirring frequently. Do not allow the sauce to simmer or boil.

chocolate note Cocoas vary. If using a brand other than Scharffen Berger, taste and adjust the flavor with extra sugar if it is too harsh or bitter, or tone down the intensity with a little extra butter or cream.

COCOA SYRUP

MAKES 1¾ CUPS

This flavorful bittersweet syrup tastes better than store-bought. It's far less rich than cream- or butter-based chocolate sauces, takes just minutes to make, and keeps well. Serve it over ice cream or keep it on hand (in a squeeze bottle) to produce a Truly Creamy Egg Cream (page 289) at a moment's notice.

¾ cup unsweetened cocoa powder (natural or Dutch-process)

1 cup sugar

Pinch of salt

1 cup boiling water

1 teaspoon pure vanilla extract (optional)

Mix the cocoa powder, sugar, and salt in a small saucepan. Stir in enough boiling water to form a smooth paste; stir in the remaining water. Bring the mixture to a simmer over low heat, stirring constantly. Let the syrup simmer for about 2 minutes. Remove from the heat, stir in the vanilla, if using, and let cool. Scrape into a squeeze bottle or jar and store in the refrigerator for up to 3 weeks.

chocolate note Any cocoa that you love will make great cocoa syrup.

The Sweet and the Savory

Playing with Nibs
            and Dining on Chocolate

Making footprints where there are none (or very few) is more fun than almost anything I can think of. Imagine enjoying orange juice yet never having tasted an orange. Or imagine being intimately familiar with peanut butter without ever having eaten peanuts. Although chocolate reigns supreme in the **WHAT I LEARNED FROM THE BEANS** dessert pantheon, most cooks and chocolate lovers have had no contact with cocoa beans, the purest, most elemental type of chocolate.

Cocoa beans are now available to chefs and to home cooks in the form of cocoa nibs. Nibs are cocoa beans on the brink of becoming chocolate. They are tiny nuggets of roasted, shelled, and cracked beans, not yet crushed or ground to homogeneity, not yet transformed into chocolate liquor or further processed into the smoother and more refined forms of sweetened chocolate we are used to. Cocoa beans are about the size and shape of kidney beans. Nibs, which are broken rather than uniformly chopped, resemble pecan shells shattered by a nutcracker, and they vary in size from bits that are less than one eighth inch to shards sometimes one half inch long. These are often jagged on one side and smooth and curved on the other. In one handful of nibs, you will see shades of mahogany and charcoal brown, slatey grays, and hints of mauve.

Chocolatiers have begun to incorporate nibs into fine chocolate and some pretty sophisticated chocolate bars; but only a few pastry chefs have started to explore their uses. When I got my first handful of cocoa nibs, I was excited about working with a very-high-quality but less-processed form of a familiar ingredient. This chance to work with "primitive" chocolate, I thought, would allow me to rethink, redefine, and reinvent chocolate desserts, and savory dishes too (see Chocolate for Dinner, page 320).

When you smell and taste cocoa nibs for the first time, you know at once they must be some form of chocolate. Yet nibs are most intriguing for the ways in which they are different from the chocolate we know. They are dry and crunchy, even crunchier and noisier than toasted nuts. They are unsweetened and austere to a palate that expects "chocolate."

Nibs taste bitter at first: Remember your first cup of espresso. Then remember how you got used to it, perhaps learned to love it. If your nibs are a blend of different cocoa beans, each little piece will taste different from its brothers. When you taste them one at a time, you are tasting just some of the hundreds of individual flavors that go into making the taste we think of as chocolate. Nibs range from winy or fruity and tart to earthy or nutlike. They can be tannic or astringent or taste like tea or cherries or peanuts . . . the list of comparison flavors is endless.

Although nibs can be mixed into batters or doughs like chocolate chips, they do not behave at all like chocolate chips. Chocolate chips are sweet and smooth and crowd pleasing; arguably, they improve anything from tough and doughy cookies to mediocre cakes and muffins. Cocoa nibs are much less accommodating. They don't automatically improve anything, and, at their worst, they are bitter and gritty. At their best, however, they are divinely crunchy, filled with nuance. Nibs are stubborn and complex. When used in contrast with something creamy and smooth, they can be perfection, or just a mouthful of soggy grit—it all depends. They must be coaxed and cajoled. I learned from experience that they have a definite affinity for certain flavors and textures, including nuts, raisins, blackberries, many spices, brown sugar, and cream. They seem to have an equal antipathy for egg yolks, yeast, baking soda, fresh mint, and certain moist cakes and breads.

Early on, I realized that what I wanted to do with nibs was emphasize their subtle, unique characteristics rather than transform them into a crude form of chocolate by grinding and sweetening them in the course of preparing a recipe. I wanted to work with the nutty, bitter, earthy, less familiar flavors and, where possible, the extraordinary crunch. To do this, I decided to think of the nibs as nuts instead of as chocolate. What would I do with a new kind of chocolate-flavored nut?

I started with simple butter cookies. At first I was unimpressed by the flavor. I shrugged and figured I would have to start over again. But two days after I had baked them, the same cookies had become extraordinarily tender, melt-in-your mouth delicacies with an undertone of indescribable flavor: like chocolate but not like chocolate, like nuts but like no nut I had ever tasted. They were subtle but rich, and I loved them. I concluded that cookies, especially crunchy ones with plenty of butter, are a perfect medium for nibs—butter cookies improve with age anyway. So as the flavor of the nibs is imbuing the cookie, all the other flavors, as well as the cookie's texture, are also improving. And because the nibs retain their crunch—they are so much crunchier than the cookie or any of the nuts that might be in the cookie—they make the cookie seem even more tender and delicate by contrast.

Success with dry, crunchy butter cookies led to the assumption that shortbread, Mexican wedding cakes, and biscotti would also be nib friendly. Wrong, I discovered. Baked too long, nibs get overroasted, bitter, and very unpleasant. My shortbread recipe bakes for at least an hour, Mexican wedding cakes take twenty-five to thirty minutes, and biscotti are twice-baked. I decided to stick with cookies with shorter baking times.

Even before I'd discovered that the long baking time required for crisp meringues might be a problem if I added nibs, I'd tasted a few nibs with a bite of plain crisp meringue and learned two things. First, the contrast between sweet and bitter was too extreme: The meringues tasted horribly sweet and the nibs terribly bitter. Second, the meringue dissolved much faster than the nibs, leaving a mouthful of bitter, naked nibs. Nibs work better in a medium that lasts longer in your mouth and has flavors that linger, or enough fat (such as in ice cream), to coat your palate, while you finish chewing the nibs. Disappointing in plain, sweet, crisp meringues, nibs were much more successful in a not-too-sweet soft, nutty meringue, inspired by marjolaine layers, with which I make a simple roulade filled with blackberry preserves and whipped cream.

Fat also affects the contrast between sweet and bitter when using nibs. Nibs taste fine in traditional chocolate chip cookie dough, which is plenty sweet, with both brown and white sugars, and also very rich in butter. But a nibs chocolate chip cookie really comes into its own when walnuts and currants are added, accentuating the natural fruit and nut flavors in the nibs and bringing all of the flavors together. Nibs are also delicious with coffee and thus very successful in a very rich, gooey, bittersweet chocolate cookie with freshly ground coffee beans. Here the nibs add chocolate intensity to an already over-the-top chocolate experience, much the same way they add excitement to a chocolate bar.

Next, I tried infusing nibs in liquids. They are good in coffee—just put them in the filter or the press pot with the ground coffee. They are too weird in tea. They are OK in hot milk—but not before bed unless you want to stay up. Nibs in cream turned out to be a revelation. I heated a handful in heavy cream and let it all steep, then strained the nibs out and chilled the cream. I whipped the cold infused cream with just a whisper of sugar. The result was a sort of light, whipped albino chocolate ganache, positively exquisite, and like nothing I had ever tasted. If you've ever fantasized about white chocolate that is not sweet, that has a true chocolate flavor and a fresh creamy taste, your dreams have come true.

Cocoa Bean Cream (page 304) is just the palest shade of creamy tan, so innocent that its rich flavor will take you by surprise. I use it to top hot bittersweet chocolate soufflés, or *café filtre* or hot chocolate, or as a cake filling. The possibilities are endless. My favorite bartender helped me create a Nibby Alexander: Armagnac and sweetened nib-infused cream served in a martini glass with a dusting of cocoa powder and a twist of candied orange peel. This luxurious dessert drink capped a sumptuous evening called "For the Love of Science and Chocolate," to benefit the Berkeley Lawrence Hall of Science.

Nib-infused cream also became the base for a sensational Double Cocoa Nib Ice Cream (page 81) and divine panna cotta and then a simple cornstarch pudding, which turned out to be lovely comfort food. At first I wasn't sure about the pudding. My daughter and I were taking turns dipping spoons into it, pausing to think a moment after each little taste, trying to decide whether it was really good or just very novel. Finally, observing that the dish was empty and we had begun a second, she said, "Mom, I think we like this."

While cream turned out to be a perfect medium for nibs, I discovered that adding eggs often muddied and distorted their flavor. Thus panna cotta was delicious but cream caramel was awful; cornstarch pudding was good but cup custard was terrible; and so forth. Cocoa bean ice cream with a custard base wasn't nearly as good as one with a base of pure cream.

Then I dreamed of nibby bread. In my mind, I could taste a gutsy whole-grain bread laced with nibs, or a rustic natural sourdough, or a suave brioche. But so far every cocoa bean bread has disappointed. I experimented with scones, soda bread, and banana bread. The nibs tended to absorb moisture and take on the unpleasant texture of damp nuts, and the flavors were bitter and astringent. They also seemed to react badly with the baking soda in soda bread, and the banana bread I had high hopes for somehow didn't work. The usually appealing bitter flavors in some grains brought out the worst in the nibs, and I suspect they had a bad reaction with the yeast as well. For the moment, I satisfy my desire for bread with cocoa beans by sprinkling nibs directly on my bread and butter, or even on a warm corn tortilla, sometimes with a little sugar, maybe even a little cinnamon. And I am still experimenting with nibs because you just never know.

COCOA BEAN CREAM

MAKES ABOUT 2 CUPS

This is one of the first things that made I with cocoa nibs. It is the stuff of dreams. Don't miss it.

1 cup heavy cream

2 tablespoons cocoa nibs, coarsely chopped into smaller bits

Sugar to taste

Bring the cream and nibs to a boil in a small saucepan. Remove from the heat, cover, and let stand for 20 minutes.

Strain the cream into a bowl, pressing on the solids to extract all the liquid. Discard the nibs. Chill the cream for at least 6 hours; it must be thoroughly cold in order to whip properly.

When ready to use, whip the cream, adding sugar to taste as the cream thickens.

COCOA BEAN AND COFFEE CREAM Add 1 tablespoon regular (not French- or Italian-roast) coffee beans, crushed, to the cream and nibs before heating.

COCOA NIB PANNA COTTA photograph on page 256
SERVES 6

This dreamy, delicately set dessert is flavored with an infusion of roasted cocoa beans. The taste is exotic, the texture positively sensual. But you must measure the gelatin like a miser . . . or risk turning an exquisite confection into a dish of Jell-O.

1/2 cup cocoa nibs, coarsely chopped into smaller bits

3 1/4 cups heavy cream

2 3/4 teaspoons unflavored gelatin

1 cup whole milk

1/4 cup plus 2 tablespoons sugar

Pinch of salt

Fresh blackberries or blackberry puree, well sugared

SPECIAL EQUIPMENT

Instant-read thermometer

6 wide margarita glasses
(or six 6-ounce ramekins)

Bring the nibs and cream to a boil in a medium saucepan over medium-high heat. Remove from the heat, cover, and let steep for 20 minutes.

Meanwhile, sprinkle the gelatin over the cold milk in a small bowl and set aside to let the gelatin soften.

Strain the cream, pressing lightly on the nibs to extract all the liquid. Discard the nibs. Return the cream to the saucepan, add the sugar, and bring to a simmer. Pour into a heatproof bowl. Gradually stir in the milk, then the salt. Set the bowl in a larger bowl of ice cubes and water and stir frequently until the mixture thickens and registers 50°F on an instant-read thermometer.

Divide evenly among the margarita glasses (or ramekins). Cover with plastic wrap and chill overnight.

Serve the panna cotta in their glasses or ramekins. Or, wrap each ramekin in a hot wrung-out wet towel and unmold onto dessert plates. Accompany with well-sugared berries or berry puree.

NIBBY PUDDING
SERVES 6

Ooooh—this pudding is creamy, smooth, and comforting. It's also quite sensual. The earthy but delicate flavor of roasted cocoa beans infused in light cream is quietly exciting.

3 cups half-and-half

1/4 cup plus 2 tablespoons cocoa nibs

1/2 cup sugar

1/4 cup minus 1 teaspoon cornstarch

Scant 1/4 teaspoon salt

SPECIAL EQUIPMENT

Six 4- to 6-ounce ramekins or custard cups

In a small saucepan, bring the half-and-half and nibs to a gentle boil over medium heat. Remove from the heat, cover, and let steep for 20 minutes.

Strain the half-and-half into a bowl, pressing on the nibs to extract most of the liquid. Discard the nibs.

In a medium heavy saucepan, mix the sugar, cornstarch, and salt with about 1/3 cup of the infused half-and-half to form a smooth paste. Stir in the remaining half-and-half. Place over medium heat and stir constantly with a heatproof rubber spatuala or wooden spoon until the mixture begins to thicken. Reduce the heat to low and continue stirring until the pudding begins to simmer. Simmer, stirring, for 1 more minute.

Remove from the heat and pour into the ramekins or custard cups. Serve warm, cool, or chilled.

NIBBY PECAN COOKIES photograph on page 15

MAKES ABOUT FORTY-EIGHT 2-INCH COOKIES

The dough for these looks like a beautiful piece of granite flecked with bits of russet and burnt umber as you roll it out. The cookies are exquisitely tender and crunchy. The flavor of the cocoa beans develops and infuses the cookies over time, so I strongly recommend that you make the dough a day before baking and bake the cookies at least twenty-four hours before you serve them—longer is even better.

1 cup (3 1/2 ounces) pecan halves	1 tablespoon plus 1 teaspoon bourbon (optional)
1/2 pound (2 sticks) unsalted butter, softened	1 1/2 teaspoons pure vanilla extract
3/4 cup sugar	1/3 cup cocoa nibs
1/4 teaspoon salt (slightly rounded if you like)	2 cups all-purpose flour

Preheat the oven to 325°F.

Spread the pecans on a cookie sheet. Toast them in the oven for 7 to 8 minutes, or until fragrant and lightly colored. Let cool, then chop.

Combine the butter, the sugar, salt, bourbon, if using, and vanilla in a medium bowl and, using a large spoon or an electric mixer on high speed, beat until smooth and creamy but not fluffy (about 1 minute with a mixer). Stir or beat in the pecans and cocoa nibs. Turn off the mixer, if you are using one, and add all the flour at once. Beat on low speed to prevent the flour from flying out, just until the flour is fully incorporated. Or stir in the flour until incorporated. If necessary, finish mixing with your hands.

For slice-and-bake cookies: Form the dough into a 12-inch log about 2 inches thick. *For rolled and cut cookies:* Divide it in half and form into two flat patties. Wrap the dough and refrigerate for at least 2 hours, preferably overnight. (The dough can be frozen for up to 3 months.)

Position the racks in the upper and lower thirds of the oven and preheat the oven to 350°F.

continued

To slice and bake: Use a sharp knife to cut the cold dough log into ¼-inch-thick slices. Place the cookies at least 1½ inches apart on ungreased cookie sheets.

To roll and cut cookies: Remove one patty from the refrigerator and let it sit at room temperature until supple enough to roll but still quite firm—it will continue to soften as you work. Roll the dough out between two pieces of wax paper or between heavy plastic sheets (from a heavy-duty plastic bag) to a thickness of ¼ inch. Turn the dough over once or twice while you are rolling it out to check for deep wrinkles; if necessary, peel off and smooth the paper or plastic over the dough before continuing to roll it. Peel off the top sheet of paper or plastic and place it in front of you. Invert the dough onto the paper and peel off the second sheet. Cut out cookies as close together as possible to minimize scraps, dipping the edges of cookie cutters in flour as necessary to prevent sticking. Use the point of a paring knife to lift and remove scraps as you transfer cookies, using a narrow metal spatula, to ungreased cookie sheets, placing the cookies at least 1½ inches apart. (If the dough gets too soft at any time while you are working, slide a cookie sheet underneath the paper or plastic and refrigerate the dough for a few minutes until it firms up again.) Repeat with the second piece of dough. Press all of the dough scraps together gently (don't overwork them with too much kneading), reroll, and cut out more cookies.

Bake for 12 to 14 minutes, or until the cookies are light golden brown at the edges, rotating the cookie sheets from top to bottom and front to back halfway through the baking. Let the cookies firm up on the pans for about 1 minute before transferring them to a rack with a metal pancake turner. Let cool completely. For best flavor and texture, store the cookies in an airtight container for at least 24 hours before serving. (They can be stored airtight for at least 1 month.)

NIBBY COCOA COOKIES If you omit the nuts, increase the nibs, and add cocoa, you get these tender, crunchy cookies with even more complex but subtle chocolate flavors.

Omit the pecans and bourbon. Decrease the vanilla to 1 teaspoon. Whisk ¼ cup unsweetened cocoa powder (natural or Dutch-process) into the flour before adding it to the dough. Increase the nibs to ½ cup. Bake the cookies for 10 to 12 minutes, or until they have puffed slightly, fallen, and feel firm to the touch.

SUBSTITUTIONS I like this recipe with walnuts, or with toasted skinned hazelnuts (page 40) instead of pecans, or substitute ¼ teaspoon ground vanilla beans, which you can do yourself or buy (see page 42), for 1 teaspoon of the vanilla extract. I also like to use sea salt that is slightly coarser than table salt—then I often use a tad more than ¼ teaspoon, as this adds a little extra flavor excitement.

NIBBY ESPRESSO COOKIES

MAKES SIXTY 1¾-INCH COOKIES

This is an intense and sophisticated chocolate experience, best enjoyed in the form of tiny cookies—and probably not appreciated by children. I love them.

⅓ cup all-purpose flour

¼ teaspoon baking powder

¼ teaspoon salt

5 tablespoons unsalted butter

6 ounces unsweetened chocolate (preferably the very highest quality), coarsely chopped

2 large eggs, at room temperature

1⅓ cups sugar

1½ teaspoons finely ground coffee beans (freshly ground)

1 teaspoon pure vanilla extract

½ cup cocoa nibs

Combine the flour, baking powder, and salt in a small bowl and mix together thoroughly with a whisk or fork. Set aside.

Place the butter and chocolate in a medium heatproof bowl in a wide skillet of barely simmering water and stir occasionally until melted and smooth. Remove from the heat and set aside.

In a large bowl, using an electric mixer, beat the eggs, sugar, coffee beans, and vanilla until pale and thick, about 5 minutes. Stir in the chocolate mixture. Stir in the flour mixture and, finally, the nibs. Cover the dough and refrigerate until firm, about 1 hour, or up to 4 days.

Position the racks in the upper and lower thirds of the oven and preheat the oven to 350°F. Line two cookie sheets with parchment or wax paper.

Drop rounded teaspoonfuls of batter 1½ inches apart on the lined cookie sheets. Bake, rotating the sheets from top to bottom and front to back halfway through the baking time to ensure even baking, until the cookies are puffed and dry on the surface but still soft and gooey within, 7 to 9 minutes. Carefully slide the cookies, still on the parchment, onto racks. Let cool completely. (The cookies can be stored, airtight, at room temperature for 2 days or frozen for longer storage.)

ALMOND STICKS WITH COCOA NIBS photograph on page 19

MAKES ABOUT THIRTY-TWO 6-INCH STICKS

Crunchy, subtle, and not too sweet, these cookies look like extra-thin miniature biscotti and have the intriguing nutty flavor of roasted cocoa nibs.

3/4 cup (3 3/4 ounces) whole blanched almonds

1 cup plus 2 tablespoons all-purpose flour

2/3 cup sugar

1/4 teaspoon salt

6 tablespoons unsalted butter, cut into chunks

2 tablespoons water

1 teaspoon pure vanilla extract

1/8 teaspoon pure almond extract

1/4 cup cocoa nibs

Combine the almonds, flour, sugar, and salt in a food processor, and pulse until the almonds are reduced to a fine meal. Add the butter and pulse until the mixture looks like a mass of crumbs. Combine the water, vanilla, and almond extract, drizzle them into the processor bowl, and pulse just until the dough looks damp. Add the cocoa nibs and pulse only until evenly dispersed.

The dough will not form a smooth cohesive mass—it will be crumbly, but it will stick together when you press it. Turn it out on a large sheet of foil and form it into a 6-by-9-inch rectangle a scant 1/2 inch thick. Fold the foil over the dough and press firmly with your hands to compress it, then wrap it airtight. Slide a cookie sheet under the package and refrigerate for at least 2 hours, or overnight.

Position the racks in the upper and lower thirds of the oven and preheat the oven to 350°F. Line two cookie sheets with parchment or wax paper.

Use a long sharp knife to trim one short edge of the dough rectangle to even it. Then cut a slice a scant 3/8 inch wide and use the knife to transfer the delicate slice to the cookie sheet. Repeat with the rest of the dough, transferring each slice as it is cut and placing them at least 1 inch apart. If some break, just push them back together, or bake them broken—they will look and taste great anyway.

Bake, rotating the cookie sheets from top to bottom and front to back half way through the baking time, 12 to 14 minutes, or until the cookies are golden at the edges. Set the pans on the racks to cool completely. (The cookies can be stored, airtight, for several days.)

NIBBY NUT AND RAISIN COOKIES photograph on page 15

MAKES ABOUT 60 COOKIES

These cookies are especially delicious if you chill the dough overnight before baking. And, for the best cookies of all—that is, ones that are brown and crunchy at the edges and chewy in the centers—eschew parchment paper, silicone-coated pan liners, and/or cushioned pans, and simply bake on unlined, ungreased baking sheets.

2¼ cups all-purpose flour	2 large eggs
1 teaspoon baking soda	1 teaspoon pure vanilla extract
½ pound (2 sticks) unsalted butter, melted and still warm	⅔ cup cocoa nibs
¾ cup granulated sugar	1 cup (4 ounces) finely chopped walnuts
¾ cup packed brown sugar	1 cup dried currants or raisins
¾ teaspoon salt	

Mix the flour and baking soda together thoroughly. Set aside.

In a large bowl, combine the melted butter, sugars, and salt. Stir in the eggs and vanilla. Stir in the flour mixture just until all of the dry ingredients are moistened, then stir in the nibs, nuts, and currants. If possible, cover and chill the dough for at least 2 hours, preferably overnight.

Position the oven racks in the upper and lower thirds of the oven and preheat the oven to 375°F. Remove the dough from the refrigerator to soften.

Scoop up level tablespoonfuls of dough and place them 2 inches apart on ungreased cookie sheets. Bake, rotating the cookie sheets from top to bottom and front to back about halfway through the baking time, for 8 to 10 minutes, or until the cookies are golden brown at the edges and no longer look wet on top.

Use a metal pancake turner to transfer the cookies to a wire rack and let cool completely. (The cookies keep, in a tightly sealed container, for several days.)

COCOA BEAN TASSIES

MAKES 24 SMALL PASTRIES

I applied my own sleight of hand to a long-remembered delicacy called pecan tassies from Margaret Fox's *Café Beaujolais Cookbook*. Even Margaret approves of these miniature tartlets filled with a sweet gooey sauce offset with cracked cocoa beans.

FOR THE PASTRY

12 tablespoons (1½ sticks) unsalted butter, melted

¼ cup plus 2 tablespoons sugar

1 teaspoon pure vanilla extract

Scant ¼ teaspoon salt

1½ cups all-purpose flour

FOR THE FILLING

1 large egg white

¾ cup packed light brown or golden brown sugar

1 tablespoon unsalted butter, melted

1 cup cocoa nibs, chopped into small bits

1 teaspoon pure vanilla extract

Generous pinch of salt

SPECIAL EQUIPMENT

Two 12-cup miniature muffin pans

Position a rack in the lower third of the oven and preheat the oven to 400°F.

To make the pastry: Combine the melted butter, sugar, vanilla, and salt in a medium bowl. Add the flour and mix just until incorporated.

Divide the dough in half and press each half into a flattened 4-inch square. Cut each square into 12 equal pieces and shape each piece into a ball. Place one dough ball in each muffin cup and press it evenly over the bottom and all the way up the sides of the cup, forming a neat rim. Set aside.

To make the filling: In a medium bowl, beat the egg white until foamy. Stir in the brown sugar, melted butter, cocoa nibs, vanilla, and salt. Divide the filling evenly among the tartlet shells, using about 1 teaspoon for each.

Bake the tassies for 10 minutes, then reduce the oven temperature to 250°F and bake for 20 minutes more, or until the pastry is well browned on the edges and underneath (lift one out with the point of a knife to check). Let cool in the pans on a rack. (Stored in an airtight container, these remain delicious for about 3 days, with the chocolate flavor intensifying from day to day.)

CURRANT AND NIB RUGELACH photograph on page 15

MAKES 48 COOKIES

Rugelach at its best is a wondrously flaky, yet unbelievably foolproof little horn of pastry pretending to be a cookie. There are various fillings, of which I have always loved the classic, cinnamon, nuts, and raisins, best. So, when it turned out that nibs are also good with raisins (or currants), I had to make room for a new favorite.

FOR THE PASTRY

2 1/2 cups all-purpose flour

2 tablespoons sugar

1/4 teaspoon salt

1/2 pound (2 sticks) cold unsalted butter, each stick cut into 8 pieces

One 8-ounce package cream cheese, chilled, cut into 8 pieces

FOR THE FILLING

2 tablespoons granulated sugar

1/2 cup packed light brown or golden brown sugar

1 teaspoon ground cinnamon

1/2 cup cocoa nibs, finely chopped into small bits

1/2 cup dried currants

To make the pastry: Combine the flour, sugar, and salt in a food processor and pulse a few times to mix. Add the butter and pulse until the butter pieces are about the size of bread crumbs. Add the cream cheese and process until the dough begins to clump together, about 30 seconds. Turn the dough out onto a work surface and divide it into 4 pieces. Press each piece into a flat patty about 4 inches in diameter, wrap in plastic wrap, and refrigerate until firm, about 4 hours.

Position the racks in the upper and lower thirds of the oven and preheat the oven to 350°F. Line two cookie sheets with parchment or wax paper or aluminum foil.

To make the filling: Mix the sugars, cinnamon, nibs, and currants together in a medium bowl.

Remove one piece of dough from the refrigerator. Roll it out between two pieces of wax paper into a 12-inch circle a scant $\frac{1}{8}$ inch thick. Peel off the top sheet of wax paper, and place the paper on the counter or a cutting board. Flip the dough onto the paper and peel off the second sheet. Sprinkle a quarter of the filling over the dough. Gently roll over the filling with a rolling pin to press it into the dough. Cut the dough into 12 equal wedges like a pie. Starting at the wide end of one wedge, roll it up and place it, with the dough point underneath to prevent it from unrolling, on one of the cookie sheets. Repeat with the remaining wedges, placing them $1\frac{1}{2}$ inches apart.

Repeat with the remaining dough and filling. (If at any time the dough becomes too soft to roll, return it to the refrigerator to firm up.)

Bake, rotating the sheets from top to bottom and front to back halfway through the baking time, for about 25 minutes, or until light golden brown at the edges. Set the sheets on racks to cool completely. (The rugelach are best on the day they are baked, but they can be stored, airtight, for about 5 days.)

COCOA BEAN ALMOND ROULADE

SERVES 10 TO 12

A simple filling of blackberry or black raspberry preserves and fresh whipped cream in a soft meringue studded with toasted nuts and lots of toasted cocoa beans makes a light and sophisticated dessert with intriguing flavors and textures. Or dress it up with a cloak of chocolate ganache glaze. Don't miss the variation with Cocoa Bean Cream.

FOR THE ROULADE

1 1/2 cups (7 1/2 ounces) unblanched whole almonds

1 1/2 tablespoons all-purpose flour

3/4 cup sugar

1/4 cup plus 2 tablespoons cocoa nibs

6 large egg whites (about 3/4 cup), at room temperature

1/2 teaspoon cream of tartar

Powdered sugar for dusting

FOR THE FILLING

Scant 1/2 cup blackberry or black raspberry fruit spread (see Note) or jam

1 cup heavy cream

1/2 teaspoon pure vanilla extract

Ganache Glaze (page 234) (optional)

SPECIAL EQUIPMENT

An 11-by-17-inch or 12-by-17-inch jelly-roll pan or half sheet pan

Position a rack in the center of the oven and preheat the oven to 325°F. Line the baking pan with parchment paper.

Spread the almonds on a cookie sheet. Toast them in the oven for 7 to 8 minutes, or until fragrant and lightly colored. Let cool completely.

Combine the toasted almonds, flour, and 1/2 cup of the sugar in a food processor and pulse to a medium-fine texture. Add the nibs and pulse to a fine meal. Set aside.

In a clean, dry mixer bowl or other large bowl, combine the egg whites with the cream of tartar and beat with an electric mixer at medium speed until soft peaks form when the beaters are lifted. Increase the speed and gradually add the remaining 1/4 cup sugar, then beat until the meringue forms stiff but not dry peaks. Pour the nut mixture over the meringue, and fold it in with a large rubber spatula just until evenly dispersed. Spread the batter evenly in the lined pan.

Bake for 25 to 30 minutes, or until the cake is golden brown and springy to the touch. Let cool completely in the pan on a rack. (The cake can be prepared up to 2 days ahead; cover the pan tightly with foil or plastic wrap and store at room temperature.)

To assemble the cake: Using a fine-mesh sieve, shake a very light dusting of powdered sugar over the cake. Run a small knife around the edges of the cake to release it from the pan. Cover with a sheet of foil. Holding the foil and pan edges together at both ends, invert the pan onto the counter. Remove the pan and peel off the parchment liner.

Spread a very thin layer of fruit spread evenly over the cake. In a large bowl, whip the cream with the vanilla until it holds a good shape without being stiff (it will stiffen further when you spread it). Spread the cream over the jam. Starting at one short edge, roll the cake up like a jelly roll. Wrap the roll in the foil and refrigerate until ready to serve. (The roulade can be refrigerated for up to 24 hours.)

To serve, unwrap the roulade and transfer to a serving platter. Sift additional powdered sugar over the top, if desired, or frost with the ganache glaze, pouring it or spreading it over the roll.

NOTE: Choose a fruit spread labeled "100% fruit," sweetened with fruit syrup rather than sugar.

COCOA BEAN CREAM ALMOND ROULADE Substitute Cocoa Bean Cream (page 304) for the heavy cream and omit the vanilla extract.

BUCKWHEAT COCOA CREPES WITH HONEY

MAKES ABOUT 14 CREPES

After eating a bowl of hot leftover kasha with warm milk and crushed cocoa nibs for breakfast one morning, I thought nibs might add a little shading and depth to the toasty earthy flavor of traditional Breton buckwheat crepes. But the nibs turned soggy in the crepes, so I turned to cocoa powder and was rewarded with these flavorful wraps, which are delicious with honey. Add a little vanilla ice cream or crème fraîche and make them a dressy dessert, sprinkled with nibs, of course.

FOR THE CREPES

1/2 cup buckwheat flour

1/2 cup plus 2 tablespoons
all-purpose flour

1/4 cup natural cocoa powder

1 cup milk

3/4 cup water plus more if necessary

3 large eggs

3 tablespoons vegetable oil

1/2 teaspoon salt

Vegetable oil for cooking the crepes

1/2 to 2/3 cup honey for drizzling

Vanilla ice cream, crème fraîche,
or sour cream (optional

3 to 4 tablespoons cocoa nibs,
lightly crushed

To make the crepe batter: Combine all the ingredients in a blender or food processor and blend until perfectly smooth. Transfer to a bowl, cover, and refrigerate for at least 1 hour, or up to 1 day.

When it is ready to cook, the batter should be the consistency of buttermilk. If it is too thick, stir in 1 to 2 tablespoons water. Lay a sheet of wax paper on the counter, or oil a baking sheet.

Heat an 8-inch crepe pan or frying pan over medium heat. Film the pan with about 1 teaspoon vegetable oil. Stir the batter, pour a scant $\frac{1}{3}$ cup into the crepe pan, and immediately swirl and tilt the pan to cover the bottom evenly. Cook for about 1 minute, until the surface looks set, then loosen the crepe at one edge. Peek to see if the crepe is golden brown underneath. Turn it over and cook for another 30 seconds, then flip the crepe out of the pan onto the wax paper or baking sheet.

Repeat with the remaining batter, oiling the pan as necessary. Stack the cooked crepes, separating them with wax paper. If serving immediately, keep the crepes warm in a 250°F oven; or let cool, wrap, and refrigerate for up to 2 days (or freeze for up to 1 month).

To reheat stored crepes, warm each one in a hot lightly buttered pan for about 30 seconds, on one side only.

To serve, drizzle each hot crepe with about 2 teaspoons honey and roll up or fold into quarters. If you like, gild the lily with vanilla ice cream (or crème fraîche or sour cream). Sprinkle with the nibs and serve, two per person.

chocolate note I like the flavor of these crepes best with natural cocoa powder, but there is no reason you can't make them with Dutch-process cocoa if you prefer it.

laying with cocoa nibs encouraged me to rethink my prior assumptions about chocolate. Because they were new to me, I had approached the nibs with a little of the Buddhist "beginner's mind": open curiosity and conscious rejection of preconceived notions. When I began paying the same attention to the true flavors in chocolate, rather than expecting those of dessert or candy, I went quite naturally to savory dishes, just as had European cooks who tasted chocolate for the first time several hundred years ago.

CHOCOLATE FOR DINNER

It became less hard to imagine the ways in which we might be using chocolate had the king of Spain not sweetened this exotic new food with almost equally exotic sugar. When he put those two stimulants together, he unleashed a force of nature. Sweetened chocolate is so compelling that we've ignored savory chocolate dishes, with the exception of a few surviving icons such as mole poblano. I have been guilty of thinking it simply academic, weird, or gimicky to put chocolate with meat or vegetables. With chicken livers? I would once have dismissed that as a blatant bid for attention.

But playing with chocolate in savory dishes changed my attitude from dismissive to curious and excited. It was like learning what to do with nibs in desserts, or my two-day marathon with capuacu, the cousin of chocolate, or creating low-fat desserts without other people's rules. Experiments that began with an open mind, then drew on the sum of my knowledge and experience, became a challenge for my palate and imagination.

And because I was playing with an open mind, I was led directly to, yes, chicken livers and chocolate even before I found a historical precedent for the combination! In the same way, I was drawn to try chocolate with various types of olives, cheeses, fresh and cured meats, and certain vegetables such as squash, eggplant, and green beans. I was mostly following my own palate, rather than reading or doing research, but I was not surprised later to see that other chefs had landed on similar shores, both before and after me. I realized that for years I had cherished Giuliano Bugialli's pasta recipe for meat sauce with savory chocolate without exploring the topic further!

What I learned from playing with chocolate in savory dishes is that these are more likely to be subtle and sophisticated than weird or contrived. Chocolate adds a luxurious texture to sauces, for example, in coq au vin, mushrooms in wine sauce, meat sauces for pasta, and mole (of course). And cocoa nibs, the most primitive chocolate ingredient, add intriguing earthy flavors and an appealing crunch to myriad savory dishes. There is a much larger world of chocolate—in terms of both form and function—than we have known. These recipes are just a beginning.

CRUNCHY BABY GREENS photograph on page 249

A recipe that's not a recipe at all. Salad was the first savory dish I tried with roasted cocoa nibs. Like toasted hazelnuts or walnuts, cocoa beans add a fine crunch and rich earthy flavor to a perfect minimalist salad. From here you can go on to add intrigue: perhaps with a handful of dried currants, shaved fennel, Niçoise olives, or paper-thin rings of sweet red onion. Or serve the salad with a hot round of goat cheese, accompanied by toasted baguette slices brushed with olive oil.

Mixed baby greens, such as mesclun or spring salad mix, rinsed and spun or patted dry

Your best extra virgin olive oil

Good red wine vinegar

Sea salt

Freshly ground black pepper

Cocoa nibs

Toss the greens with just enough oil to coat, and splash judiciously with vinegar. Then toss again. Season with salt and pepper to taste. Sprinkle with nibs and serve.

CHOPPED EGGPLANT WITH COCOA NIBS

MAKES ABOUT 4 CUPS

Guessing that the flavors of eggplant and cocoa beans might be sympathetic, I adapted a popular Middle Eastern appetizer, often called eggplant chopped liver(!). I omitted the chopped egg called for (as eggs bring out the worst in nibs) and baked the eggplant with olive oil instead of frying (too much oil) or grilling (adds smoke flavors). The nibs add a nutty, almost meaty dimension to the dish. Delicious.

2 large eggplants

Salt

Olive oil

1 medium yellow onion, coarsely chopped

¼ cup chopped Italian parsley

¼ cup cocoa nibs, finely chopped into small bits

Freshly ground black pepper

Wash the eggplants and trim off the stem ends. I leave the skin on, but you can remove it if you prefer. Cut the eggplants into ⅓-inch-thick slices. Sprinkle salt liberally over both sides of each slice and stand the slices on their edges in a colander on a deep plate or in the sink. Allow the juices to drain for at least 30 minutes.

Preheat the oven to 450°F. Grease two baking sheets with olive oil.

Rinse the eggplant slices briefly to remove excess salt, then blot dry with paper towels. Brush both sides of each slice with olive oil and arrange them in one layer on the baking sheets. (If they don't fit, cut some in half and arrange them like a jigsaw puzzle.) Bake, turning once, until browned and very soft, about 10 minutes per side.

While the eggplant is baking, film a large frying pan with olive oil, add the onion, and cook slowly, over medium-low heat, until it is deep golden brown (the slower the cooking, the more flavor you will get). Sprinkle the onion with a little salt and set aside.

When the eggplant is done, transfer it to a cutting board and coarsely chop with a large sharp knife, taking care not to leave any long pieces of skin. Transfer to a bowl. Add the onions, mashing and stirring with a fork. Mix in the parsley and chopped nibs. Taste and adjust the salt, and add a little freshly ground pepper to taste.

CHOPPED EGGPLANT WITH COCOA NIBS AND WALNUTS Add ⅓ cup chopped walnuts with the cocoa nibs.

CHOPPED CHICKEN LIVERS
WITH SHERRY-COCOA PAN SAUCE

MAKES 1⅓ CUPS

Don't be shocked at the idea of liver and chocolate. It's a natural if you just stop thinking of chocolate as being only for dessert. In *A True History of Chocolate,* Michael and Sophie Coe cite an eighteenth-century cookbook by the priest Felici Libera that includes a recipe for sliced liver dipped in chocolate and fried. Instead, I've sautéed chicken livers and finished them with a velvety little pan sauce thickened with cocoa. If you don't want *chopped* liver, serve the dish hot, directly from the sauté pan over egg noodles or strips of fried polenta.

¼ cup raisins	Freshly ground black pepper
¼ cup dry amontillado or other medium-dry sherry	2 teaspoons natural cocoa powder
	2 tablespoons water
Olive oil	
½ cup diced yellow onion	Coarsely chopped Italian parsley for garnish (optional)
Salt	
10 ounces chicken livers, rinsed, trimmed, and cut into quarters	

Coarsely chop the raisins and put them in a cup with the sherry. Set aside.

Film the bottom of a medium nonstick frying pan with olive oil. Add the onions and cook slowly, over medium-low heat, allowing them to turn soft and translucent and then brown. Sprinkle with a pinch or two of salt. Scrape into a bowl and reserve.

Add a little more oil to the pan and sauté the chicken livers gently until brown on the outside but still red within. Sprinkle with salt and pepper. Pour the sherry and raisins over the livers. Add the cocoa and water and stir to blend. Cook, stirring, until the liquid is reduced and thickened and the livers are barely pink inside. Scrape the mixture into the bowl with the onions and let cool slightly.

On a cutting board, with a large knife or in a mezzaluna, chop the livers to a coarse paste. Taste and adjust the salt and pepper. Sprinkle with chopped parsley, if desired. Serve warm or chilled on crackers or warm pita bread.

ROASTED SQUASH SOUP WITH COCOA BEAN CREAM

SERVES 4 TO 6 photograph on page 249

A perfectly simple and delicious fall soup with the added delight of drizzled cream infused with crushed cocoa beans.

One 2$\frac{1}{2}$- to 3-pound butternut squash	1 tablespoon chopped sage leaves
1 medium yellow onion, cut into eighths	Freshly ground white pepper
2 tablespoons olive oil	3 tablespoons cocoa nibs
$\frac{1}{2}$ teaspoon salt	$\frac{1}{2}$ cup heavy cream
4 cups chicken stock or vegetable broth, or water	

Preheat the oven to 450°F. Line a baking sheet with aluminum foil.

Quarter and seed the squash. Peel it and cut it into 2-inch pieces. Put the squash and onion on the baking sheet, drizzle with the olive oil, and sprinkle with the salt. With your hands, toss to coat the squash and onions with the oil. Roast for about 25 minutes, turning the pieces once or twice, until the squash is quite tender and a little browned at the edges.

Transfer the roasted vegetables and any juices to a blender or food processor. Add about 1 cup of the stock and puree until smooth. Transfer to a medium saucepan and add the remaining stock and the sage. Cover and bring to a simmer over medium heat. Correct the salt and season with pepper.

Meanwhile, just before serving, use a rolling pin to crush the cocoa nibs lightly between sheets of parchment or wax paper, or crush them in a mortar. Combine the nibs and cream in a small saucepan, bring to a simmer, and simmer for 1 or 2 minutes to infuse the nibs' flavor into the cream. Ladle the soup into bowls and spoon a drizzle of cream and cocoa nibs over each bowl.

NIBBY ASPARAGUS WITH PROSCIUTTO photograph on page 248

SERVES 4 TO 6

Elegant finger food or a plated first course. It is at its most aromatic and delicious when served hot or warm.

1 to 1¹/₂ pounds asparagus

2 tablespoons fruity extra virgin olive oil

2 tablespoons cocoa nibs, lightly crushed with a rolling pin

2 to 3 thin slices prosciutto, trimmed of excess fat and sliced into long slender shreds

Bring a large pot of salted water to a boil. Snap the woody ends from the asparagus, rinse, and peel the stems (if you like). Cook the asparagus in boiling water just until barely tender and still bright green, 3 to 5 minutes.

Meanwhile, in a very small saucepan, warm the oil and crushed cocoa nibs over the lowest heat for 2 to 3 minutes to infuse the oil with the nibs' flavor; do not simmer.

When the asparagus is ready, drain and spread out on layers of paper towels; let stand for a minute to evaporate the excess moisture. Transfer the asparagus to a platter and toss with the crushed nibs, warm oil, and prosciutto shreds. Serve hot or warm.

NIBBY GREEN BEANS This simple and superb dish celebrates fresh green beans instead of asparagus and calls for balsamic vinegar and sea salt instead of salty prosciutto. A first course unto itself, or a splendid vegetable dish. We often end up eating the warm beans with our fingers before we even get to the table.

Substitute green beans, rinsed and ends trimmed, for the asparagus. Omit the prosciutto. Toss the beans with the warm olive oil and nibs, then toss again with 2 to 3 teaspoons balsamic vinegar and a sprinkling of fleur de sel or coarsely ground sea salt, to taste.

WILD MUSHROOM RAGOUT photograph on page 247

MAKES 4 SMALL MAIN-COURSE SERVINGS, OR 4 TO 6 APPETIZER SERVINGS,
SERVED WITH POLENTA OR NOODLES

I had a little Rioja and a bag of wild mushrooms in the fridge, and I was about to go out of town. Thinking about fall flavors and woodsy mushrooms reminded me of the unopened bottle of quatre épices (nutmeg, pepper, clove, and cardamom) I brought home from France and put in the spice drawer.

Guilt over the mushrooms that would otherwise spoil, nostalgia for a French autumn, and the opportunity to open the spices resulted in a princely ragout that I have "translated" so that you needn't own a bottle of quatre épices. This robust savory dish tastes big and rich enough that you might believe it contains meat or game, although it has none. The sauce is dark and velvety with a depth that suggests hours of long, slow simmering when, in fact, it is fairly quick to make. *Bon appétit.*

1 pound mixed wild (and cultivated) mushrooms, such as portobellos, chanterelles, shiitake, cèpes, and cremini

About 2 tablespoons olive oil

2 garlic cloves, finely minced

2/3 cup dry red wine (I have used Rioja, merlot, and Chateâuneuf-du-Pape)

A scant 1/8 teaspoon each of ground nutmeg, ground cardamom, and white pepper

A pinch or two of ground cloves

1/4 teaspoon salt

1/4 cup water

1 tablespoon finely chopped unsweetened chocolate

Keeping the different mushrooms separate, rinse briefly and dry them, then slice 1/4 inch thick; discard the stems if they seem tough. Heat a large skillet over medium-high heat and add about a teaspoon of olive oil. Add one type of mushroom and sauté, stirring frequently until browned, 2 to 3 minutes. Scrape them into a bowl and set aside. Repeat with each mushroom type, scraping them into the same bowl. If you are not using a nonstick pan, between batches you may dissolve the browned bits from the pan with a little water, then scrape the juices into the bowl.

continued

Remove the pan from the heat to cool slightly, then set over medium-low heat. Add 1 more tablespoon olive oil and the garlic; sauté until soft but not browned. Return the mushrooms and any accumulated juices to the pan, add the wine, spices, and salt, and simmer for 2 to 3 minutes to evaporate the alcohol in the wine.

Add ¼ cup water, cover, and simmer for 6 to 10 minutes to cook the mushrooms and release their juices into the sauce. Uncover and cook until the sauce is reduced and slightly syrupy. Stir in the chocolate until it melts and smoothes the sauce. Taste and correct the seasonings, if necessary. Serve over fried or soft polenta or egg noodles.

chocolate note You can substitute 2½ teaspoons natural cocoa powder for the unsweetened chocolate.

GIULIANO'S SWEET AND SAVORY MEAT SAUCE WITH CHOCOLATE

SERVES 6

This recipe from Giuliano Bugialli, which appeared in his *Classic Techniques of Italian Cooking,* was, many years ago, my first taste of chocolate in a memorable savory dish. The finishing flavor combination of sweet raisins, "sour" vinegar, pine nuts, and chocolate is called *dolce-forte* in Italian, as it is both sweet and strong—or sour. Although the dish is said to be Florentine, the pine nuts and raisins suggest a sixteenth-century Sicilian provenance and the culinary influence of Spanish Jews escaping the Inquisition. Please don't conjure up hot fudge sauce over pasta: The chocolate adds an earthy depth and complexity, richness, and a voluptuous texture that is completely in harmony with the meaty flavor of the sauce.

I have taken small liberties: Giuliano uses $1/2$ cup olive oil instead of my 3 to 4 tablespoons, and he originally called for chocolate chips instead of bittersweet or semisweet chocolate. And he serves the sauce over homemade tagliatelle made with cocoa powder. The optional cocoa nibs are my addition.

1 medium red onion

3 celery stalks

2 medium carrots

1 medium garlic clove

10 sprigs Italian parsley, leaves only

4 ounces pancetta, or 2 ounces boiled ham plus 2 ounces salt pork

3 to 4 tablespoons olive oil

1 pound lean ground beef

$1^1/4$ cups dry red wine

1 cup drained canned Italian tomatoes, or $3/4$ cup tomato puree

Salt and freshly ground black pepper to taste

$1/2$ cup red wine vinegar

$1/4$ cup raisins

2 tablespoons pine nuts

$3/4$ ounce bittersweet or semisweet chocolate, finely chopped

1 tablespoon sugar

1 pound dried or fresh tagliatelle or other egg pasta

Cocoa nibs, crushed with a rolling pin or coarsely chopped into bits, to pass at the table (optional)

continued

Finely chop the onion, celery, carrots, garlic, and parsley. Dice the pancetta. In a large sauté pan, heat the olive oil. Add the chopped vegetables, parsley, and pancetta, and sauté slowly over low heat for about 15 minutes, until the vegetables are translucent and beginning to brown. Add the ground meat and stir it into the sautéed ingredients with a fork or wooden spoon. When the meat is no longer pink, add the wine and simmer to evaporate it, about 5 minutes.

Meanwhile, unless using puree, pass the tomatoes through a food mill.

When the wine has evaporated, add the tomato puree to the pan. Season lightly with salt and pepper, and simmer slowly for about 25 minutes.

Meanwhile, prepare the *dolce-forte*: Combine the wine vinegar, raisins, pine nuts, chocolate, and sugar in a small bowl; set aside.

Bring a large pot of salted water to a boil.

When the sauce is ready, stir in the dolce-forte and simmer 5 minutes longer. Correct the seasoning with salt and pepper, and add additional vinegar or sugar if necessary.

Cook the pasta just until al dente. Reserve some of the cooking water, then drain the pasta. Pour a little sauce into the bottom of a serving dish and top with the pasta and the remaining sauce. Toss the pasta and sauce together, moistening it with a little of the reserved pasta water if necessary. If you like, pass a bowl of cocoa nibs at the table to sprinkle over the pasta.

chocolate notes You can use standard bittersweet or semisweet chocolate (without a percentage on the label), or any marked 50% to 62%. Or use higher-percentage chocolates as follows:

To use chocolate marked 66% to 72% instead of standard bittersweet: Use $1/2$ ounce chocolate.

To use unsweetened chocolate or chocolate marked 99% instead of standard bittersweet: Use $1/3$ ounce chocolate.

In all cases, when the sauce is finished, you can correct with pinches of sugar as necessary to balance the sweet and savory character of the dish.

A LITTLE SAUCE FOR PASTA photograph on page 249

SERVES 6

Another pasta sauce using chocolate as a flavor—but this time it's nibs. In the time that it takes to boil the water and cook the pasta, you can prepare this simple sauce, which is really no more than a harmonious assortment of flavorful ingredients and textures warmed in garlicky olive oil. As always with this genre of sauce, exact amounts are subject to your mood and taste, and their availability. In other words, if you like the sauce, eventually you will make it with handfuls of ingredients and without a recipe in front of you. Cocoa nibs, of course, are not authentic to the Mediterranean cuisine evoked by the other flavors in this dish, but tomatoes are not indigenous to Italy either! While the idea of it may push the envelope, the actual flavor of unsweetened chocolate readily complements the sweet caramelized carrots, robust olives, garlic, and parsley, and that nibby crunch is so appealing.

1 pound dried pasta	1/2 cup pine nuts
Flavorful extra virgin olive oil	1/3 to 1/2 cup chopped pitted Niçoise olives
1 cup diced carrots	
8 garlic cloves, finely diced (not minced)	Salt and freshly ground black pepper
1/4 cup cocoa nibs	1 cup coarsely chopped Italian parsley
2 ounces thinly sliced prosciutto, cut into small dice	

Bring a large pot of water with a handful of salt to a boil. Add the pasta and cook just until al dente.

While the pasta is cooking, film a large skillet with a little olive oil and heat over medium-high heat. When the oil is hot, cook the carrots until slightly browned and tender, about 5 minutes. Scrape the carrots into a bowl, return the skillet to the heat, and add a little more olive oil. Cook the garlic slowly until soft and beginning to brown. Turn off the heat and stir in the nibs, prosciutto, pine nuts, olives, and carrots. Sprinkle with salt, if necessary, and a few grinds of fresh pepper. Set the skillet aside.

continued

When the pasta is ready, scoop out and reserve a cup of the cooking water; drain the pasta. Rewarm the contents of the skillet over medium heat, add the drained pasta and the parsley, and stir for a minute or two to combine everything and blend the flavors; add a little of the reserved pasta water as necessary to moisten the mixture. Taste and correct the salt and pepper, drizzle with a little olive oil, and serve immediately.

COQ (OR LAPIN) AU VIN

SERVES 8

Coq au vin is normally enriched and flavored with smoky bacon, which I have omitted here, as I do not like smoky flavors with chocolate. Chocolate adds its own rich meaty flavor and nuance to this superb dish. It also thickens the sauce without additional flour and deepens the color.

Even a purely classic coq au vin (i.e., *sans chocolate*) is improved by taking care to remove excess fat along the way. This defines and brightens the flavors and makes the dish at the same time both more elegant and less rich. I stretch the "work" pleasantly over four days. I usually marinate for two days and cook on day three, remembering to sip the leftover wine as I sauté, simmer, and skim. On the fourth day, there's nothing left to do but remove and discard the solidified fat and reheat the whole business with a little chocolate while boiling some noodles.

If you like rabbit, the substitution is easy and excellent. However, since the rabbit has no protective skin, the browning step must be done over gentler heat to avoid toughening the flesh.

1½ bottles drinkable red wine (such as merlot, zinfandel, or Rioja)

2 large yellow onions, thinly sliced

2 large carrots, sliced

8 garlic cloves, chopped

4 sprigs Italian parsley, plus chopped parsley for garnish

4 sprigs thyme, or ½ teaspoon dried thyme

2 bay leaves

2 large chickens (each 3½ to 4 pounds), each cut into 8 serving pieces

1 teaspoon salt, plus more to taste

¼ cup all-purpose flour

About ¼ cup olive oil

1 pound small button mushrooms, rinsed and patted dry, stems removed and reserved

½ cup cognac or other brandy

3 cups chicken stock

1½ pounds pearl onions (about 4½ cups), blanched briefly in boiling water for easier peeling

½ ounce unsweetened chocolate, finely chopped

Freshly ground black pepper

continued

At least 1 day, or up to 4 days, before you plan to serve, marinate the chicken: In a medium nonreactive saucepan, combine the wine, onions, carrots, garlic, parsley sprigs, thyme, and bay leaves. To evaporate the alcohol, bring to a simmer and cook until the marinade no longer smells harsh or tastes of alcohol, 3 to 5 minutes. (You can hasten the evaporation by carefully igniting the surface of the simmering wine with a long match or wooden skewer; if you can't get it to ignite, it's OK to give up.) Remove from the heat and let cool completely.

Divide the chicken pieces between two large zipper-lock freezer bags. Add half the cold marinade (with its vegetables and herbs) to each. Press to expel the air and seal the bags. Place the bags in a large bowl (in case of leakage) and refrigerate for 24 to 48 hours, turning them from time to time.

One day before serving, if possible, remove the chicken pieces from the marinade and set aside. Strain the marinade, and reserve the liquid and the vegetables separately. Pour the liquid into a large saucepan and bring just to a simmer over low heat. Let barely simmer for about 5 minutes to allow the proteins to rise and coagulate on the surface. Set a large strainer lined with a paper towel over a bowl. Without stirring or disturbing the marinade more than necessary, ladle it gently into the strainer. Discard the coagulated scum in the towel and reserve the strained liquid.

Dry the chicken pieces with paper towels. Sprinkle with the salt and dust with flour. Heat 2 tablespoons of the oil in a large skillet over high heat. When the oil is very hot but not smoking, brown the chicken pieces a few at a time, transferring them to a bowl as they brown. Then brown the reserved vegetables and the mushroom stems in the oil remaining in the skillet.

Pour the brandy over the vegetables and scrape up the brown crusty bits from the bottom of the pan. When the brandy has nearly evaporated, scrape the mixture into a large heavy pot or Dutch oven (set the skillet aside). Add the strained marinade, chicken stock, and chicken pieces. Cover and simmer until the chicken is tender, 1 to 1½ hours.

While the chicken is cooking, add a little more oil to the skillet. Sauté the onions until golden brown and tender. Scrape them into a bowl. Sauté the mushroom caps and add them to the onions. Set aside.

When the chicken is tender, scrape off any marinated vegetables from the pieces and transfer the chicken to the bowl with the mushrooms and onions. Strain the sauce into a bowl, pressing lightly on the solids to extract as much liquid as possible, then discard the vegetables. Skim as much fat from the sauce as you can. Return the sauce to the pot and simmer until it is reduced to 4 cups. If you are serving the chicken within a short time, skip the next paragraph.

If you are working ahead, cover and refrigerate the chicken. Pour the sauce into a separate container, cover, and refrigerate for as long as overnight. When ready to continue the recipe, remove and discard the congealed fat from the top of the sauce, and reheat the sauce in the Dutch oven.

To serve, combine the chocolate and a couple of spoonfuls of the heated sauce in a cup and stir until the chocolate is melted and smooth. Scrape the chocolate mixture into the pot. Add the chicken, onions, and mushrooms and heat through (this takes longer, of course, if the chicken was refrigerated; I sometimes warm it slightly in the microwave before adding it to the sauce). Taste and correct the salt, and add a few grinds of pepper to taste. Serve with egg noodles and a generous handful of chopped parsley.

chocolate note You can substitute 1 1/2 tablespoons natural cocoa powder for the unsweetened chocolate.

MOLE COLORADITO

MAKES ABOUT 1 QUART, OR ENOUGH FOR 8 SERVINGS

This recipe is author Nancy Zaslavsky's marvelous mole, finished, of course, with chocolate. After tasting it in San Miguel de Allende, I reproduced it at home in Berkeley to make sure that it wasn't just the margaritas and Mexican mountain air that made it taste so good. It wasn't.

The recipe here is for the sauce. For the chicken, you have several options. Nancy serves a quarter of a small chicken in a pool of sauce on each plate, drizzled with a little sauce and a generous sprinkling of sesame seeds. Or, for a crowd, poach lots of half chicken breasts (bone in and skin left on) in water or light stock with a few herbs until almost cooked through. When the chicken is cool enough to handle, pull the skin off and discard. Remove the meat from the bones, tearing the meat into big shreds. Put the shreds in a big pot with the mole. By the time the mole is reheated, the chicken will be cooked through but still marvelously moist and juicy. Any way you serve it, have lots of hot corn tortillas on hand for sopping, mopping, or wrapping.

Ancho and guajillo chiles (or the suggested alternatives) are available in Mexican markets and some supermarkets. Nancy uses Mexican chocolate, naturally. I abandon authenticity in that department and use the best bittersweet 70 percent that I can find.

8 dried ancho chiles
or dried mulato chiles

8 dried guajillo chiles
or dried New Mexico chiles

1/2 cup raisins

1 large unpeeled white onion,
quartered

8 unpeeled garlic cloves

A 2-inch cinnamon stick
(*canela* or true Ceylon cinnamon,
if possible; see page 41)

1/2 cup unblanched whole almonds

1/2 teaspoon dried thyme

1 teaspoon dried oregano,
preferably Mexican

1 teaspoon salt (Nancy uses kosher)

Freshly ground black pepper

3 ripe plum tomatoes

2 tablespoons vegetable oil

One 2-ounce tablet Mexican chocolate,
broken up, or 1 1/2 ounces bittersweet or
semisweet chocolate, chopped

About 3 cups hot chicken stock

Sugar to taste (optional)

Toasted sesame seeds for garnish

To make the chile paste, slit the chiles open down the side and remove the seeds and stems. On a hot griddle or in a hot cast-iron skillet, toast the chiles on both sides, flattening them with a spatula, until their skins blister and change color. Put the chiles in a bowl, add the raisins, and cover with hot water. Let soak for 30 minutes.

Drain the chiles and raisins, puree them in a blender, adding a little water as necessary (no more than 1/2 cup) to make a puree. Strain the puree through a medium sieve into a bowl.

Reheat the griddle or the skillet and toast the onion quarters and garlic cloves, turning them from time to time, until they have just a few blackened spots. Put the onions in a clean blender. Peel the garlic and add to the blender. Toast the cinnamon briefly on the hot griddle, until fragrant, and add to the blender.

Toast the almonds in a small skillet over medium heat until fragrant and the insides are golden brown. Add the almonds to the onion and garlic in the blender, then add the thyme, oregano, salt, and about 6 grinds of pepper. Puree, adding water as necessary. Strain into the chiles.

Place the tomatoes on the hot griddle and turn them from time to time, just until they have a few blackened spots—they should not be completely soft or falling apart. Peel the tomatoes, puree in the blender, and strain.

Heat the oil in a wide deep pot until hot. Add the chile mixture (watch out, it will splatter) and cook, stirring, for a few minutes to further toast the ingredients and concentrate the flavors. Add the chocolate, lower the heat, and simmer for 15 minutes, or until thickened. Taste and adjust the seasonings (if you've used a strong bittersweet chocolate instead of Mexican chocolate, you can add a few small pinches of sugar when you finish the sauce, as necessary). (The chile paste can be made ahead, cooled, covered, and refrigerated for up to 3 months or frozen for up to 6 months. Reheat before continuing.)

continued

To finish the sauce, add the tomato puree and stir for a few more minutes. Thin to the desired consistency with the broth, adjust the seasonings, and heat through. (The sauce can be cooled, covered, and refrigerated for up to 3 days; reheat before serving.)

Serve over chicken, sprinkled with toasted sesame seeds.

chocolate note If you do not use Mexican chocolate, which is flavored with cinnamon and fairly sweet, start with the $1\frac{1}{2}$ ounces of bittersweet or semisweet chocolate, and add a little more to taste if necessary. You can use any good chocolate you like; I most often use a bittersweet 70% and find that $1\frac{1}{2}$ ounces is the perfect amount. Whatever cinnamon and/or sugar is missing can be taken care of, if necessary, when you taste and correct the sauce at the end.

I love tasting chocolate, but I'm impatient with chocolate tastings that are designed to select the "best" from a group of chocolates. It's not that I think there are no bad chocolates. But there are too many different interesting chocolates to put them on a one-dimensional scale. We have, in fact, begun to talk about chocolate the way we talk about wine. Both can be ambrosial, "food of the gods."

Both begin with raw materials from the soil, and both require an almost magical fusion of art and science to transform them into the products that we know and love. Details of cultivation and climate make a difference in the characteristics and quality of chocolate, as does each step in the manufacturing process. We discuss bean varieties and sources, and blending versus the merits of chocolate from a single source. However, unlike wine and other sophisticated foods that we love (like caviar), chocolate is not an acquired taste. Most of us grew up with it and aren't likely to need someone else to tell us what is best, regardless of whether or not our tastes have changed since childhood. When it comes to chocolate, I don't think expert opinions carry that much weight. People have to have their own experience.

I lost faith in blind tastings a while back. After organizing a blind chocolate tasting for a magazine several years ago, I realized that the results said less about the chocolate and more about the experience and demographics of the twelve tasters and the challenge of selecting what should be tasted in the first place. Here's what happened. The highest-ranking chocolate turned out to be the one produced locally: Its familiar taste sent it right up the chart. An impressive but unfamiliar European chocolate that was a tad fruitier and more tart than everyone was then accustomed to didn't show too well: Its unfamiliar "foreign" flavor and comparative acidity cost it points. Another chocolate that was slightly sweeter than the rest of the samples also got a low rating. The tasting taught me that regional tastes and familiarity exert strong influences on our preferences, and it showed me that outliers are likely to lose points just for being different from the rest of the group. If tasters trying to rank ten oranges encounter a tangerine among them, they are likely to be confused. The tangerine will probably do poorly (even if it's a delicious tangerine) because it doesn't seem to be part of the group. I concluded that blind panel tastings may be fascinating from a sociological and psychological perspective but are flawed instruments for judging something as complex as chocolate (or anything else I care a lot about).

We nibblers, home cooks, chefs, and chocolatiers use chocolate in so many different ways. Sometimes it stands on its own—a plain bar of chocolate unwrapped and savored. Sometimes we combine it in recipes for confections and desserts and, in doing so, pair it with myriad flavors and ingredients that vary in texture, taste, and sweetness. A chocolate-covered caramel is different from a chocolate-coated nut cluster, which is, in turn, different from a chocolate mousse or chocolate ganache flavored with liqueurs or infused with herbs or spices, or a chocolate chip cookie, a piece of fudge, or a slice of chocolate cake. And there is no single chocolate that does all of these things best, thank heavens!

I eventually designed a tasting that resembles a food and wine pairing: We taste a small selection of chocolates with a sweet fruity ingredient (raisins), a nutty ingredient (toasted almonds), and something salty (pretzels). Instead of searching for the "best" chocolate, we explore flavor combinations that might actually occur in desserts, candies, or snacks. The exercise is fun, and it suggests a fresh approach to choosing chocolate for recipes—by taste! You can try it by making the simple seasonal chocolates called mendiants.

MENDIANTS photograph on page 22

MAKES ABOUT ONE HUNDRED ½-INCH MENDIANTS

Soon after the *rentrée,* when Parisians return to work and school after the long summer holiday, shop windows burst with fall colors and chocolatiers set out trays of thin satiny rounds of crisp, perfectly tempered chocolate garnished with a harvest of dried fruit and nuts. These are mendiants. The word *mendiant* literally means "beggar of alms," and it refers to the four orders of mendicant monks. Classically, chocolate mendiants are decorated with blanched almonds, raisins, hazelnuts, and dried figs to represent the white, gray, brown, and purple robes worn, respectively, by Dominican, Franciscan, Carmelite, and Augustinian friars. Of course, today's mendiants flaunt bright green pistachios and myriad jewel-toned dried and candied fruits. I even season them with pinches of spice. Mendiants may be as small as a quarter (easy to pop right in your mouth) or as big as a coaster (nice for nibblers).

A perfect mendiant is an ode to simplicity: delightful to look at and delicious to eat. Yet, once upon a time, in my youthful desire to sample every rich creamy truffle in my path, I dismissed the mendiant. It seemed too basic and I thought the garnish beggarly—rarely more than two or three bits of fruit or nut. I didn't realize I would one day find mendiants as tempting as truffles, precisely for their minimalist perfection of taste and texture.

Making mendiants is a meditation for the eye and palate. Select toppings for shape, color, and taste. There is no precise recipe; it is all up to you. Rest assured, in general, that all kinds of nuts and dried and candied fruits and peels taste good with chocolate. But "in specific," different flavors taste good, better, or best, depending upon the chocolate. If you take the time to taste your chocolate with several garnishes, first singly, then in duets and trios, you will notice how some combinations sing to you. You will make perfect mendiants.

Mendiants keep well at room temperature, which makes them easier and more convenient than filled chocolates or truffles. Make them in advance and pack them in gift boxes with clear plastic covers to show off your artistry.

continued

1 pound bittersweet, semisweet, milk, or white chocolate

ABOUT 2 OUNCES *EACH* OF THREE OR MORE OF THE FOLLOWING

Toasted or untoasted almonds or hazelnuts, walnut or pecan halves, macadamias, or pistachios (see page 40)

Sunflower or pumpkin seeds

Dried fruits such as raisins, currants, or cherries

Candied citrus peel, crystallized ginger, or glacéed fruit

Spices, preferably freshly ground, such as dried chiles, black pepper, cardamom seeds, nutmeg, or anise seeds (optional)

SPECIAL EQUIPMENT

Several baking sheets or other trays (they need not be heatproof)

Portable fan (optional)

Prepare the garnishes first. Once the chocolate is ready, you will not have time. For example, cut whole nuts in half (if desired) or chop them; dice or slice crystallized ginger or citrus peels, etc.

Line the baking sheets with parchment paper and tape down the edges if you plan to cool with a fan.

Melt and temper the chocolate according to the instructions on page 357–361. Spoon a dozen or so equal-sized pools of chocolate, at least 2 inches apart to allow for spreading, onto one of the lined baking sheets. Rap the baking sheet firmly on the counter to spread and thin the puddles of chocolate. Garnish each puddle artistically, before it sets, with 2 to 3 ingredient pieces. (If you are working with a helper, you can spoon out more puddles of chocolate at a time; do not exceed the number of puddles you can decorate before the chocolate sets.) Sprinkle some of the mendiants with pinches of spice, if desired. Let set in a cool (not cold) place, preferably in front of a fan, for at least an hour.

Pack in a covered container with wax paper between the layers. Store in a cool dry place.

chocolate note Perhaps it is obvious that you can use any chocolate or any percentage that you desire, or that you can use white chocolate or milk chocolate. As long as it tastes good to you, any chocolate will make splendid mendiants.

Appendix

Chocolate by the Numbers

A Dessert Maker's Guide to High-Percentage Chocolates

Compared even with just a few years ago, the variety of chocolate available to chocolate lovers and home cooks is astonishing. If you love bittersweet chocolate, you are probably already nibbling more brands than you used to, including intense chocolates with the percentage of pure chocolate content marked right on the label. As your palate becomes more demanding and more accustomed to stronger and more complex chocolate flavors, you naturally want to use new chocolates in recipes as well. Perhaps you've already tried substituting high-percentage chocolates in your favorite desserts. If you've been lucky in your recipe choice, you've had great results. But it is more likely that you've had some disasters. Here's why.

Once upon a time, the bittersweet or semisweet chocolate called for in recipes— those that you have clipped over the years, jotted down on index cards, or marked in favorite books—contained about half chocolate liquor and half sugar. For decades this was the unofficial standard for the bittersweet and semisweet chocolate used by home cooks. But today chocolates called bittersweet can differ so much in chocolate liquor and sugar content that they may not even be interchangeable in a recipe (see Bittersweet and Semisweet Chocolates, page 51)!

Any chocolate labeled with a percentage over 60 is already stronger—increasingly so as the percentage grows—and less sweet than the standard chocolate for which most recipes are written. High-percentage chocolates offer an exciting choice of flavors and quality and considerable creative flexibility, but they definitely require continuing education for the cook. Stronger chocolates can affect the taste and texture of recipes in unexpected, often unpleasant ways.

You might anticipate that using a higher-percentage chocolate would simply make a dessert more chocolatey and less sweet—which might be your reason for using a 70 percent chocolate in the first place. But it is more complicated than that. If you look at the diagram on page 346 you will see, for example, that a bar of bittersweet chocolate with 70 percent chocolate liquor is only 30 percent sugar. It has almost

40 percent more chocolate liquor and 40 percent less sugar than standard American bittersweet chocolates. In recipes, a 70 percent chocolate behaves like a different animal! The effect of increasing liquor and decreasing sugar is exaggerated because manufacturers usually add less extra cocoa butter to chocolate when they increase the total amount of chocolate liquor (which has cocoa butter in it), so the amount of nonfat dry cocoa solids increases more than the fat as the percentage of chocolate liquor goes up. The effect of using a higher-percentage chocolate is a little like adding cocoa powder to a recipe and subtracting sugar at the same time. That just begins to explain dry cake batters, dense gummy mousses, and ganache that curdles.

I have been creating and adapting recipes for high-percentage chocolates for more than a decade. I began experimenting by trial and error, as I always do. Eventually I created formulas for substitution. But then I began to stray from the formulas, for even more exciting results—often to get the increase in flavor and reduction in sweetness I originally sought by using stronger chocolate in the first place, but without disappointments and failures.

CHOCOLATE COMPONENTS

Let's review the three main components of a bittersweet or semisweet bar and what each contributes. Chocolate liquor is made up of nonfat dry cocoa solids and cocoa butter, which are shown separately on each diagram. The third component is sugar. Some (often the most inexpensive) semisweet chocolates may also contain a very small amount of milk solids and butterfat—both of which I have ignored here.

The nonfat dry cocoa solids (imagine entirely fat-free unsweetened cocoa powder) contribute virtually all of the chocolate flavor. Because they are a dry ingredient and contain carbohydrates, they act a little like flour: They absorb moisture and liquid. Because nonfat dry cocoa solids are the main source of chocolate flavor, my formulas for substituting chocolates are based on comparing the average amounts of these solids in different chocolates. You can see that about $1\frac{2}{3}$ ounces of bittersweet 70 percent chocolate has about the same amount of nonfat dry cocoa solids as 1 ounce of unsweetened chocolate, so that becomes my formula— along with a sugar and butter adjustment in the recipe.

Cocoa butter is fat. It contributes smoothness, richness, and body to the chocolate liquor. It melts at a higher temperature than dairy butter, so it is not as soft and does not melt in your mouth as quickly, but it does carry the chocolate flavor.

Sugar contributes sweetness and also keeps baked goods moist. It may also contribute chewiness, in brownies, for example, or (seemingly contradictorily) crispness in cookies—or caramelized flavor in anything.

Whether or not it is necessary to modify a recipe when you substitute a high-percentage bittersweet chocolate for a standard semisweet depends on the type of recipe, the percentage of chocolate liquor in the chocolate you want to use, and your goal in using a stronger chocolate in the first place.

COMPOSITION OF UNSWEETENED, BITTERSWEET, AND SEMISWEET CHOCOLATE BARS

AN AMERICAN BITTERSWEET OR SEMISWEET BAKING SQUARE	= **50% CHOCOLATE LIQUOR** 18% to 22% nonfat dry cocoa solids + 28% to 32% cocoa butter (may include some milk fat)	+	**50% SUGAR** 50% or more sugar
A STANDARD BITTERSWEET OR SEMISWEET BAR	= **55% CHOCOLATE LIQUOR** 20% to 22% nonfat dry cocoa solids + 33% to 35% cocoa butter	+	**45% SUGAR** 45% sugar
A BITTERSWEET BAR LABELED 70%	= **70% CHOCOLATE LIQUOR** 28% to 30% nonfat dry cocoa solids + 40% to 42% cocoa butter	+	**30% SUGAR** 30% sugar
UNSWEETENED BAKING CHOCOLATE	= **99% CHOCOLATE LIQUOR** 46% to 50% nonfat dry cocoa solids + 50% to 54% cocoa butter		

Notice that as the percentage of chocolate liquor increases, the percentage of nonfat dry cocoa solids increases proportionately more than the percentage of cocoa butter. Many chefs cite the increase in fat to explain problems that arise in using high-percentage chocolates in recipes designed for standard bittersweet and semisweet chocolate. But, in fact, the proportionately larger increase in nonfat dry cocoa solids affects the outcome far more than the increase in fat.

ABOUT THE CHOCOLATE BAR DIAGRAM Data for percentage-labeled chocolate came from manufacturers' spec sheets (when available), conversations with manufacturers, and/or from label math as follows: The percentage of chocolate liquor on the label, subtracted from 100 percent, equals the sugar percentage. The fat percentage is derived from the nutrition label: Divide the grams of fat by the grams per serving. The percentage of nonfat dry cocoa solids is obtained by subtracting the fat percentage from the chocolate liquor percentage. Percentages of sugar, fat, and nonfat dry solids should add up to 99 percent to 100 percent, as vanilla and lecithin make up less than 1 percent. Label math is most accurate when chocolate does not contain milk solids (of which 12 percent is allowed) or milk fat (of which up to 5 percent is allowed). Fortunately, the higher-percentage chocolates do not usually contain milk products.

Chocolates that are not labeled with percentages are trickier to break down. Manufacturers of the standard baking squares, and even some premium bars of American bittersweet and semisweet chocolate, consider percentage information proprietary. They won't divulge the chocolate liquor percentage, much less the specific percentage of cocoa butter, nonfat dry cocoa solids, or sugar. I used label math to get a rough idea of these percentages. Grams of sugar per serving, divided by grams per serving, gives us the percentage of sugar in the chocolate. Then the percentage of chocolate liquor is obtained by subtracting the sugar percentage from 100 percent, unless the chocolate contains milk solids or milk fat (listed on the ingredient statement), which is common among standard chocolates and baking squares. If the chocolate contains milk solids, your label math may overstate the actual chocolate liquor by up to 12 percent. If the chocolate contains milk fat instead of milk solids, the actual liquor percentage may be up to 5 percent less than your calculation indicates. Divide the fat grams per serving by the serving size to find the percentage of cocoa butter (plus other fats, if any, on the ingredient list). Subtract the fat percentage from the liquor percentage to find the percentage of nonfat dry cocoa solids.

Using label math experience and a general knowledge of manufacturing, a few well-placed questions, and just a little guessing, I determined that, with the exception of one brand, bittersweet and semisweet baking squares contain 48 to 50 percent chocolate liquor, with an average of about 18 percent dry cocoa solids. Standard bittersweet and semisweet bars for baking and eating (without a percentage on the label) have 50 to 55 percent liquor, usually with 20 to 23 percent nonfat dry solids. If the numbers are not completely accurate, they are close enough to be useful.

Formulas for Converting Recipes from One Chocolate to Another

Imagine you have a great brownie recipe that calls for 4 ounces of unsweetened chocolate. You love the recipe because it is perfectly balanced in terms of sweetness, richness, and flavor—but instead of using unsweetened grocery store baking chocolate, you want to substitute that delicious 70 percent chocolate you have been snacking on lately. How much 70 percent chocolate should you use and what other changes, if any, should you make in the recipe? I figured that out in order to create the quartet of brownies (pages 93–94), each using a different kind of chocolate or cocoa in the same basic recipe. Meanwhile, I derived several formulas with which you can convert your own favorite recipes from one chocolate to another without risking unhappy surprises. However, just because you have a formula doesn't always mean you have to stick to it slavishly—I often use these as a point of departure only.

TO SUBSTITUTE BITTERSWEET AND SEMISWEET CHOCOLATE FOR UNSWEETENED CHOCOLATE

In order to substitute sweetened chocolate for unsweetened chocolate, you must subtract sugar and butter from the original recipe. Recipes that do not contain enough sugar and butter in the first place cannot be converted this way. Brownies work beautifully (see pages 93–99), as do ice creams and cheesecakes. Scan the specific formula for the chocolate you want to use and check the recipe for sugar and butter before trying the conversion.

To substitute standard bittersweet or semisweet chocolate (without a percentage on the label or any labeled 50 to 58 percent) for unsweetened chocolate

For every ounce of unsweetened chocolate called for, substitute 2½ ounces of standard bittersweet or semisweet chocolate and decrease the sugar in the recipe by 2½ to 3 tablespoons and the butter in the recipe by ½ tablespoon.

EXAMPLE: If the original recipe calls for 4 ounces unsweetened chocolate: Use 10 ounces (4 × 2½) standard bittersweet or semisweet chocolate, decrease the sugar by 10 to 12 tablespoons (4 × 2½ or 3), or ⅔ cup, and decrease the butter by 2 tablespoons (4 × ½).

To substitute chocolate labeled 62 to 64 percent for unsweetened chocolate

For every ounce of unsweetened chocolate called for, use 2 ounces chocolate labeled 62 to 64 percent and decrease the sugar in the recipe by 1½ to 2 tablespoons and decrease butter in the recipe by ½ tablespoon.

To substitute chocolate labeled 66 percent for unsweetened chocolate

For every ounce of unsweetened chocolate called for, use 1¾ ounces chocolate labeled 66 percent, decrease the sugar by 1⅓ tablespoons (4 teaspoons), and decrease butter by ½ tablespoon.

To substitute chocolate labeled 70 to 72 percent for unsweetened chocolate

For every ounce of unsweetened chocolate called for, use 1⅔ ounces chocolate labeled 70 or 72 percent, decrease sugar by 1 tablespoon, and decrease butter by 1 teaspoon.

TO SUBSTITUTE HIGH-PERCENTAGE CHOCOLATE FOR STANDARD BITTERSWEET OR SEMISWEET BARS OR BAKING SQUARES

To substitute high-percentage chocolate for standard chocolate, use less chocolate and adjust the sugar. The formulas in this section give a range for reducing the quantity of chocolate called for in a recipe. If you normally use bittersweet or semisweet baking squares, reduce the chocolate by the greater amount to get results that are similar in chocolate intensity to desserts you are accustomed to. If you normally use bars (which average a little more chocolate liquor than squares) or if you want a more bittersweet chocolate flavor, reduce the chocolate by the smaller amount. In either case, you can also increase the intensity of bittersweet chocolate flavor by using less of the sugar adjustment.

To substitute chocolate labeled 62 percent for standard bittersweet or semisweet bars or baking squares

For every ounce of chocolate called for in the original recipe, use 10 to 15 percent less chocolate and add 1 teaspoon sugar.

EXAMPLE: If the original recipe calls for 10 ounces chocolate: Use $8\frac{1}{2}$ to 9 ounces chocolate labeled 62 percent and add 10 teaspoons (10×1), or 3 tablespoons plus 1 teaspoon, sugar to the original recipe.

To substitute chocolate labeled 64 percent for standard bittersweet or semisweet bars or baking squares

For every ounce of chocolate called for in the original recipe, use 20 to 25 percent less chocolate and add $1\frac{1}{4}$ teaspoons sugar.

To substitute chocolate labeled 66 percent for standard bittersweet or semisweet bars or baking squares

For every ounce of chocolate called for in the original recipe, use 25 to 30 percent less chocolate and add $1\frac{1}{2}$ teaspoons sugar.

To substitute chocolate labeled 70 or 72 percent for standard bittersweet or semisweet bars or baking squares

For every ounce of chocolate called for in the original recipe, use 30 to 35 percent less chocolate and add $1\frac{1}{2}$ teaspoons sugar.

ARE THE FORMULAS ALWAYS NECESSARY?

One of the biggest attractions of chocolate with more chocolate liquor is its strength and relatively low proportion of sugar. Rather than using a formula to compensate for these characteristics—using less chocolate and adding sugar—you might be tempted to substitute the stronger chocolate ounce for ounce to make a dessert more chocolatey and less sweet. But only a few recipes adapt to straight substitution with only minor fine-tuning. In the baking repertoire, "nearly flourless" chocolate nut tortes like the Queen of Sheba (page 109), because of their enormous flexibility and lack of formal structure, and the lower-fat recipes sprinkled throughout this book, because they are less densely chocolate in the first place, permit this kind of substitution. They require only a little less baking time to succeed brilliantly. And in candy making, of course, you are free to use chocolate of any percentage for dipping.

However, most recipes are not so permissive. If you change the chocolate, you must make other adjustments to the recipe for a successful outcome.

Recipes that are essentially combinations of chocolate and liquid, or that have a chocolate and liquid component, are particularly sensitive to variation in chocolate. Ganache, the combination of chocolate and cream used for truffle centers and for chocolate glazes and sauces, will break (look curdled) or separate unless there is enough liquid (from the cream) available for the nonfat dry cocoa solids in the chocolate to absorb. There also has to be enough liquid to surround the fat droplets that are formed when the ingredients are mixed or whisked together into an emulsion (see page 147).

Chocolates with a higher percentage of chocolate liquor have more nonfat cocoa solids competing with the other ingredients in the ganache recipe to absorb the liquid needed to surround the fat droplets. These chocolates also contain less sugar, which competes with the solids to "drink" the liquid. In a ganache, eventually the sugar dissolves and increases the volume of the liquid available to coat the fat droplets; thus the sugar helps form the emulsion. But if chocolate that contains more dry cocoa solids and less sugar is substituted, ounce for ounce, for a lower-percentage chocolate, more liquid will be needed to form the emulsion and keep the ganache from breaking or separating.

Thus, for 10 ounces standard bittersweet or semisweet, you need at least 5 ounces cream to make ganache for truffles (I prefer 6 ounces) and 8 or more ounces for a glaze you can pour. But for 10 ounces of bittersweet 70 percent chocolate, you need at least 8 ounces cream (9 is much more dependable) and 10 ounces or more make a good fluid glaze.

In addition to ganache, chocolate mousse or any recipe that begins by melting chocolate together with a relatively small amount of liquid (before the two are mixed with other ingredients) will also require more liquid (or less chocolate) if you substitute a higher-percentage chocolate for a standard one. For example: Standard bittersweet or semisweet chocolate melts well using 1 tablespoon of liquid for every 2 ounces of chocolate. If you substitute a 70 percent chocolate, you must increase the water to at least $1\frac{1}{2}$ tablespoons per each 2 ounces of chocolate for it to melt smoothly.

Even if there is no curdling or other outward sign of trouble as you are preparing the recipe, a 70 percent chocolate substituted for ordinary bittersweet or semisweet chocolate often yields a dense, dry mousse with an unpleasantly intense flavor. Rather than increasing the liquid in recipes of this kind, you can accomplish the same result by decreasing the amount of chocolate. Use the formula for substituting a 70 percent chocolate for one that contains 50 to 55 percent chocolate liquor (see page 351). You will use less chocolate to achieve the same amount of flavor without ruining the texture. Then, if you want a more bittersweet mousse, use less (or none) of the sugar adjustment called for in the formula.

TO SUBSTITUTE COCOA POWDER FOR CHOCOLATE

I have had success converting recipes for brownies, ice creams, cheesecakes, and chocolate custards from cocoa to chocolate. Although I did not explore this type of conversion in depth throughout this book, the information that follows will allow you to experiment.

Each substitution is given two ways: for mainstream cocoa powder, such as Hershey's, Nestlé, or Ghirardelli (which contain 10 to 11 percent fat), and for high-fat specialty professional brands, such as Scharffen Berger, Valrhona, or Pernigotti (which contain 22 to 24 percent fat).

Cocoa powder is very potent, so sloppy measuring can make a bigger difference that you might think. Before you measure, stir the cocoa and press out any lumps with the back of a spoon, then spoon the cocoa loosely into the measure, heap it, and sweep it level. Do not pack or tap the cup or spoon to settle the cocoa.

To substitute unsweetened cocoa powder for chocolate

For each ounce of unsweetened baking chocolate, substitute 2 tablespoons plus 2$\frac{1}{2}$ teaspoons ordinary unsweetened cocoa powder plus 1 tablespoon butter. Or substitute 3 tablespoons high-fat cocoa powder plus 2 teaspoons butter.

For each ounce of standard bittersweet or semisweet chocolate (50 to 55 percent), substitute 1 tablespoon ordinary unsweetened cocoa powder plus 1 tablespoon sugar and 1$\frac{1}{2}$ teaspoons butter. Or substitute 1 tablespoon plus 1 teaspoon high-fat cocoa powder plus 1 tablespoon sugar and 1$\frac{1}{2}$ teaspoons butter.

For each ounce of bittersweet (70 percent) chocolate, substitute 1 tablespoon plus 2$\frac{1}{4}$ teaspoons ordinary unsweetened cocoa powder plus 2 teaspoons sugar and 2$\frac{1}{4}$ teaspoons butter. Or substitute 2 tablespoons unsweetened high-fat cocoa powder plus 2 teaspoons sugar and 2 teaspoons butter.

Like Water for Chocolate: Dangerous Liaisons

One of the first lessons culinary students are taught about chocolate is that water is its enemy. Home cooks learn the same lesson the hard way when a bowl of melted chocolate becomes inexplicably thick and dull. With this lesson comes a series of rules: Chocolate must be melted in a perfectly dry bowl and stirred with a perfectly dry spatula; no water must ever be inadvertently splashed into the chocolate; stray wisps of steam are to be feared. But, like so many absolute rules, there is more to be said. It is true that chocolate melted alone (without significant quantities of butter or cream) can be transformed from a gloriously glossy melted fluid into an intractable thick, dull, grainy paste if it comes into contact with just a little moisture or water (or liquid such as milk, coffee, juice, wine, or even vanilla extract). When this happens, we say that the chocolate has "seized." Seized chocolate, because it neither melts nor flows, becomes useless for most purposes. Seizing does happen if you splash or drip water accidentally into the melting bowl or stir with a wet spoon. It also happens if you try to melt several ounces of chocolate with only a tablespoon or two of butter or cream. You would expect that a little fat in the form of butter or cream would thin the chocolate, but instead the chocolate thickens up because of the small amount of water in the cream, or the even smaller amount of water in the butter.

The problem is chocolate and *a little* water. Chocolate is composed of sugar and chocolate liquor, which is dry particles dispersed in fat (cocoa butter). When chocolate is melted, the dry particles float around easily in the liquid fat and the chocolate becomes beautifully fluid. If only a small amount of water is added, it is absorbed immediately into some of the dry chocolate particles. That makes those particles tacky and prone to sticking together. The more the particles stick together, the less fluid the chocolate becomes, even though it is supposedly melted. Additional water (like the hair of the dog that bit you) can be the solution that makes the chocolate fluid again. Once there is enough water to saturate all the dry particles in the chocolate, the particles lose their stickiness and release each other to float freely once again in the melted fat. So, if melted chocolate and liquid seize in the course of preparing a recipe, it is probably because there is not enough liquid; you can usually fix it by adding a bit more.

A CAUTIONARY NOTE: Although more water is a good fix for seized chocolate that is already mixed with a little water or liquid, you can't fix seized "straight" chocolate by adding liquid if you are planning to temper the chocolate or use it in a pure form for dipping. If chocolate melted alone and intended for these purposes seizes because it accidentally comes into contact with moisture, it should be set aside for another use. It will work fine as an ingredient in a cake batter or a glaze or a ganache that calls for plenty of cream or butter, or a safe quantity of liquid.

OK, so, chocolate is perfectly compatible with quantities of liquid that exceed a certain "safe" ratio of liquid to cocoa fat and dry cocoa solids in the chocolate. But, how much is enough? Milk chocolate, white chocolate, and standard bittersweet and semisweet chocolate (unless their percentage exceeds 60 percent) require at least 1 tablespoon of water for each 2 ounces of chocolate. Higher-percentage chocolates, because they contain more dry particles, require more water. A 70 percent chocolate needs at least 1½ tablespoons of water per 2 ounces of chocolate, and unsweetened chocolate will not melt fluidly with water unless there are at least 2 tablespoons of water for every 2 ounces of chocolate (or 1 tablespoon per ounce).

Be aware that even a "safe" amount of liquid can cause trouble. For instance, if cold liquid is added to warm or tepid chocolate, the chocolate can thicken or form little gritty chocolate chips. One way to avoid this is to melt the chocolate with the liquid so they warm up together. Or, if you must add liquid to chocolate that is already melted, warm the liquid first to avoid the cold-to-warm shock. Another method, and one that saves a step, is to pour hot liquid over finely chopped chocolate, then stir until the chocolate melts.

Understanding the relationship of water to chocolate—identifying the dangerous part of that liaison—is essential to a dessert maker's success. So many chocolate desserts and confections have a chocolate and liquid component, and problems with high-percentage chocolates show up there first.

Tempering Chocolate

A piece of tempered chocolate has a shiny reflective surface (unless it has been scuffed or jumbled with other pieces of chocolate) and an even interior color and texture. It is brittle enough to snap audibly when broken or bitten. Melted chocolate that has been tempered shrinks slightly as it cools and so it releases perfectly from molds, and it mirrors any surface with which it has been in contact. Any bar or piece of chocolate that you buy was tempered at the factory and, unless it has been damaged by heat in transit or in storage, will still be tempered when you unwrap it to eat or cook with it.

Heat-damaged chocolate or chocolate that has melted and cooled without being retempered looks dull and gray, perhaps mottled or streaky. It may be soft and cakey at first, but it will eventually become dry and gritty with a stratified interior texture. When that happens the chocolate actually tastes less flavorful and melts less smoothly in your mouth.

Whether in perfect temper or damaged to start with, each time chocolate is melted, it can be tempered again to regain its glossy surface and crisp texture. Of course, there is no need to temper melted chocolate used as an ingredient in a batter or dessert, sauce, or glaze. However, if you want to dip cookies in chocolate that will dry hard and glossy, or if you want to make a molded chocolate rabbit, or if you want dipped chocolates to dry beautifully and keep at room temperature, you must temper the chocolate.

Melted chocolate solidifies as it cools because the fat molecules link together and form crystals that, in turn, connect to form a sturdy network. Cocoa butter is a complex fat capable of taking several different crystal forms, but only one of the crystal forms is stable and will cause the chocolate to contract and harden with the desired shiny reflective surface and brittle snap. The stable crystal form is called *beta*. The goal of tempering is to create beta crystals. It takes only a small percentage of beta crystals to ensure that subsequent crystals will also take the beta form as the chocolate cools. The process of tempering involves a sequence of heating, cooling, and stirring steps designed to produce enough beta crystals to set the pattern for the rest of the crystals that will form as the chocolate cools.

Under the right conditions, beta crystals form and survive at temperature between 82° and 91°F; they melt and are destroyed at higher temperatures. Most tempering methods involve heating the chocolate well above 91°F so that all crystals (stable and unstable) are melted and destroyed, and you start with a kind of crystal-free blank slate. Then, as the chocolate cools, you create brand-new beta crystals. Once there are enough beta crystals, the chocolate is tempered. You can use a simple test to determine when this has happened.

Before you begin to practice and learn tempering, there is one important mantra to keep in mind: Tempering is not simply a matter of taking chocolate from one prescribed temperature to another, although most instruction focuses mostly on that activity. Tempering is really a function of three interrelated factors: time, temperature, and agitation (stirring). In practical terms, this means that your chocolate may not be in temper the moment you have completed the steps to get your chocolate to the "correct" temperature. That does not mean that you have failed. Almost always, the chocolate will be tempered after just a few more minutes of stirring. Do not get so involved with temperature that you forget the necessity for time and stirring. Use the test for temper as feedback as you work, and be prepared to practice, go slow, observe, and adjust (Zen and the art of chocolate tempering).

There are several methods for tempering chocolate. I have chosen this one because it is convenient to use and easy to learn.

THE CHUNK METHOD FOR TEMPERING CHOCOLATE

This particular method requires at least 20 percent of the chocolate you start with to be solid chocolate that is already in temper—a nice shiny bar in the same condition that it was in when it left the chocolate factory. Do not be concerned about tempering more chocolate than you need for a recipe or project; leftover tempered chocolate can be reused, or eaten. Also, a large bowl of tempered chocolate is easier to keep warm and in good working condition than a small one. I like to work with at least 1¼ pounds of chocolate, but you can temper less.

Temper any amount of chocolate that you like, using the following guidelines.
- Choose good-tasting chocolate, not chocolate chips or coatings that are not truly chocolate (other than white chocolate coating made with cocoa butter).
- Do not work in a hot room.
- Before tempering, prepare whatever is to be dipped and measure out any other ingredients needed and have them at room temperature (cool or cold centers will cause the chocolate to crack when it cools).
- Do not allow moisture to come in direct contact with the chocolate: Make sure that the inside of the bowl, the spatula, and the thermometer stem are all clean and dry.
- Whenever you take the temperature of the chocolate or the water, wipe the thermometer stem clean with a paper towel.

continued

1¼ pounds bittersweet, semisweet, milk, or white chocolate (of which at least ¼ pound is solid, in one or two big pieces, and in temper)

Instant-read thermometer

Set aside one or two large pieces of the solid tempered chocolate, equal to ¼ pound (or 20 percent of the total amount of chocolate you are starting with). Chop the remaining chocolate into small pieces (½ inch or smaller) and place them in a heat-proof bowl with a 2- to 3-quart capacity (use stainless steel if you are melting on top of the stove, glass if you are using the microwave). Warm the chocolate slowly, using one of the following methods, so that it registers only about 100°F by the time it is entirely melted.

To melt the chocolate in a water bath: Set the bowl in a large wide skillet of barely simmering water and stir frequently at first, and then constantly, until about three-quarters of the chocolate is melted. Remove the chocolate from the heat and stir for 1 to 2 minutes to melt the remaining chocolate. If the chocolate it not entirely melted, replace the bowl in the skillet and continue to stir, then remove from the pan.

To melt the chocolate in the microwave: Heat the chocolate for 2 to 3 minutes at Medium (50%) power. Stir well—even though the chocolate will be only partially melted. Then heat for decreasing time increments, stirring well after each zap. Stop when there is still some unmelted chocolate in the bowl. Stir well to allow the warm melted chocolate to finish melting the pieces.

If the temperature of the chocolate exceeds 100°F, let it cool to about 100°F (no need to be exact here). Drop the reserved tempered chunks of chocolate into the bowl and stir constantly until the chocolate registers 90°F for dark chocolate, or 88°F for white or milk. As you stir, you are simultaneously cooling the melted chocolate and melting the surface of the tempered chocolate chunks. As the temperature of the melted chocolate approaches 90°F, stable beta crystals from the surface of the tempered chunks start to mingle with the melted chocolate and form the "seed" to create more beta crystals. When there are enough beta crystals, the chocolate is tempered. The object is not to melt the chunks completely, but to use them to provide the beta "seed" to produce more beta crystals. In fact, if your chunks are completely melted by the time the chocolate reaches 90°F, the necessary beta crystals are likely to have been destroyed; add another chunk of chocolate and continue to stir.

When the chocolate is at the desired temperature, it may or may not yet contain enough beta crystals to be tempered. Use the Test for Temper (see below) to check. If the chocolate is not in temper, continue to stir for a few minutes longer, then test again. When the chocolate is in temper, remove the unmelted chunk(s) and chill them in the refrigerator for 10 minutes, then store at room temperature to be used again. Use the tempered chocolate immediately.

If you are using the tempered chocolate for dipping, stir it from time to time and scrape down the bowl to prevent chocolate from building up around the sides. The chocolate will cool and thicken as you work. You can set the bowl in a pan of warm water for a few seconds at a time, or you can warm the sides of the bowl with a hair dryer, and stir until the chocolate regains fluidity, as long as you do not let it exceed a maximum temperature of 91°F for dark chocolate or 88°F for milk and white chocolate. Or you can keep the bowl in a container of warm water just 2 degrees warmer than the maximum temperature for the type of chocolate you are using. Or set the bowl on a heating pad covered with several layers of towel so that it is barely warm.

THE TEST FOR TEMPER

Drizzle some of the chocolate onto a knife blade or a piece of wax paper. Set the test in front of a fan (preferably) or in a cool place. If the chocolate starts to set within 3 minutes, it is tempered. If it remains soft and wet looking even after 3 minutes, it is not yet tempered.

KEEPING TEMPERED CHOCOLATE IN WORKING CONDITION

Once chocolate has been tempered, it will thicken as you work with it. Intuitively, it would seem that the thickening is due to cooling, but that is only partially true. In the course of dipping centers, for example, tempered chocolate will thicken even if maintained at its "ceiling temperature" in a water bath or on a heating pad covered with towels. Why does this happen? Remember that the formation of the necessary beta crystals in the tempering process required time and agitation, in addition to temperature. Once the chocolate is in temper, time and agitation (caused by dipping, scraping the bowl, and occasional stirring) continue to create more and more beta crystals, whether or not you want them. More beta crystals make the chocolate thicker and eventually harder to work with. The chocolate is still in temper, but there are too many beta crystals; the chocolate sets even faster than before and the gloss is a little duller. Chocolate is said to be "overseeded" or "overtempered" when it is very thick and sludgy from too many beta crystals.

The remedy? If the chocolate has cooled, rewarm it to its ceiling temperature by setting the bowl in the skillet of warm water for a few seconds at a time, or in the microwave (10-second bursts at Medium [50%]) or with a hair dryer, with thorough stirring after each burst. If the chocolate is at the maximum temperature recommended but it is still too thick, you have to intentionally melt and destroy some of the excess beta crystals by allowing some of the chocolate to exceed the maximum temperature. Use the water bath or microwave or hair dryer as before, but let the chocolate get a little hotter around the edges of the bowl (or in the center, if using the microwave). Then stir the chocolate well to mix in the warmer chocolate; otherwise your shiny tempered chocolate will show some fine streaks after it cools. This should return your chocolate to a more fluid and, with luck, still tempered state. After this maneuver, always test for temper again to make sure that you haven't melted too many beta crystals and lost the temper of your whole batch.

Another way to fix overseeded chocolate is to add a little "virgin" chocolate (chocolate that has been heated to 125°F and cooled to 90° to 92°F but is not seeded or in temper) to the thick chocolate and stir it in thoroughly. This rewarms the chocolate, reduces the ratio of tempered crystals, and puts you back in business.

Glossary

ALKALIZED COCOA *See* Dutch-process cocoa.

ALKALIZING A chemical process applied to cocoa nibs or to chocolate liquor to reduce acidity. *See also* Dutch-process cocoa.

BITTERSWEET OR SEMISWEET CHOCOLATE Sweet chocolates that contain a minimum of 35 percent by weight of chocolate liquor. Bittersweet and semisweet chocolates may also contain up to 12 percent milk solids, which may include milk fat. See page 55 for more about bittersweet or semisweet chocolate.

BLOOM Streaks, graying, or discoloration on the surface of chocolate caused by poor tempering, temperature fluctuations, and/or moisture in storage. Finely crystallized sugar on the surface of chocolate (caused by moisture) is called sugar bloom. A dull appearance or streaks on the surface of the chocolate caused by poor tempering or too much heat in storage is called fat bloom. See Qualities to Look For, page 59, for a fuller discussion.

CACAO The source of all chocolate and chocolate products. The term *cacao* refers to the tree and its fruit and the seeds inside the fruit (also called cacao beans or cocoa beans), which are processed to make chocolate. When it appears on a chocolate label, cacao refers to the total cocoa bean content of the bar.

CACAO BEANS *See* Cocoa beans.

CHOCOLATE LIQUOR Cocoa nibs ground into a fine paste, i.e., pure unsweetened chocolate. Different types of chocolate are defined by the minimum percentage of chocolate liquor they contain. When the term *chocolate liquor* appears with a percentage on a chocolate label, it also includes any cocoa or cocoa butter added separately to adjust the flavor or texture of the chocolate. When chocolate liquor appears in the ingredient list on the chocolate package, it may or may not be listed separately from any added cocoa butter or nonfat dry cocoa solids.

COCOA (OR COCOA POWDER) Chocolate liquor that has most of the fat extracted from it, then is pulverized to a powder. Cocoa powder is unsweetened and may be natural or treated with alkali (Dutch-process). See page 48 for more about cocoa powder. The term *cocoa* is also used in a broader sense in the commodity market to mean cocoa beans. The British use the term *cocoa* to mean chocolate liquor, and, as such, it may appear on chocolate labels with a percentage. See Understanding Bittersweet and Semisweet Chocolate Labels, page 55.

COCOA BEANS The seeds of the fruit of the cacao tree, *Theobroma cacao*. All chocolate and cocoa is made from cocoa beans that have been dried, roasted, and hulled (the latter process breaks the beans into pieces).

COCOA BUTTER The ivory-colored fat that constitutes 50 to 54 percent of the weight of hulled roasted cocoa beans; also called *cocoa fat*. Cocoa butter is extracted from chocolate liquor (ground roasted cocoa beans) in the making of cocoa powder. Extra cocoa butter is usually added to chocolate liquor to make fine chocolate. Although it has very little flavor of its own, cocoa butter melts readily in the mouth and makes chocolate taste smooth, rich, and long lasting on the palate.

COCOA MASS Another term for chocolate liquor.

COCOA MASSE The French term for chocolate liquor.

COCOA NIBS Hulled roasted cocoa bean pieces.

COCOA SOLIDS; DRY COCOA SOLIDS Both terms are used inconsistently. They may refer to chocolate liquor, inclusive of any added cocoa butter or dry cocoa solids. But both terms are sometimes used to mean only nonfat dry cocoa solids (chocolate liquor minus all fat). See Understanding Bittersweet and Semisweet Chocolate Labels, page 55.

CONCHING A prolonged, heated mixing and scraping process during the last stages of manufacture that results in chocolate's smoothness of flavor and texture. Conching grinds chocolate particles to a size undetectable by the human palate, smoothes their microscopic rough edges, and mixes and coats them intimately with fat. In the process, undesirable aromas and flavors are released through timed and controlled aeration. Fine chocolates may be conched for 24 to 36 hours, or even up to 72 hours

COUVERTURE Chocolate that contains a minimum of 32 percent cocoa butter. Couverture is smooth on the palate and fluid enough (due to the cocoa butter) when melted to coat candies with the relatively thin layer of chocolate considered a hallmark of fine confections. As an indicator of quality, the term *couverture* had more meaning in the past, when standard chocolate bars and cooking chocolate often contained less cocoa butter. Today, with the exception of some baking squares, most bittersweet and semisweet chocolate bars (and milk chocolate bars) that home cooks buy for eating and cooking are, in fact, couverture. Chocolate chips, morsels, and chunks (with few exceptions) have less than 32 percent cocoa butter and, therefore, are not couverture.

DUTCH-PROCESS COCOA Dutch-processed, or alkalized, cocoa powder made from chocolate liquor or cocoa nibs that have been chemically treated (usually with potassium carbonate) to reduce acidity and harshness. See page 48 for fuller a discussion.

GANACHE The generic term for any combination of chocolate mixed with cream (with or without flavoring or the occasional addition of butter or egg). Ganache may take the form of a flowing sauce or glaze, a firm or soft truffle center, a spreadable frosting, or a fluffy filling. The flavor and texture of ganache varies with the ratio of chocolate to cream, the method of mixing them together, the conditions of cooling, and how the mixture is ultimately handled after cooling.

LECITHIN A soy-based fat that is used in tiny quantities to emulsify the fats in chocolate.

MILK CHOCOLATE Sweet chocolate that contains a minimum of 10 percent by weight of chocolate liquor. Milk chocolate must also contain a minimum of 3.39 percent milk fat and a minimum of 12 percent milk solids (inclusive of milk fat).

NATURAL COCOA Cocoa made from chocolate liquor that has not been chemically treated to reduce acidity. See page 48 for a fuller discussion.

NONFAT DRY COCOA SOLIDS The fat-free component of chocolate liquor, which represents 46 to 50 percent of its weight. Imagine dry cocoa solids as completely fat-free cocoa powder. Virtually all the chocolate flavor resides in the dry cocoa solids.

TEMPERING Tempering is a controlled heating, cooling, and stirring process that creates stable fat crystals in chocolate. Tempered chocolate hardens uniformly, with an even color, brittle texture, and glossy surface.

UNSWEETENED BAKING CHOCOLATE Pure chocolate liquor to which a little vanilla and/or lecithin may have been added.

Sources

**BERYL'S CAKE DECORATING
AND PASTRY SUPPLIES**
P.O. BOX 1584
NORTH SPRINGFIELD, VA 22151
800–488–2749
www.beryls.com

An awesome collection of professional tools, ingredients, books, and supplies for pastry chefs, dessert makers, cake decorators, and confectioners. Among other things: digital thermometers (including Polder, with the probe on a cable), silica gel (desiccant), custom cookie cutters, chocolate dipping forks, and Valrhona and Callebaut chocolates. Catalog available.

**KING ARTHUR FLOUR
THE BAKER'S CATALOGUE**
P.O. BOX 876
NORWICH, VT 05055-0876
800–827–6836
www.bakerscatalogue.com

Everything for the baker and dessert maker, including, among other ingredients, Merckens Dutch-process and natural cocoas (formerly De Zaan cocoas), the best natural cocoa I know other than Scharffen Berger, and digital thermometers.

PARRISH'S CAKE DECORATING SUPPLY, INC.
225 WEST 146TH STREET
GARDENA, CA 90248
800–736–8443

www.parrishsmagicline.com

Everything for the baker, including Magic Line pans with solid or removable bottoms in every conceivable size, and both 2 inches and 3 inches deep. Catalog available.

THE PASTA SHOP
5655 COLLEGE AVENUE
OAKLAND, CA 94618
888–952–4005
www.rockridgemarkethall.com

A fabulous gourmet retail store that has a second location in Berkeley. The buyer and owners solicit advice from an impressive list of local cookbook authors and professional bakers (who happen to be friends): Thus the store has a subspecialty in baking and decoration ingredients and chocolate. Chocolate and cocoa from Scharffen Berger, Valrhona, Michel Cluizel, and Callebaut; Madagascar and Tahitian vanilla extracts and whole and ground vanilla beans; the best candied fruits and citrus peels; honeys; chestnuts in a variety of forms, including chestnut flour; nut pastes; and more.

PENZEYS SPICES
P.O. BOX 933
WI9362 APOLLO DRIVE
MUSKEGO, WI 53150
800–741–7787
www.penzeys.com

All kinds of spices; Madagascar, Tahitian, and Mexican vanilla beans; and several types of cinnamon, including Ceylon cinnamon (also known as Mexican cinnamon, or *canela*). Reading the catalog is a real education about flavor ingredients and their uses.

SCHARFFEN BERGER CHOCOLATE MAKER
914 HEINZ STREET
BERKELEY, CA 94710
800–930–4528
www.scharffenberger.com

Exquisite bittersweet, semisweet, and unsweetened chocolates, cocoa nibs, and the best natural cocoa powder.

SPUN SUGAR CHOCOLATES
1611 UNIVERSITY AVENUE
BERKELEY, CA 94703
510–843–9192

"Professional" chocolates, such as Callebaut and Ghirardelli, can be ordered in less than 10-pound quantities (often the minimum elsewhere), perfect for the home cook; Scharffen Berger chocolates, as well as the new Étienne Guittard line of European-style and single-origin chocolates from Venezuela with 58, 61, and 72 percent chocolate liquor; cake-decorating supplies.

SUGAR AND SPICE
2965 JUNIPERO SERRA BOULEVARD
DALEY CITY, CA 94014
650–994–4911

Cake-decorating and candy-making supplies.

SUR LA TABLE
1765 SIXTH AVENUE S
SEATTLE, WA 98134-1608
800–243–0852
www.surlatable.com

Premium source for quality tools and equipment for home bakers; ingredients including Scharffen Berger and Valrhona chocolates. Catalog available.

SWEET CELEBRATIONS
(FORMERLY MAID OF SCANDINAVIA)
7009 WASHINGTON AVENUE S
EDINA, MN 55439
800–328–6722
www.sweetc.com

Ingredients and equipment of all sorts for the home baker. Catalog available.

WILLIAMS-SONOMA
P.O. BOX 7456
SAN FRANCISCO, CA 94120
800–541–2233
www.williamssonoma.com

Baking tools and equipment; ingredients including Pernigotti cocoa and Scharffen Berger, Valrhona, and Callebaut chocolates. Catalog available.

IN ADDITION

Ceramics supply stores sell banding wheels that can be used as decorating turntables.

Restaurant supply stores sell commercial half sheet pans and cake pans, Ateco decorating turntables, and more.

Acknowledgments

A book takes more than an author. Maya Klein was my assistant through the early phases of this book, and her intelligence and creativity enriched it. Robert Steinberg and John Scharffenberger of Scharffen Berger Chocolate Maker allowed me to have an intimate look at the creation of a new American chocolate. Robert's friendship came with challenging questions, discussion, argument, and tasting, all of which brought clarity to my thinking. Maricel Presilla introduced me to Jorge Redmond and Rand Turner of El Rey chocolates; I thank them all for the opportunity to visit the world of cacao at the source, in Venezuela. Edith McClure was a frequent and beloved tasting partner. Jennifer Chin spent two weeks with me knee-deep in ganache. Over the years, even brief conversations with Shirley Corriher, Hal McGee, Thalia Howenthal, Jim Graham, Veronica Bowers, Elaine Gonzalez, Terry Richardson, Michael Recchiuti, Flo Braker, and Marion Cunningham added to my knowledge.

Thanks to everyone at Artisan, in particular Ann Bramson, for her brilliance and warmth, and her loyalty to a project that turned out to be more challenging than we imagined. I thank Deborah Weiss Geline for her impressive ability to understand complexity *and* remain focused in a sea of notes and corrections, Judith Sutton for her vast knowledge and meticulous copyediting, Vivian Ghazarian for her design talents, Nancy Murray's production expertise, Amy Corley's and Pamela Cannon's publicity and marketing efforts, and typesetter Barbara Peragine. Thanks, too, to Nancy Nicholas for her encouragement and help with organization and writing. As always, I thank my agent and friend, Jane Dystel, for her support and good counsel.

I have always enjoyed preparing desserts for the camera. Deborah Jones is an inspired photographer and a joy to work with. Stylist Sara Slavin brought magic, as usual, to our fifth book together. Sandra Cook did beautiful work styling the ice cream and the savory photos. Special thanks to Jeri Jones and Brooke Buchanan for being part of the team.

Writing a book takes place in the real life of the author. I can't close the last chapter of *Bittersweet* without thanking the people who make a difference to me with their love and encouragement, wisdom and insight. Thus, to my family, friends, and teachers of every kind—in particular Joan Nackerud, Edith McClure, Beryl Radin, Christine Blaine, Amelia Saltsman, Barbara and Bob Blackburn, Suzanne Samson, Steve Keneipp, Kelly Dobbins, Sarah Leverett, Christina Lapides, Bev Frances, Albert Abrams, and of course my daughter, Lucy Medrich—thank you.

Index

A

Albert's mousse, 166–67
Alice's chocolate sauce, 292
alkali, in cocoa powder, 50–51
almond(s):
    in fallen chocolate soufflé cake, 112–13
    in grappa, currant, and pine nut torte, 118–19
    in Queen of Sheba torte, 109–11
    sticks with cocoa nibs, 311
ancho chile(s):
    and cherry tartlets, 281
    hot chocolate, 205
    in mole coloradito, 336–38
anise, bittersweet tartlets with hazelnuts, orange and,
    280–81
Armagnac, white chocolate ice cream with prunes and,
    85
aroma, of chocolate, 59
asparagus, nibby, with prosciutto, 326

B

baby greens, crunchy, 322
baking sheets, 31
Baking with Julia, 218
bars, black-bottom pecan praline, 98
beans, green, nibby, 326
Beard, James, 125
Beck, Simone, 102, 105
Bergeaud, Suzanne, 101–2, 122
Berkeley Lawrence Hall of Science, 302
berries:
    chocolate meringues with, and cream, 182
    in meringues glacées with the works, 183
    see also specific berries
best cocoa brownies, 95–96
bittersweet chocolate, 51–53, 57–58
    brownies, classic, 94
    decadence cookies, 286–87
    deception, 170–71
    ganache truffles, extra-, 155–57
    glaze, 235
    hot fudge sauce, 293
    ice cream, 77–78
    mousse, warm, 168–69
    pavé, 201
    roulade, 200–201
    soufflés, intensely, 198–99
    tartlets with hazelnuts, orange, and anise, 280–81
    see also high-percentage chocolates; semisweet
        chocolate
bittersweet deception, 170–71
blackberry(ies):
    jam, in cocoa bean almond roulade, 316–17
    and walnut praline sundae, 89
black-bottom pecan praline bars, 98
black cocoa, 49
black raspberry jam, in cocoa bean almond roulade,
    316–17
blending, of cocoa beans, 44, 45–47
bloom, on chocolate, 59
Book of Jewish Food (Roden), 108
bowls, 30
Braker, Flo, 125, 214–15
brandy:
    in grappa, currant, and pine nut torte, 118–19
    use of, 40
    in white chocolate ice cream with prunes and
        Armagnac, 85
brownies:
    about, 90–92
    best cocoa, 95–96
    black-bottom pecan praline bars, 98
    cakier classic unsweetened, 94
    classic bittersweet, 94
    classic semisweet, 94
    classic unsweetened, 93–94
    lacy coconut-topped, 99
    macadamia shortbread, 97
brown sugars, use of, 42
buckwheat cocoa crepes with honey, 318–19
budini, 120–21
Bugialli, Giuliano, 321, 329
butter:
    in tortes, 107
    use of, 37
butternut squash soup with cocoa bean cream, roasted,
    325
buttons, chocolate, 55

C

cacao trees, 43
    as Third World crop, 46–47
cakes:
    bittersweet deception, 170–71
    bittersweet roulade, 200–201
    chocolate génoise, 229–30

liqueur(s):
    raspberry, in Julia's cake, 218–20
    in tortes, 107
    use of, 40, 186
liquid measures, 27
little sauce for pasta, a, 331–32
livers, chicken, chopped, with sherry-cocoa pan sauce, 324
low-fat recipes, about, 67, 191–93

M

macadamia shortbread brownies, 97
macaroons, coconut saras, 224–25
manufacture, of chocolate, 43–47
marble cheesecake, 266–68
mascarpone cheese, in strawberry celebration cake, 211–13
measuring, 25–27
measuring cups, 32
meat sauce, Giuliano's sweet and savory, with chocolate, 329–30
Medrich, Lucy, 68, 69, 126
melting chocolate:
    cookie tartlets, 282–83
    meringues, 202–3
melting of chocolate, methods for, 60–64
mendiants, 341–42
meringue(s):
    about, 179
    chocolate, 180–81
    chocolate, with berries and cream, 182
    gâteau Diane, 184
    glacées with the works, 183
    melting chocolate, 202–3
    nutty chocolate, 181
    strawberry chocolate, cinnamon ganache with, 182
    white, 181
    white, in Carmen meringay, 226–27
Mexican chocolate, in mole coloradito, 336–38
Microplane zester, 36
microwave ovens, 32
    melting chocolate in, 60, 62, 64
milk chocolate:
    about, 53
    in gianduja truffles, 159
    lover's ice cream, 82–83
    in mendiants, 341–42
    mousse, 174–76
    truffles, 158–59

mint:
    in bittersweet chocolate ice cream, 78
    chocolate chip ice cream, 79
    classic ganache truffles with, 153
    whipped ganache filling with, 233
    white chocolate mousse with, 175
mise en place, 25
mixers, 32
mixing, 27–29
mocha:
    ganache filling, whipped, 232
    hot chocolate, 204
    latte ice cream, 83
    mousse, 175
    tart, warm, 278–79
moisture, melting of chocolate and, 63
mole coloradito, 336–38
molten chocolate–raspberry cakes, 221–22
molten raspberry–chocolate cupcakes with marbled glaze, 273
morsels, chocolate, 54–55
mousse:
    Albert's, 166–67
    chocolate marquise, 172–73
    gianduja, 175
    milk chocolate, 174–76
    mocha, 177
    triple, 177–78
    warm bittersweet, 168–69
    white chocolate, 174–76
        with fresh mint, 175
        –citrus, 176
mouthfeel, 59–60
mushroom, wild, ragout, 327–28

N

National Confectioners Association, 6
natural cocoa powder, 48–49, 50
Neufchâtel cream cheese, in marble cheesecake, 266–68
New York magazine, 4
nibby:
    asparagus with prosciutto, 326
    cocoa cookies, 309
    espresso cookies, 310
    green beans, 326
    nut and raisin cookies, 312
    pecan cookies, 307–8
    pudding, 306
Nibby Alexander, 302
nibs, *see* cocoa nib(s)
nonfat dry cocoa solids, 44, 53, 55, 345–48

roasted squash soup with cocoa bean cream, 325
Roden, Claudia, 108
rolling pins, 33
roulade:
    bittersweet, 200–201
    cocoa bean almond, 316–17
ruffled fans, chocolate, 238–39
ruffles, chocolate, 240
rugelach, currant and nib, 314–15
rum:
    in strawberry celebration cake, 211–15
    use of, 40
rum raisin–white chocolate ice cream, 85

S

salad, crunchy baby greens, 322
salmonella, raw eggs and, 164, 165
Sarah Bernhardt chocolate glaze, 236
sauce:
    Alice's chocolate, 292
    bittersweet hot fudge, 293
    blackberry-raspberry, walnut praline and blackberry
        sundae with, 89
    chocolate, 290–91
    Giuliano's sweet and savory meat, with chocolate,
        329–30
    a little, for pasta, 331–32
    mole coloradito, 336–38
    Scharffen Berger cocoa fudge, 294
    sherry-cocoa pan, chopped chicken livers with, 324
    strawberry, peanut butter–chocolate torte with, 114–15
saucepan fudge drops, 285
scales, 33
Scharffen Berger cocoa fudge sauce, 294
Schmidt, Steven, 275
Schulze, Joan, 160
scones, cream, with chocolate chunks, 288
seeds, sunflower or pumpkin, in mendiants, 341–42
semisweet chocolate, 51–53, 57–58
    brownies, classic, 94
    Giuliano's sweet and savory meat sauce with, 329–30
    in mole coloradito, 336–38
    mousse, warm, 168–69
    see also bittersweet chocolate; high-percentage
        chocolates
serrated knives, 34
sherry-cocoa pan sauce, chopped chicken livers with, 324
shortbread:
    crust, in tarts and tartlets, 276–83
    -macadamia brownies, 97
Sicilian chocolate gelato, 88

silica gel, 31
single-origin chocolates, 44, 45–47
skewers, 34
soufflé(s):
    bittersweet, with cocoa bean cream, 199
    cake, fallen chocolate, 112–13
    chocolate-flecked cocoa, 194–95
    intensely bittersweet, 198–99
soup, roasted squash, with cocoa bean cream, 325
Spain, king of, sweetened chocolate and, 320
spatulas, 34
spiced hot chocolate, 205
spices, use of, 41
spirits, use of, 40
spun sugar, 244
squash, soup, roasted, with cocoa bean cream, 325
stirring, to melt chocolate, 63–64
storing, of chocolate and cocoa, 56
strainers, 34–35
strawberry(ies):
    celebration cake, 211–13
    chocolate meringue with cinnamon ganache, 182
    sauce, peanut butter–chocolate torte with, 114–15
substitutions, in recipes, 349–54
sugar, use of, 41–42
    spun, 244
sundae, walnut praline and blackberry, 89
sunflower seeds, in mendiants, 341–42
sweet chocolate, 53
syrup, cocoa, 295

T

tarts and tartlets, 278–83
    ancho chile and cherry, 281
    bittersweet, with hazelnuts, orange, and anise,
        280–81
    cocoa bean tassies, 313
    espresso walnut, 279
    melting chocolate cookie, 282–83
    pans for, 35
    warm mocha, 278–79
tassies, cocoa bean, 313
tea, jasmine, classic ganache truffles with, 153–54
temperature:
    of ingredients, 28–29
    of oven, 28, 29, 193
tempering chocolate, 357–62
terroir, 46–47
texture, of chocolate, 59
Thanksgiving, chocolate for, 274–77
thermometers, 35

tiger cake, 269–70
timers, 36
toasted coconut–white chocolate ice cream, 86–87
toothpicks, 34
tortes, 107–21
    chestnut, 116–17
    fallen chocolate soufflé cake, 112
    grappa, currant, and pine nut, 118–19
    peanut butter–chocolate, with strawberry sauce,
        114–15
    Queen of Sheba, 109–11
tribute cake, 214–17
    canela, 217
    espresso, 217
    gianduja, 217
    raspberry, 217
triple mousses, 177–78
True History of Chocolate, A (Michael and Sophie Coe),
        324
truffles:
    au Cocolat, 140–41
    classic ganache, 151–54
    classic ginger, 153
    classic jasmine, 153
    classic mint, 153
    cold creamy, 142–45
    dipping and finishing of, 161–62
    extra-bittersweet ganache, 155–57
    gianduja, 159
    handling of, 146–50
    milk chocolate, 158–59
    white chocolate, 158–59
    white chocolate–lemon, 159
    women of taste, 160
truly creamy egg cream, 289
types of chocolate, 47–55

U

United States:
    chocolate consumption in, 5–6, 7
    chocolate industry standards in, 51–52, 347
unsweetened chocolate, 48
    classic brownies with, 93–94
    in coq (or lapin) au vin, 333–35
    in wild mushroom ragout, 327–28

V

Van Houten, Conrad, 49
vanilla, use of, 42
varietal chocolates, 45–47

W

wafers, real chocolate, 284
walnut(s):
    chopped eggplant with cocoa nibs and, 323
    esspresso tart, 279
    praline and blackberry sundae, 89
warm bittersweet mousse, 168–69
warm mocha tart, 278–79
water:
    in chocolate mousse, 165
    and seizing of chocolate, 355–56
water bath, 60, 61, 63
Waters, Alice, 160
wax paper, 32
whipped:
    chocolate ganache filling, 231–33
    cream, chocolate meringues with berries and, 182
    Mexican cinnamon ganache filling, 233
    mint-infused white chocolate ganache filling, 233
    mocha ganache filling, 232
whisks, 36
white chocolate, 45, 53–54, 64
    in cold creamy truffles, 142–45
    ganache filling, whipped, with mint, 233
    ice cream, 84–87, 89, 114
    –lemon truffles, 159
    in mendiants, 341–42
    mousse, 174–76
    –orange mousse, in triple mousses, 177–78
    truffles, 158–59
white confectionery coating, 53–54, 64
white meringue, 181
    in Carmen meringay, 226–27
wild mushroom ragout, 327–28
Williams, Chuck, 125, 214
wine, red, in coq (or lapin) au vin, 333–35
wire whisks, 36
women of taste truffles, 160

Y

Year in Chocolate, A (Medrich), 275

Z

Zabar's, 4
Zaslavsky, Nancy, 336
zest, citrus, white chocolate mousse with, 176
zester, 36